Computer Scenographics

Darwin Reid Payne

Southern Illinois University Press
Carbondale and Edwardsville

97 96 95 94   4 3 2 1

Library of Congress Cataloging-in-Publication Data

Payne, Darwin Reid.
        Computer scenographics / Darwin Reid Payne.
            p.   cm.
        Includes index.
            1. Theaters—Stage-setting and scenery—Computer programs.
        2. Motion pictures—Setting and scenery—Computer programs.
        I. Title.
        PN2091.S8P349   1994
        792′.025—dc20   93-39696
        ISBN 0-8093-1904-7 (cloth)   CIP
        ISBN 0-8093-1905-5 (paper)

The paper used in this publication meets the minimum requirements of American
National Standard for Information Sciences—Permanence of Paper for Printed Library
Materials, ANSI Z39.48-1984. ∞

Contents

Figures   vii
Preface   xi

Introduction   1

1   Basic Computer Graphics Technical Requirements and Concepts   9
The Computer Scenographics Studio   9
Basic Hardware and Equipment   22
Computer Graphics Programs   37

2   The Computer as a Design Research Tool   62
Advantages and Limits of Computer Graphics   63
Interactive Image Files: Libraries and Templates   71

3   The Computer Drawing Board   96
Computer Drawing   97
Templates   133

4   The Computer Scenographic Model   157
Computer Three-Dimensional Graphics   161
Computer Modeling for Cinema and Television   199
Rendering Scenographic PICT Images on the Computer   214

Conclusion   225

Index   231

Figures

1.   Man drawing a lute   2
2.   Diagram of Leonardo's drawing machine   3
3.   Diagram of scenographic studio   11
4.   Diagram of manual graphics area   14
5.   Computer workstation   20
6.   Diagram of computer workstation   21
7.   Macintosh computer screen sizes   26
8.   Monitor control panel   28
9.   Graphics tablet and keyboard   30
10.   Computer input devices   31
11.   Diagram of graphics tablet   33
12.   Pressure-sensitive graphics tool   34
13.   Use of pressure-sensitive tool   35
14.   ThunderScan hand scanner   36
15.   Diagram of computer programs   43
16.   Bit-mapped scenographic rendering   45
17.   Capture 4.0 screen   52
18.   Utility program screens   54
19.   Inspiration 4.0 diagram   56
20.   Hierarchical file diagram   58
21.   Norton Fast Find screen   59
22.   Ergonomic factors diagram   61
23.   Computer graphics screen   65
24.   Computer graphics diagram   66
25.   Chart of scenographic emphasis   68
26.   Computer drawing diagram   70
27.   Bit map scenographic drawing   71
28.   Bit map tools and palettes   72
29.   Photoshop 2.5 scenographic drawing: *Hamlet*—act 5, scene 1   73
30.   Picture objects diagram   76

31.   Progress of scanned image diagram   77

32.   Library image file   79

33.   Library image files   80

34.   Macro image window diagram   81

35.   Bit-mapped costume images   82

36.   Bit-mapped costume drawing   83

37.   Object-oriented costume images   84

38.   Object-oriented costume drawing   85

39.   Scanned costume image diagram   86

40.   Clip-art library images   87

41.   Clip-art images in working drawings   88

42.   Clip-art images in working drawings   89

43.   Printer ornaments as graphic elements   91

44.   Converting printer ornaments into graphic elements   92

45.   Scenographic design from printer ornament graphic elements   93

46.   Scaling graphic elements diagram   94

47.   Diagram of computer theater layers   99

48.   Canvas 3.5 layer specifications diagram   100

49.   Diagram as scenographic concept   102

50.   Steps in perspective grid construction   105

51.   Steps in perspective grid construction   106

52.   Computer-made perspective grid   107

53.   Scenographic concept from library elements   108

54.   Scenographic perspective drawing: *Night of the Iguana*   109

55.   Making plank units in Canvas 3.5   110

56.   Object-oriented and bit-mapped graphics   111

57.   Drawing object-oriented graphics   113

58.   Drawing polygon and Bézier objects   114

59.   Object-oriented image information dialog boxes   115

60.   PowerDraw 5.0 arc tools   116

61.   PowerDraw 5.0 faired curve tool   117

62.   PowerDraw 5.0 ellipse protractor tool   118

63.   Object-oriented image-scaling dialog box   119

64.   Line possibilities in Canvas 3.5   121

65.   Automatic alignment in CAD programs   124

66.   Drawing objects with guidelines in Canvas 3.5   125

67.   Computer calculators   128

68.   Drawing complex object-oriented images   129

69.   Drawing and altering complex object-oriented images   130

70.   Manipulating object-oriented images in Canvas 3.5   131

71.   Diagram showing graphic image construction differences   132

72.   Constructing complex objects from basic forms in Canvas 3.5   133

73.   Altering complex objects in Canvas 3.5   134

74.   Aldus IntelliDraw 2.0 combine option   135

75.   Aldus IntelliDraw 2.0 symmetrigon objects   136
76.   Generic floor plan template   140
77.   Theater-specific floor plan   141
78.   Computer furniture template   143
79.   Rotating scenic units in Canvas 3.5   145
80.   Moving scenic units by arrow keys   149
81.   Computer front elevation: *Pajama Game*   150
82.   Elevation detail: *The Beaux Stratagem*   151
83.   Working drawing detail with model view: *1776*   152
84.   Converting bit-mapped image to object-oriented graphic   153
85.   Computer light plot diagram   154
86.   MiniCad+ 5.0 two-dimensional screen diagram   159
87.   MiniCad+ 5.0 three-dimensional screen diagram   160
88.   Diagram of three-dimensional coordinates   163
89.   Diagram of Virtus WalkThrough basic windows   164
90.   Real-life scenographic model view   169
91.   Virtual reality model view   170
92.   Printout of computer paper model parts   173
93.   Virtual reality model image: *Incident at Vichy*   174
94.   Scenographic model: *Incident at Vichy*   175
95.   Virtual reality arena theater views   176
96.   Virtus WalkThrough top views   177
97.   Virtus WalkThrough front views   178
98.   Virtus WalkThrough bird's-eye perspective view   179
99.   Virtus WalkThrough virtual reality model   180
100. Virtus WalkThrough model offstage view   181
101. Virtus WalkThrough model view   182
102. Virtus WalkThrough model stage-right view   183
103. Virtual reality model auditorium viewing positions   184
104. Virtus WalkThrough basic screens   185
105. Virtus WalkThrough model-rendering options   186
106. Virtus WalkThrough magnetic guidelines diagram   190
107. Virtus WalkThrough surface options   192
108. FreeHand 4.0 PICT model rendering   193
109. Virtus WalkThrough library screen   196
110. Virtus WalkThrough library object   197
111. Virtus WalkThrough wall thickness diagram   198
112. Cinema studio functions diagram   202
113. Diagram of virtual reality film studio   203
114. Diagram of virtual reality television studio   204
115. Filmed media storyboards   206
116. Diagram of aspect ratio options for filmed media   207
117. Scenographic sketch using FreeHand 4.0   210
118. High-resolution graphic construction   211

119.   High-resolution graphic construction   212

120.   Diagram of materials for scenographic renderings   214

121.   Diagram for scenographic sketches from PICT images   215

122.   Scenographic model rendered as object-oriented graphics   216

123.   Adobe PhotoShop 2.5 scan of Gordon Craig model: *Hamlet*   217

124.   Adobe PhotoShop 2.5 variation of Gordon Craig model: *Hamlet*   218

125.   Adobe PhotoShop 2.5 variation of Gordon Craig model: *Hamlet*   219

126.   Gallery Effects Texturizer filter   220

127.   Gallery Effects alternate Texturizer images   221

128.   Overhead projection of Virtus WalkThrough images   222

129.   Diagram of Virtus Voyager options   223

Preface

The title of this book is *Computer Scenographics*. While the first word of the title—*computer*—is ubiquitous in the present-day world, the second—*scenographics*—is not found in any dictionary to date. While *scenography*, *scenographic*, and *scenographer* do exist, *scenographics* has yet to find a place. (Perhaps when this orphan word finds its niche in future lexicons—as it is likely to do—I will claim the credit.)

And yet, I can think of no better word—coined or not—to describe the subject of the book that follows. *Scenographics* seems to me to be an apt description of the kinds of drawings scenographers make, and *computer scenographics* the best designation for the drawings computer users create. This brings us to the underlying question the present text addresses: *Do scenographers trained in traditionally grounded crafts, skills, and production philosophies need computers and computer technology?* This book is a highly personal answer to that question from one who thinks they do.

As a graphic artist with a traditional art school education, I do not envision the day I throw out my pencils and pastels, pens and ink, paints and brushes, or clear from my studio the countless items of equipment, files of images, or the physical records of past projects. Nor will I relegate to the dumpster those many boxes of impedimenta accumulated during the past forty years of scenographic practice. I have lived too long with these possessions to do without them now; they form too great a part of my life to casually give them over. These material things are integral parts of daily work. They are trusted for what they have done before, for what they still do today. More importantly, these tangible materials and tools link me to artists of the past and to their accomplishments.

Too often, however, the pace of traditional scenographic craft runs counter to the demands of modern theater production. Present-day scenography requires not only artistic skill but also an ability to communicate quickly and accurately abstract ideas to others in visual form. By adopting computer technology into my studio, I have found ways to communicate my ideas to others not only as accomplished facts but as changeable options. More important, the computer provides me with methods to better incorporate the opinions and desires of others into the evolution of my own concepts and decisions. These interchanges, moreover, are accomplished more quickly than previously possible. The computer, I have discovered, facilitates communication. For this main reason, I have incorporated the computer into my everyday scenographic practice.

In my previous books—*Scenographic Imagination* and *Theory and Craft of the Scenographic Model*—I concentrated on the ways a scenographer's mind works during conceptual stages of design projects; in both books practicalities of scenographic craft were secondary to that main intention. Using the methods proposed in those works, it was often possible to separate conceptual work from craft accomplishment. In computer graphics, however, concept and technology are interdependent; conceptual investigation and practical application cannot easily be separated. There is little doubt that the scenographer using computers must be prepared to jettison old patterns of thought and learn new ways of working.

In the past, computers were too expensive to own and too difficult for use in day-to-day scenographic work. This situation has changed dramatically; increasingly computers play a vital part in scenographic work. Since the mid-1980s, computer graphics have become practical options for working scenographers. Mirroring this trend, schools, colleges, and universities continue to add instruction to their curriculum and equipment to their facilities using computers in every area of design research, technical drawing, and scenographic craft.

Although I am convinced that computers will play an increasingly greater part during the training and in the practice of future scenographers, thus far little information as to how computers aid scenographic design exists. It is my hope that the present work adds to that now available. While this book gives general information, its main purpose is to instruct scenographic students now in training. It does not, however, demonstrate the *how to* of computer graphics; nor does it address all computer programs. No such book is possible. No encyclopedic view of computer graphics is given or intended. Such a project is not feasible in a book of any length much less the present one. A general introduction *to,* and an appreciation *of,* computer graphics for both student and working scenographers is, on the other hand, attainable; that is the present goal. To accomplish this objective, the text addresses four major areas. These are:

1. How computer studios are set up. Suggestions for equipment and recommendations of specific programs are also discussed.

2. How computers are used both as conceptual tools and as storage for visual ideas and research materials. Computers have been used primarily as recordkeepers and word processors. They now extend these capabilities to include design experimentation.

3. How technical information needed for producing a scenographer's ideas on stage is created with computers. In this section, various forms of scaled working drawings—floor plans, elevations, orthographic projections—are also discussed. The use of templates to facilitate scenographic design is explained and demonstrated.

4. How modelmaking has been changed by computer-generated three-dimensional possibilities, especially by the introduction of *virtual reality* onto the small computer platform. In many ways, chapter 4 is a sequel to *Theory and Craft of the Scenographic Model;* both concern the making and use of scenographic models.

The images accompanying the text were created on a Macintosh IIci and a Macintosh IIsi with 8 megabytes (MB) of RAM (with a math coprocessor added to the IIsi to increase its power to more quickly process computer graphic equations) displayed on a Radius monochrome two-page monitor. The text of the book was written on a Macintosh SE and IIci.

Use of this book assumes that both equipment and programs suggested in the following chapters are available to the reader.

Computer
Scenographics

Introduction

Although Filippo Brunelleschi, in about 1413, was the first artist to demonstrate to a wide audience how perspective is calculated in two-dimensional drawings, it was not until 1435 that a systematic set of principles was assembled in written form. These principles, articulated by Leon Baptista Alberti—architect, painter, writer, and scientist—anticipate the investigations of Leonardo da Vinci, born seventeen years after Alberti's work appeared. It will take almost a century, however, from Brunelleschi's first experiments before Albrecht Dürer produces a book—*The Art of Measurement,* 1525—detailing mechanical devices that show artists how perspective works. Prominent in Dürer's study are four plates showing these mechanical drawing devices. To the modern eye, these contrivances—like that shown in *A Man Drawing a Lute* (fig. 1)—have a curiously antiquated charm; they appear to our modern eye more toys for play than seriously intended tools for drawing. Nor do we actually know how artists of the day used them in their work.

The fact that Dürer devoted considerable time in his treatise to illustrating these machines gives credence to the assumption that he—along with his contemporaries—considered mechanical aids as legitimate extensions to drawing practices. To what extent he considered them alternatives to traditional drawing practices is not entirely clear; nor do we know if he actually used such devices in his own work. It is very possible that Leonardo da Vinci's *perspectograph*—a machine documented in his notebooks—was the prototypical model for those Dürer includes in *The Art of Measurement*. Figure 2 shows a modern diagrammatic view of the device Dürer probably saw during his visit to Leonardo in Venice in 1498.

To what extent, it is legitimate to ask, have these long-dead experimenters influenced the thought of modern-day computer technologists? Did these machines produce more *accurate* drawings—if indeed that was the sole purpose behind the experimentation evidenced—or did other motives exist? The most important of the possible reasons is that many important artists of the Renaissance—as Dürer and Leonardo demonstrate—sought every way to extend the craft of drawing. They searched out, it is evident, the most advanced technological solutions at the time in order to provide better explanations of drawing principles. It was certainly not from artistic inadequacy that Dürer or Leonardo needed aid, since both were consummate draftsmen. Dürer even notes in the text of his

Fig. 1. Man drawing a lute

book that *"such* [a device] *is good for all those who wish to make a portrait, but who cannot trust their skill."*

What purpose, then, lay behind the need to devise and use these admittedly cumbersome machines? Why should any artist invest valuable time and effort to seek out mechanical solutions to artistic problems? Why not, in short, simply rely on the trained eye and the skilled hand?

The answers to these questions are not nearly as important as the fact that the documents that have come down to us are the very first instances in the history of graphic art where artists attempt to produce accurately perceived images through technological procedures. These machines predict the modern computer. They anticipate by nearly half a millennium the techniques we know today as digitizing of information and ray-tracing of images; in figure 1 these fundamental principles of computer graphics drawing are prophetically apparent.

Some five hundred years later, graphic artists use computers for basically the same reasons that captured the attention of Dürer and Leonardo: the ability to achieve more accurately on two-dimensional planes objects that exist in three-dimensional worlds. It is especially important to note that the intention of artists using any machines is not to produce artistically edited expressions of what is seen but, rather, to *reproduce* a mechanically accurate view of what the physical eye sees. This is not, of course, the goal of all graphic artists, but it is the main thrust of scenographic drawing inasmuch as drawing for scenographic design is a means to an end, not the end itself. In *Drawing Systems,* by Fred Dubery and John Willats, we are reminded that

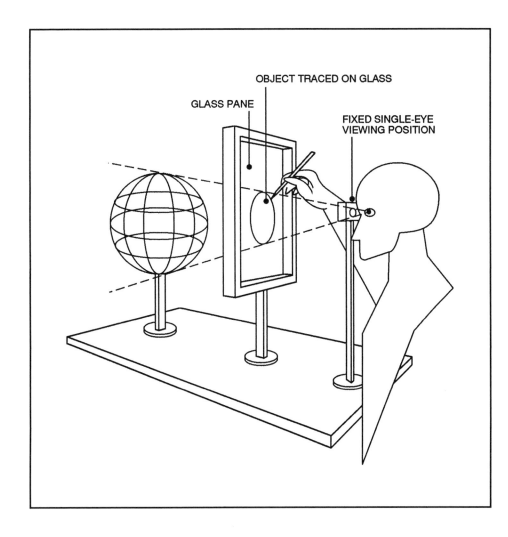

OBJECT TRACED ON GLASS

GLASS PANE

FIXED SINGLE-EYE
VIEWING POSITION

Fig. 2. Diagram of Leonardo's drawing machine

Students in the fields of engineering, architecture, industrial design, cartography, painting and sculpture—that is, fields whose language is partly or wholly visual—are inclined to use drawing systems traditional to those fields, without considering how appropriate they may be to a particular problem. The great changes which have occurred in these fields, together with changes in the mechanics of visual presentation through photography *and the computer, seem to call for a critical re-examination of the utility of the various drawing systems*. (Italics mine.) (Fred Dubery and John Willats, *Drawing Systems* [New York: Studio Vista, 1972])

In the past, the scenographer's tools and materials have been all-but-invisible interfaces bridging ephemeral concepts and physical results; usually they are considered in terms of immediate usefulness, if considered at all. That tools could also be important participants in the creative processes linking these worlds did not consciously surface before the advent of the computer. Is such a hypothesis reasonable to pursue? Can machines actively participate in human creativity? These are questions we need to consider carefully if not answer fully.

The ability of the computer to quickly and efficiently organize information is well known and widely accepted; its capability to use information creatively is less appreciated and remains a largely unexplored area of study. Computers have not, it is fair to say, been considered integral to the artist's conceptual processes; they have been more at home in business offices than in artist's studios. A computer's phenomenal speed and reliability, in fact, blinds many potential users to the ways these machines are able to explore the random possibilities of vision and thinking that are central to creative work. There are many scenographers—myself among them—who would not want to use computers exclusively in the preparation of their design; most of us continue to place value on the manual skills of drawing and painting learned and perfected over time and see no value in abandoning these skills entirely. The direct pen or brush stroke leaves personal marks on the papers and boards we use that we have come to trust. It is doubtful that the most powerful computer or most sophisticated computer program can supplant that intimate interaction of hand and mind physical tools and materials provide. Seductive as the precision and speed of computer graphics are, the best computer graphics program cannot replace those feelings of accomplishment experienced when renderings turn out well or finished models provide new insights. There are no good reasons, however, why a balance between old methods of work inherited from the past cannot be incorporated into the new capabilities that computer technology provides.

Will scenographers who master computer graphics complete projects more quickly than they have in the past? Do computers actually save time? Probably not; a design for the stage has built into it internal clocks that begin at the start of a project and that run until the project is complete. These time spans are not altered significantly by technological intervention. To determine whether time is saved or wasted depends more on the effectiveness of the individual artist than it does with arbitrary assignments of time allocations to steps in a process. Hypothetical stopwatches by which these steps are accurately measured simply do not exist. The real value of computers lies not in their ability to *save* hypothetical quantities of time but in the ways they allow graphic information to be presented to others more effectively.

The concerns we should address are to what extent will computers permit abstract concepts of the scenographer to be captured in communicative form and, subsequently, to what extent are resulting images modifiable as necessity demands. To find how these aims are accomplished, we must first clear away some of myths and preconceptions that became established as computer technology evolved.

From its inception, the computer has had the reputation of incomprehensible complexity accompanied by an innate malevolence. Those who remember Stanley Kubrick's *2001* may forget many details of its plot; few, however, can forget HAL, the malevolent computer. From their beginnings, computers have seemed inhumanly aloof and remote from human concerns. As the butt of myriad cartoons and as the all-too-frequently blamed source of most of our present-day ills, computers and the arcane technology that supports them have provided the main metaphor for that hostile world of the future where authoritarian commands are executed at incredible speeds while human concerns are lost in vast electronic labyrinths. At the start of our study, therefore, we need to understand that both *computer* and *technology* are simply words describing important aspects of twentieth-century human ingenuity, not negative code words to mysterious and arcane worlds controlled by selected initiates. *Technique* and *technology* are, in fact, closely linked; they both come from the Greek words *technikon* and *technikos*. *Technique* is a word, moreover, crucial to every working artist's vocabulary; as a concept it bears no particularly hostile implication as is frequently attributed to the concept of technology. *Technology*, on the other hand, is more apt to bear sinister overtones; often it is considered as an independent entity brought into being by faceless persons disdainful of those who rely on it. *Technology* means nothing more than adopting suitable tools and practices to achieve specific goals. We should never forget that artists have always sought new ways to do old tasks.

Will this new technology actually help the scenographer to be more creative or to work more quickly and effectively? In the past, scenographers accomplished their work in two primary ways: showing ideas as hand-drawn graphic images or, using other materials and techniques, creating three-dimensional forms as models of external realities. Unlike most other visual artists, scenographers do not have as an ultimate goal the making of self-contained creative works of art; their primary skill lies in assembling or fashioning objects and materials that simulate experiences perceived in time and space by living performers. In *The Empty Space,* Peter Brook defines the scenographer's task in this way:

> Art lovers can never understand why all stage designing isn't done by "great" painters and sculptors. What is necessary, however, is an incomplete design: a design that has clarity without rigidity; one that could be called "open" as against "shut." This is the essence of theatrical thinking: a true theatre designer will think of his designs as being all the time in motion, in action, in relation to what the actor brings to a scene as it unfolds. In other words, unlike the easel painter, in two dimensions, or the sculptor in three, the designer thinks in terms of the fourth dimension, the passage of time—not the stage picture, but the stage moving picture. A film editor shapes his material after the event: the stage designer is often like the editor of an Alice-Through-the-Looking-Glass film, cutting dynamic material in shapes, before this material has yet come into being. The later he makes his decisions the better. (Peter Brook, *The Empty Space* [New York: Avon Books, 1969])

All scenographers and directors know that the ability to alter images quickly and accurately is as important as it is to imagine them in the first place. Until recently, scenographers have relied on skill with pen or pencil to show coworkers the graphic processes that underlie a scenographic design. The relationship of these drawn images to proposed ideas has been only as effective as the individual scenographer's drawing skill. Even the best drawers, however, produce crude approximations of proposed schemes at these conferences. With the advent of the computer, new effective ways become available to scenographers, directors, and technical staff needing to explore ideas. Computers have given scenographers not only ways to draw in two dimensions but also a means to create accurate representations of the third. The computer makes the interaction of concept and image as flexible and as fluid as the conversations that engender them. How this desired result is reached—what tools are required and what skills need to be learned—is the main subject of this book.

To some extent, the concept of *drawing* will have to be redefined, since the essence of this book's message is that the computer is not simply an·alternative tool to make static images but is also a means to explore three-dimensional spaces simultaneously as we create two-dimensional graphics. Entirely new ways of working, it is clear, must be learned if scenographers are to successfully master these new possibilities, because, unlike drawing on paper with pencil or pen and ink, the computer screen is as mutable as our thoughts and can alternate seamlessly between the "flat" ideas of working plans and photographically correct three-dimensional images.

During the late 1980s computers began to lose much of their inscrutable mystique as graphics programs increasingly became more intuitive and accessible. Only since 1985 have graphic artists been able to obtain programs that allow them to freely experiment. Although sophisticated technology lies at the heart of any computer activity, until recently truly creative programs have not been available to graphic artists. In tandem with the development of sophisticated programs has been a revolution in the interface design that makes these programs easier to understand and use. Computers are becoming more comprehensible to those who, until now, were confused with the often Byzantine routines computers of the past required. As a result of constantly improved interface design, graphic artists are increasingly finding they can transfer drawing skills learned in art school classrooms to computer screens.

A primary goal of this book is to draw attention to some significant changes to traditional scenographic procedures that computer technology causes. To be candid, I have encountered designers who consider the use of any electronic device in the design process a degradation of scenographic art; a betrayal of the traditional consort of hand and mind. Although trained as a traditional painter and sculptor, I obviously take exception to this view. Further, I believe that the speculations and procedures advanced in the following pages are worthy of careful attention and study by all innovative scenographers, especially those now in training. I also hold that since the mechanism of thinking is fundamentally a matter of electrical impulses fired in the brain, the use of the computer is a defensibly logical means to access the creative imagination, not an abrogation of it. Nor am I alone in this assessment.

In *Opera News*, Denise Tilles reports that the British scenographer William Dudley sees the possibilities of the computer as a creative tool. She writes, "When scenic designer Bill Dudley speaks about the work he creates on the computer for companies such as the Metropolitan Opera and Bayreuth, he speaks in religious metaphors. 'When I first saw a graphic designer work on the Macintosh two years ago,' Dudley recalls, 'it was like Saul on the road to Damascus.' Dudley, who always had worked in the traditional scenic artist's manner—making a sketch, putting a grid over it, drawing by hand over that and then tediously hand-painting—is taken completely with computer designing. 'In my first year of owning a Macintosh system, I became almost an evangelist for it,' the designer says. 'It's my pleasure and delight, really. I've almost had to be dragged away from the screen to go out into the real world.' . . . Dudley credits his use of the computer as artistically liberating, as well as saving both time and money. Since 1990 he has been using his Macintosh IIFX and various . . . software programs for both opera and theater. Specifically, he uses 'image manipulation' software, with which a designer can create two-dimensional representations. . . . Dudley's ardent support of the computer, he sadly notes, is not shared by most of his peers. 'I would tell colleagues about working with the computer, but nobody was interested. I've told people, particularly young designers, "Don't be afraid of using the computer," and they say, "I'd rather use my pencil, thank you very much," like an ostrich that's buried its head in the sand. My thesis is that you can actually loosen up and be freer, experiment more and use more ideas. People say, "But I like the accidental things that happen while designing." On the computer, you've got an incredible amount of accidental things that can happen.'"

Like William Dudley, I am convinced that the computer is an important addition to the scenographer's art and craft; I also share his childlike fascination with the possibilities of this amazing machine. Yet my admiration is tempered with the realization that I remain bounded by the limits of the creative abilities learned in traditional painting and drawing classes fashioned by traditional tools and traditional techniques. Nor do I ever forget that no matter how much my computer gives a gloss of accuracy to drawing or how much it increases the raw speed of work done, as an artist I am not much changed. Computers can improve working skills; they do, for example, make many irritatingly tedious mechanical tasks less onerous. To these gains, it must be admitted, is added a serendipitous pleasure of *play;* an element most creative artists not only share but count upon. The random nature of electronic patterns formed on the screen invites experimentation. In addition, computers let the mind wander along paths it might not take using more traditional materials and techniques. To that extent, computers can be considered *conceptual tools*; tools that widen the spectrum of imagination. I am especially pleased that others are beginning to share my enthusiasm for this aspect of computer possibility.

Although this book is introductory in nature, only demonstrations showing how traditional relationships between theater artists can be made more productive by using computer technology will be included. These new relationships exist under a general rubric of *interactive scenographics*. What does this term—*interactive scenographics*—mean? How do these new working relationships differ from those of the past? These are basic questions we address in the pages that follow.

We who work for the theater live in a time not unlike that of the Renaissance; great changes are taking place. It would be shortsighted for scenographers working in today's theater not to seek out any new technological means that makes the hand more responsive to the mind's direction. Still, we should never forget that the computer is only a tool. It is a highly sophisticated tool; a tool whose speed and accuracy cannot be matched by the most skillful of those who use it. It is also a fascinatingly complex piece of technology, a marvel of electronic engineering, a machine that continually surprises and frequently astounds its users by performing thousands of intricately complex calculations at the speed of light. And yet, for all the marvelous things it is able to do, there is one thing beyond the most sophisticated of computers: *it cannot think*. At the door of a new millennium, there are still many who have an unreasonable fear of the computer's potentialities. Of its own volition, a computer is unable to type a single letter or draw the shortest line without some human mind telling it to do so. Without a human mind to determine a purpose or write a program to instruct it how to accomplish the task, the computer has no more intellect than an equally sized lump of stone. At the start of our study, therefore, let us constantly keep in view that no matter how much the computer aids us today, no matter how much it infiltrates our working lives tomorrow, the best of computers employing the most complex of programs will not make our work more creative than the mind that guides it. What is presented in the following pages cannot make one a better scenographer; what is found there may, however, help to become a more productive one.

A NOTE ON COMPUTER TERMS: At the present time there are more than forty-five hundred computer terms in existence. The list grows daily. Many of these terms are familiar words used in new, often unfamiliar contexts. Many of these terms are acronyms; words that compress whole concepts into a single new term: RAM and ROM are good examples as are *modem* (an abbreviation of a modulator/demodulator device) and *PostScript* (a page-description language developed by Adobe Systems that offers flexible font capability and high-quality graphics). Some words result from the dismantlement and reassembly of common words, the common computer term *pixel* being a good example (it is composed of two words: *picture* and *element*). The entire world of computer terminology borders on conditions that must have prevailed in the Tower of Babel. Those who happen onto a group of computer devotees invariably find their common interchange to be a freely composed language of letters, numbers, and code words—an arcane jargon to the uninitiated.

How then, does one keep up with the ever-shifting semantic landscape computer users cannot avoid? One cannot. Still, as with any other foreign tongue, it must be learned if understanding is to be achieved. Much of this necessary education happens as familiarity with computers and programs increases; the most important part of a computer erudition takes place as an absorption process that mirrors the way we learn as children. Performing actions imparted through a program's tutorial instruction is the chief way we learn; we come to know a term, an action, or a concept often without consciously realizing that we have done so. At other times, however, nothing will do but to look up what we need to know in a written source. Most traditional dictionaries do not help much. What is needed, instead, is a dictionary exclusively devoted to computer terms and concepts. Fortunately, such works are increasingly available. As in any other developing field, these works vary in usefulness. Among the best of these computer dictionaries available is a Microsoft Press publication simply called *Computer Dictionary* (Redmond, WA, 1991). It is a recommended adjunct text for this book.

Basic Computer Graphics Technical Requirements and Concepts

1

The physical scenographic studio is a place large enough to hold drawings boards, chairs, tables, and storage cabinets along with requisite tools and supplies needed to create two-dimensional and three-dimensional scenographic design information. Normally, over time, these work areas increase to accommodate the scenographer's ever-growing accumulations of physical things.

Electronic studios, on the other hand, run counter to this trend. Defined in terms of programs, computer memory, and relatively small peripheral devices that extend a computer's basic possibilities, these studios exist in spaces no larger than typically sized desk tops. As equipment becomes more sophisticated and powerful, these studios actually shrink in size rather than grow. In the computer studio, screens become drawing boards. They also serve as—sometimes replace—traditional light boxes for tracing images. Program interfaces become the doors to electronic tool rooms, making physical workshop areas sometimes unnecessary. Within small areas of space, electronic three-dimensional models are constructed, dismantled and reassembled, or replaced with newer models. The electronic studio also functions as an extensive filing system; it is a library storing vast collections of images and written texts; it imports, creates, and stores records of every kind. In tandem with CD-ROMs players, computers give access to libraries—both physical and electronic—in distant places. A computer shows its stored materials to a single person, a network of others, or—using external projection equipment—display words and images to an auditorium of viewers. Moreover, computer images can be static or animated; with peripheral equipment, television signals can be captured. And if all these marvels were not enough, with additional accessories, computer studios become communications centers capable of communicating words and images around the world at the speed of light.

The question is, Will the computer studio of the future replace entirely the physical studio of the the past? The answer is, Not for the foreseeable future; perhaps not as long

The Computer Scenographics Studio

as scenographic design is practiced. Despite the extensive possibilities of the electronic studios just discussed, the familiar studio of paper and paint, balsa wood, cardboard, and glue will remain the primary working environment for most scenographers. Be warned, however, that although such studios will not soon disappear, scenographers of tomorrow must expect an increasing incursion of computer technology into these traditional work-places; the studio of tomorrow will be, most certainly, a different one from those of the past. Therein lies the underlying question of this book, How best to plan for, and bring about, this new amalgamation of physical and electronic possibility; for, notwithstanding the modest spatial demands of electronic technology, the introduction of computers into the scenographer's studio requires a careful planning of the physical available space. Although computer *software* takes little physical space, the *hardware*—equipment needed to implement that *software*—is not as easily accommodated. Reconsideration of all established studio procedures is necessary for computers and their peripheral equipment. Special attention must also be given to the working environment created by electronic gear. Computer work is stressful—even dangerous to general health—when studio ergonomics are neglected. Planning of electronic studios should always begin with a detailed reexamination of the scenographer's traditional working areas and working patterns.

The General Studio Area

The working space of the scenographer is an important factor in the practice of scenographic craft, since the physical layout of the studio invariably affects the productivity of what is produced there. The physical requirements of these places are many and varied. A studio is not only a shop where physical things are made, but also a sanctuary where intentions originate, develop, and—all too often—must be discarded. Studios vary as greatly as do the scenographers working in them; no two are the same. Some are as Spartan as a Greek ruin, others as orderly as a hospital operating room; others still are as chaotically evocative as Miss Haversham's dining room. The common thread that runs through all, however, is that these are places that are fashioned to do highly specialized kinds of work.

How do these places come into being? There is no good way to predict how efficient studios evolve; no master plan assures their effectiveness. Since no two scenographers have identical work patterns, the distinctive way each designer works accounts more for the variations encountered from studio to studio than do architectural differences. Time, the random accumulation of tools and materials, the personalities of individual artists who work in them, all contribute to the creation of a successful scenographic studio. Nevertheless, most have some features in common. These are best seen as demands peculiar to scenographic work expressed in particularized work areas. In the following section we take a closer look at what some of these demands are, how they are met, and speculate on what happens to the traditional scenographic studio as electronic gear is introduced. Let us begin with a general examination of studios in general.

The Manual Graphics Studio

Figure 3 shows a diagrammatic plan of individual studio areas needed for construction of scenographic projects. The functions of the individual areas are:

A. A place to make finished sketches—watercolor, pastel, pen and ink, and so on: Storage of expendable materials should be kept in immediate proximity to the working

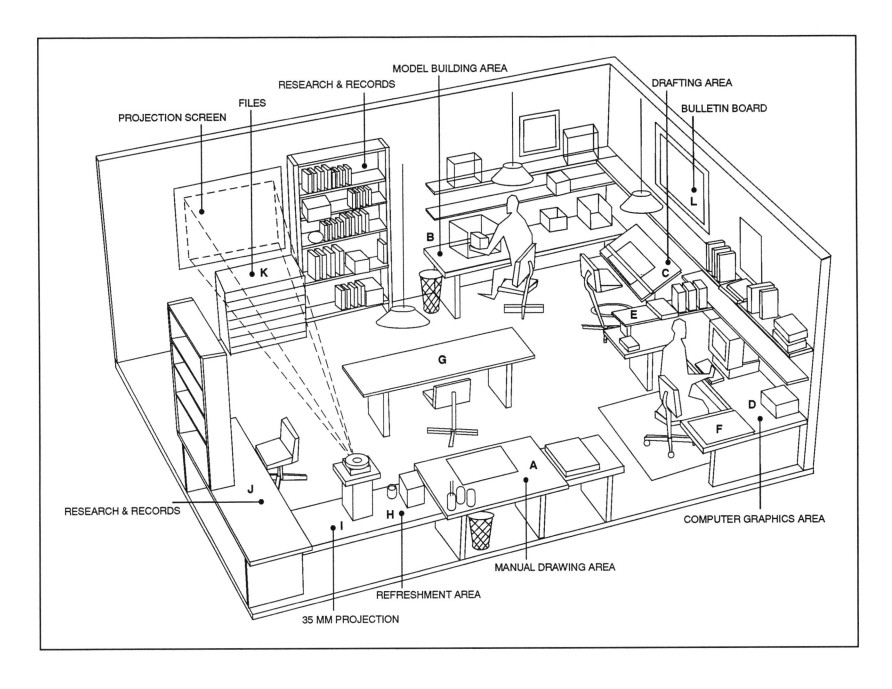

PROJECTION SCREEN

FILES

RESEARCH & RECORDS

MODEL BUILDING AREA

DRAFTING AREA

BULLETIN BOARD

RESEARCH & RECORDS

35 MM PROJECTION

REFRESHMENT AREA

MANUAL DRAWING AREA

COMPUTER GRAPHICS AREA

area but not in it. Open shelving is the most effective way to keep track of what is in stock or what is needed.

B. A place to create and experiment with scenographic models: To keep materials in stock and tools within reach is such an obvious recommendation that few scenographers think about it. Nevertheless, it is important to reiterate this recommendation, since years of instructing others in scenographic design convinces me that it is as important to teach

Fig. 3. Diagram of scenographic studio

approaches and *attitudes* to work as it is to teach *methods* of accomplishment. Instrument and material layouts are carefully planned in hospital operating rooms, even taught in medical schools, and although the consequences of sloppy procedure in a scenographer's studio are not as devastating as they would would be in a hospital operating room, a disorganized studio almost always results in haphazard approaches to projects done in it. A certain amount of creative disorder will always exist in the working scenographer's workplace, but quality work is not possible in chaotic conditions. Period.

C. A place to draft manual working specifications: The drafting table should be covered with replaceable drafting-table materials; most usually the material used is a smooth light green plastic with white backing. Drafting-table coverings have relatively soft front surfaces to facilitate manual drawing. Regardless of the drafting table's basic surface, it will be quickly and permanently damaged if used unprotected. The nature of the covering material, moreover, is such that the drawing quality of drafting done on it is improved. Some coverings are made to withstand the cutting of paper or cardboard materials. This is not advisable even if the manufacturer claims it is acceptable to do so. Although they are relatively expensive, pads especially made for cutting should be used instead. It is also advisable to keep a large roll of brown paper to be used over this covering when painting scenic sketches, for example. Covering the entire working surface with this paper is particularly necessary when using good pastels; the dust from these extremely soft materials spreads over everything not covered.

D. An area devoted to computer work: The computer graphics area is discussed in detail below under "The Computer Graphics Workstation."

E. Storage space: As recommended above, open shelving above work areas is the preferred way to keep in touch with necessary materials and frequently used tools. Keeping work spaces unencumbered is an especially annoying problem when creating complex projects. Open shelving is particularly advantageous for the computer graphics area of the studio, since even the most seasoned computer user occasionally needs to find how a little-used procedure in a program is approached. Manuals and information concerning computer graphics, for this reason, should be kept near to hand.

F. A hard-copy work area with a large-size cutting pad: Cutting and assembling images before scanning or after printing hard copies of screen graphics necessitate a work area close to the computer workstation. While the cutting area does not need to be as large as that for modelmaking or for making large working-drawing details, it should not be restricted if accurate cutting is expected and accidents avoided. Since most scenographers do not have large-page plotters, but instead assemble large drawings from smaller printed parts, this area should have plenty of elbow room.

G. An area for all-purpose working and planning: A large general worktable on which to lay out work in progress or to make large-sheet working drawings is an absolute necessity for a working studio. A centrally placed table is also necessary for conferences or discussions of work in process.

H. Refreshment area: Although not an absolute necessity, an area set aside for coffee or tea making for occasional breaks from work on a project is a highly recommended feature of any well-planned studio. These breaks are especially advised for scenographers working long hours on the computer, since they not only diffuse stress from eyestrain and repetitive wrist movement but frequently promote fresh views of work being done.

I. Area for 35-mm projector and screen for viewing 35-mm slides.

J. Areas for storage of reference books, records, file clippings, catalogs; computer disk storage; working drawings; sketches and set drawings; drawing materials, drafting supplies, model materials; finished models; slides and projections. Shelving that is adjustable and capable of expansion is a necessity for any active scenographer.

K. Storage for flat materials and finished flat work: Flat storage is essential to the professional scenographer. Most drafting tables have immediate storage for drafting paper in the table itself. It is possible to obtain—although usually quite expensive—individual drawers that stack on old units as new flat storage drawers are acquired.

L. Bulletin boards: Display areas for current ideas, works in progress, notes, schedules, etc., near working areas. In most working scenographer's studios, an important feature is a place to keep images, notes, schedules, and like materials, directly in view. At times, the materials put there are necessary to the immediate problems of a project; at other times, these materials simply act as inspirational reminders concerning projects at hand or future projects being contemplated.

Even though computers facilitate design conceptualization as well as mechanical realization, electronic studios still require many of the same tools and materials that are found in traditional scenographic studios. Every scenographic studio, therefore, should be equipped with the following (see figure 4 diagram):

A. Permanent drafting equipment (not shown): T square; triangles; architectural scales (flat scales, while having fewer scales on the unit and relatively more expensive, are preferable to triangular scales), straight edges, templates and curves, flexible curves, mechanical pencils, mechanical pencil sharpeners, mechanical drawing tools, drafting brush.

B. Drafting or technical pens in various line sizes: Most graphic artists have in their studio a set of these indispensable instruments. Within the metal sheath of the pen point is a fine metal filament tipped with a hard-wearing point. Individual pens are made to draw lines in various widths. Although these pens can be purchased individually, buying them as a matched set is advisable, since it allows the artist to draw a wide range of lines. A set of pens, however, is a sizable investment, and for that reason care should be used in their selection. Koh-I-Noor is a reliable maker of these instruments. Rapidograph 3165 Technical Pens, Series I—the trade name of Koh-I-Noor's product are obtainable in 13 separate line widths ranging from 0.13 mm to 2.00 mm. This company also offers a more expensive line of pens known as 3165 Jewel Pen. The advantage of the higher-priced pen is that it has a self-polishing abrasive resistant jewel point made of a hard acid-resistant material that makes it usable on drafting film and on other glossy surfaces like computer-generated transparencies.

C. Permanent tools for scenic sketches (see figure 120 for a diagram showing tools and materials necessary).

D. Paper-cutting tools: A good pair of paper shears and slim-barreled X-acto knife,

Equipment and Materials of the Scenographic Studio

Permanent Tools and Equipment

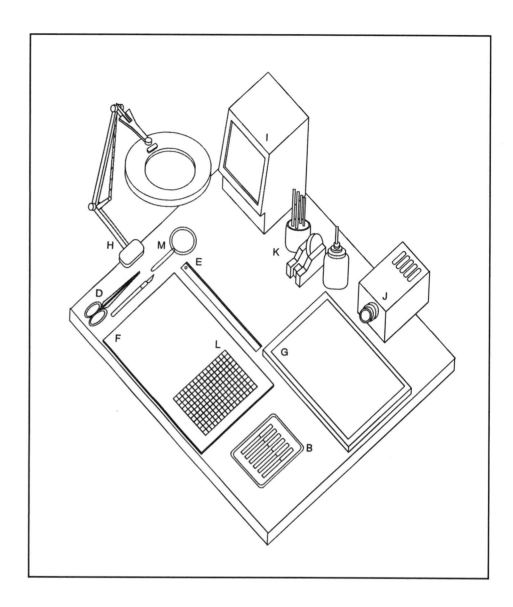

Fig. 4. Diagram of manual graphics area

using No. 11 blades, are the two most useful tools for cutting paper materials created on the computer. Since it is possible to print out paper model sections from elevation and plan files, these tools are used to cut out the model-section shapes for the paper model (fig. 92).

E. Steel-edge cutting rule: A fairly expensive tool that has only one function: to allow paper and board materials to be cut safely. Using the blade of a T square, the edges of plastic triangles, or even the metal edge of a steel ruler is courting seriously cut fingers. The steel-edged cutting rule, on the other hand, is a heavy piece of hard steel that usually has a slightly beveled edge that allows for safe, accurate cutting.

F. Self-healing cutting pad: These pads are made of a plastic substance that allow for the cutting of paper materials with sharp blades with very little damage to the surface of the pad below.

G. A portable light box: Although light boxes are more generally found in studios where traditional graphics are done, no graphic designer should be without this helpful piece of equipment. While the computer screen acts in many instances like a light box—visible layers in drawing/painting programs acting in a similar manner as with an actual light boxes—there are times when hard copies of computer-generated files are treated as traditional graphics. The light box is helpful when seminal sketches are drawn that will later be scanned into the computer for conversion from bit-mapped images into high-resolution drawings. The light box—used with a magnifying glass of a magnifier lamp—also serves as a viewer for examining 35-mm slides and other kinds of transparencies. It is also extremely useful when painting slides for onstage projections.

H. A magnifier lamp: This is another studio acquisition that proves itself extremely useful in numerous instances, especially when image details are small and indistinct. This piece of equipment also serves as an easily controlled task light.

I. A tabletop slide viewer: Although not directly related to the production of computer graphics, these viewers are a good alternative to viewing past designs or slide research materials with more expensive 35-mm projectors that require an external viewing surface. An added attraction to using these units is that slides are viewed in ordinary light. About the most practical way of showing computer designs—especially color renderings—is through the making of slides of computer images. Although this must be done by someone with a slide maker, at the present time it is more practical than color printing. Making slides of proposed designs is an economical way of creating portfolios that are easy to carry or to send through the mails.

J. An opaque image projector: This piece of equipment is frequently found in traditional graphics studios. It is also useful in the various scenic shops as a means to translate the scenographer's plans into actual scenic structures; the images a computer drawing program produces are directly practicable using opaque projectors. It is also possible for computer images to be made into 35-mm slides; these, in turn, are used with 35-mm projectors in the same way as opaque projectors.

K. Paper assembly materials (not shown): Physical models derived from the computer are predominately constructed from ordinary paper or thin-stock materials. These models are primarily—although not exclusively—used as evolutionary steps toward the creating of conventionally made models. The materials used, therefore, tend to be those that allow quick or temporary assembly of cut-out printed sections. Masking tape, invisible (Magic) tape, and rubber cement or rubber cement sprays are recommended for paper modelmaking.

L. Transparent acetate grids: These grids can be purchased from any art supply store. They tend to be, however, expensive. It is recommended, therefore, that a needed grid is individually designed by the scenographer using computer drawing programs such as Canvas 3.5, a program that has in its Toolbox a grid-making option that creates grids with specifiable numbers of horizontal or vertical lines. This allows the scenographer to create grids in specific scales or with information deemed important. Finished templates are printed directly on overhead transparency film sheets by the laser printer. It is also possible to print out odd-scaled graph paper not available in art supply stores or—using office copiers—to make gridded overhead transparencies from these graph papers. Printing outlines of working drawings onto transparency film has numerous applications. It is also possible for perspective images from three-dimensional programs such as Virtus WalkThrough—a virtual reality program discussed in chapter 4—to be used with overhead projectors as painter's elevations when intricate perspective views must be transferred from a working drawing to actual full-scale backdrops (see figure 128).

M. Hand magnifying glass: Although the magnifier lamp listed above is a useful piece of equipment, the old-fashioned hand magnifying glass remains a staple of any well-equipped graphics studio. Although not applicable to computer screen viewing—most computer programs have magnification capabilities—magnifying glasses become useful once computer graphics are printed.

Expendable Materials

To successfully integrate computer graphics with traditional graphics, the following materials and studio supplies are necessary:

1. Drafting materials: tracing papers; erasers; drafting tapes; leads
2. Materials for scenic sketches: illustration boards; drawing pads; inexpensive sketch paper; tube watercolors; tempera; metallic colors; inks; pastels; Conte crayons; drawing pencils; watercolor pencils; fixative; tissues and small cotton cleaning rags
3. Collage and assemblages: found images; found flat materials that could include metal foils, flat-textured materials (cloth, plastics, etc.), string; glue binders (white glue, multipurpose modelmaking cement, gesso, modeling paste)
4. Materials for modelmaking: balsa woods, wire, various cords, metal materials, metal foils, glues, illustration board, Styrofoam, textile and wire cloth, found objects gesso, modeling paste

Although not evident from this brief examination of traditional tools that close links between traditional studios of the past and computer studios of the future exist, in actual practice these relationships quickly emerge. In "PICT Images from WalkThrough 1.1.3 Model Views," in chapter 4, techniques for integrating computer graphics with traditional techniques of rendering are discussed more fully; basic tools and materials needed for rendering mixed-media scenographic drawings are shown (fig. 120).

Scenographic Studio Lighting

A substantial documentation exists to attest that graphic artists of the past carefully considered the quality of light in their working areas; they knew that how these areas were lighted affected any work done in them. It is surprising that many artists today do not study this important influence as closely as they should. Perhaps the very abundance of lighting devices as well as the relatively inexpensive cost of light itself causes a disregard for adequately thinking over this most important subject. In William Atkinson's informative study, *Working at Home* (New York: Dow Jones-Irwin, 1985), John Bachner—a consultant to the National Lighting Bureau in Washington, DC—notes that "there is a direct relationship between lighting and productivity. By improving the visual environment, you improve visual performance of visual tasks, which include just about every task imaginable. You'll be able to work faster and with fewer errors."

Lighting for studios housing both computer workstations and manual graphics areas need careful planning, since each area has distinct prerequisites that are not always compatible. For traditional graphics work, general light must be provided throughout the entire area. Specific-task lighting, however, should augment the general lighting if drawings are to avoid shadows, since lighting appropriate for manual drawing areas almost always reflects light sources on computer screens. These reflections are stressful to computer users; often eye strain resulting from long exposure to screen glare occurs without conscious awareness on the part of the sufferer. "Many office employees complain," Bachner notes, "of too much light. In most cases, however, the complaint is usually a reaction to poor quality of light that creates glare. Direct glare leads to eye fatigue because muscles have to keep your eyes in proper focus in spite of the light. Your eye muscles continually adapt to minimize the problem, and after a while the muscles begin to get tender. This is when you experience eyeaches and headaches."

Screen glare, however, is only one of the scenographer's problems when planning studio lighting. Another difficulty arises when different work areas have different—often conflicting—light requirements. It is imperative, therefore, that the lighting of each area be carefully considered in respect to illumination's three basic attributes: *quantity of light, direction of sources, and quality of output*.

Different disadvantages attend different light technologies; incandescent bulbs, for instance, provide warmer more natural light but also cast relatively hard shadows. Light from incandescent sources creates distinct hot spots reflected off computer screens. Florescent light has fewer shadows, but—unless corrected—distorts color. Uncorrected fluorescent light gives false color values to scenic sketches, color elevations, and costume materials. This condition is partially corrected by adopting the same practice used in many scenic studios: construction areas have fluorescent lighting, while paint areas have incandescent light sources. This allows painters to see colors more nearly as they appear under theatrical lighting; scenery painted using typical fluorescent lighting distorts color. In addition, many studies show that a direct correlation between hyperactivity and fluorescent light exists; those who work in florescent light frequently show higher levels of both stress and fatigue.

To ensure that the proper levels of lighting are attained, see the table shown on page 18, "Lighting Considerations," which is excerpted from the National Lighting Bureau's booklet, *Lighting Energy Management for Offices and Office Buildings*.

The Computer Graphics Workstation

All visual theater workers know that the tools they depend on are only as accurate as the individual who employs them. Accuracy is a state of mind, not an automatic benefit of any tool or any technology no matter how careful its construction or sophisticated its engineering. Accuracy has always been and still remains the result of considered intent; the advent of the computer has done nothing to change this. The introduction of the computer into the theater artist's studio only makes it possible to realize that intent with

Lighting Considerations

Illuminance Categories and Illuminance Values for Generic Types of Activities Interiors

Type of Activity	Ranges of Illuminances (Footcandles)	Reference Work Plane
● Working spaces where visual tasks are only occasionally performed	10–15–20	General lighting throughout spaces
● Performance of visual tasks of high contrast or large size	20–30–50	Illuminance on task
● Performance of visual tasks of medium contrast or small size	50–75–100	
● Performance of visual tasks of low contrast or very small size	100–150–200	
● Performance of visual tasks of low contrast and very small size over a prolonged period	200–300–500	Illuminance on task, obtained by a combination of general and local (supplementary) lighting
● Performance of very prolonged and exacting visual tasks	500–750–1,000	
● Performance of very special visual tasks of extremely low contrast and small size	1,000–1,500–2,000	

Courtesy of the National Lighting Bureau

greater speed. The human appreciation of exactitude, in fact, is the prime attribute that makes computers possible, not the reverse. A computer remembers only what it has been programmed to remember, does only what it is instructed to do. The best of computers mirrors the intelligence of its user; computer accuracy is never greater than its employer's ability to discern and appreciate it. It is best to disabuse ourselves early of the idea that computers will create our designs. It can no more do that than it can think for us.

It is safe to assume that most scenographers training today will devote a portion of their studio work area to a graphics workstation. But just what does this mean? And what is a *workstation*?

In the *Dictionary of Computer Terms*, a small book highly recommended for its concise explanations of many computer terms and concepts, the word *workstation* is defined as follows:

> WORKSTATION: A workstation is an extremely powerful micro-computer typically used for scientific and engineering calculations. Two of the largest manufacturers of workstations are Sun Microsystems and Apollo. (Douglas Downing and Michael Covington, *Dictionary of Computer Terms*, 2d ed. [Hauppauge, NY: Barron, 1989])

During the past few years there has come to be a broader definition of what makes up workstations. The freer use of the term now allows that any personal system of computer hardware, additional tools or equipment used with it, as well as the physical supporting structures these things require—desks, chairs, files—can be considered a workstation. This more extensive definition is adopted throughout the present text.

Even the most basic of equipment and the most inexpensive of applications represents a sizable investment for most beginning scenographers. Many students training today have access to some equipment and to some applications; many schools have invested in both hardware and graphics programs. What is shown in figure 5, is the workstation assembled in my own studio. Figure 6 gives a more diagrammatic view of a basic layout for a workstation suited to scenographic work. The basic hardware illustrated and the additional items of equipment have been selected not only for their usefulness and reliability but also for their affordability. In terms of possible equipment, what is shown in figures 5 and 6 lies near the low end of available technology; at the same time, the equipment included in this personal workstation is not the most basic: it would be possible to produce computer graphics with fewer technical resources, but only at a significant reduction in the speed of accomplishment. The layout shown seems to me a reasonable possibility for an established single scenographer; it would not serve as well for large design studios such as those found, for instance, in cinema or television production centers. In some cases the software applications (the name given to the programs that generate the actual graphics on the computer) listed represents the low end of the possibilities available for graphic design. For the most part, however, the programs recommended represent the best possible for the work discussed in this text. While the costs of hardware and software are, and will probably remain, high for sometime still, the history of both is one that should give hope to the scenographers training today; costs of hardware and applications tend to decrease as the technology that makes them possible becomes older and more widespread. Competition in the world of computers and computer technology is a force that eventually works to the advantage of the buyer, and original development costs tend to be reflected in earlier versions of any piece of technology or in any program used by such equipment. A distinct advantage of purchasing programs from a dealer is that when they are upgraded—that is, improved by additional functions or workability—the registered owner has the option of obtaining these at a fraction of the list cost of the new version. It is generally possible to order most programs from large merchandising organizations at greatly reduced costs.

The workstation is actually a graphics studio in miniature; almost all tools found there, or functions performed by them in actual physical studios, have parallel tools or

Fig. 5. Computer workstation

drawing functions residing in this physically smaller, markedly different environment. In the traditional studio, tools made of solid materials—wood, steel, aluminum, plastic,—are employed. These can be placed in immediate surroundings or stored in distant places. The "tools" used in the computer graphics studio, on the other hand, are virtually nonexistent; at best they are little more than transient electrical impulses systematically encoded into a computer program's permanent memory. As such they are employed to produce

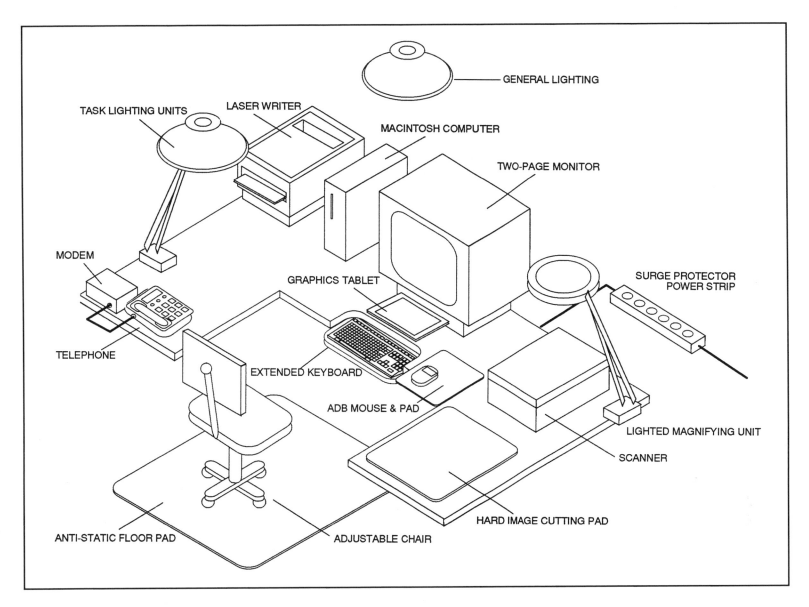

GENERAL LIGHTING

TASK LIGHTING UNITS

LASER WRITER

MACINTOSH COMPUTER

TWO-PAGE MONITOR

MODEM

GRAPHICS TABLET

SURGE PROTECTOR
POWER STRIP

TELEPHONE

EXTENDED KEYBOARD

ADB MOUSE & PAD

LIGHTED MAGNIFYING UNIT

SCANNER

ANTI-STATIC FLOOR PAD

ADJUSTABLE CHAIR

HARD IMAGE CUTTING PAD

temporary images on electronically charged viewing screens; computer tools are really only the effects of electrons that have no counterpart in the physical world. Computer tools are, in other words, only integral functions of particular software applications, which we buy, created by computer programmers who encoded them. These tools are, more precisely, sophisticated mathematical calculations traveling along electrical paths; as such they can only be understood in terms of metaphorical symbols taken from our real world of previous experiences and associations.

It is remarkable that the human brain so quickly and so completely assimilates, as well as productively uses, systems so fundamentally at odds with tactile experience and conceptual understanding. Considering just how strange the difference between physical

Fig. 6. Diagram of computer workstation

tools and electronic tools are does, however, help us appreciate, if not fully understand, why some computer programs are said to be more *intuitive* than others. *Intuitive* used in this way simply means *instinctive*. Not all graphics programs are so constructed; these less intuitive programs have—in computer terminology—*steep learning curves*. In our more detailed discussions of individual applications, we will examine more closely the relationship of tool use in different programs to those tools we use in the physical studio. This brings us to the most important tenet in this book and the one principle that underlies all explanations given here; that principle is: To become proficient and productive using computer tools to generate graphic images, *one must have a working knowledge of graphic tools and materials found in the physical studio as well as a complete understanding of their principles and use*.

The following sections outline many of the requirements of a scenographic workstation as well as recommendations for a select few software applications particularly suited to scenographic work. These recommendations represent the minimum requirements for productive scenographic design.

Basic Hardware and Equipment
Computers

In February of 1993, Apple discontinued the Mac II line, a group of computers that lasted approximately six years. At the same time, a number of new computers based on the faster Motorola 68040 processors were introduced with prices considerably below those offered before. This does not mean that only the computers currently in Apple's active list—and this changes yearly—are worthy of consideration, or that older computers have suddenly lost their value with the announcement of the new. Discontinued models remain available from dealers offering used and reconditioned models long after new models are announced. Many older models, in fact, can be upgraded into computers with the speed and capabilities of newer computers. Classified advertisement pages frequently have notices of single units for sale from previous owners.

Six computers are listed below. Although the last mentioned is the fastest and most useful of those given, it also costs the most. It is standard practice for most computer manufacturers to reduce the cost of their highest-end computer as a newer more advanced model is produced. The time period for these changes is approximately one year. All machines lose a third of their initial value a year after their manufacture. The monetary value of any one computer continues to drop year by year; there is no remedy to this situation. Unlike some items, computers never appreciate over time. Does this mean that one must always be forced to trade in this year's model for next year's product? Not necessarily. Just because it is the latest computer does not mean it is inherently superior to its predecessor. Like some models of automobiles, occasionally the newest model is a lemon; some older models become classics. Nor does a computer lose its usability simply because a newer machine is faster or has newer technology. A good machine, if properly maintained, will provide useful service for many years. There comes a time, however, when even the trustiest of computers will not keep pace with advancing software development. Then, despite the considerable costs involved, trading the old computer for a newer one becomes the only sensible course of action. When purchasing a new computer these points should be considered:

1. How critical is the basic speed of the computer to the work intended for it?

2. What are the standard on-board capabilities of the computer? Does it have a MC68882 floating-point math coprocessor? What kind of video card is resident? Are other kinds of cards capable of being installed? What is the size of its internal hard drive? What capability does the machine have for memory upgrade or additional acceleration?

3. What is the approximate time period before the next computer purchase? While this last consideration may seem too speculative to be useful, with a minimum of effort, it is possible to find reliable information that tells what computer manufacturers intend to offer over the next few years. A little forethought can save hundreds of dollars.

There is only one thing certain in the purchase of a computer: next year a better, cheaper machine is coming. Unfortunately, the work we do today cannot be accomplished on that computer.

1. Macintosh SE with dual drives (for 3.5 800K disks): This computer issued in 1987 is still a workhorse as well as a highly versatile tool; with 4MB of RAM installed (its maximum), it will run most graphic programs discussed in this book. Much of the text was written using an SE. It is—despite its age and small-screen format—the most affordable machine for creating relatively sophisticated graphics. Used in tandem with a two-page monitor, the creation of most working drawings is possible. A major drawback for SEs is that they have only one expansion slot—named a *processor direct slot* (PDS). While is possible to use a number of expansion cards with the SE—accelerators, internal modems, external monitor adaptors—the capacity to upgrade it to any significant degree is limited. The SE's CPU (the central processing unit—the chip that determines what a computer does) is a Motorola 68000 chip, which means that for many graphics programs a 68030 must be installed.

2. Macintosh SE/30: The SE/30 was issued two years after the SE. Unlike the SE, this machine possesses an 68030 CPU. The SE/30 features a high-density drive that makes it possible to read and write to floppy disks with capacities greater than 800K. Both the SE and the SE/30 are now retired from the Macintosh price list, yet both continue to have brisk sales as used machines; either—used with one-page or two-page displays—provide good performance at reasonable cost. With both the SE/30 and the IIsi, MC68882 floating point math coprocessors are available; these speed calculations for most—not necessarily all—graphics and CAD programs. RAM memory upgrades are—like the SE—limited to 4MB.

3. Mac IIsi: The IIsi has a 20MHz 68030 CPU and color video support but is limited to only one PDS slot or one NuBus slot. This gives limited capability for upgrading, even though the memory capacity is 17MB. This machine does not come with an MC68882 floating-point math coprocessor; for any serious CAD or graphics work, one should be installed. As computer applications become more advanced, we should expect file sizes to grow; the more memory available, the better. While in the late 1980s and early 1990s this amount of memory was adequate, it will not be in the future. If a math coprocessor is added to the IIsi, along with at least 9MB of memory, this machine rivals the IIci. While the IIsi is slightly faster than the LC II (a computer not recommended for serious scenographic work), the upgrade path for this machine is definitely limited. If possible,

the next two machines listed should be considered as better long-time options.

4. Macintosh IIci: One of Apple's modular CPU series based on the Motorola 68030 microprocessor, this machine was issued in 1989. It was discontinued—along with the rest of the Mac II line—in 1993. The IIci's clock speed is 25MHz and has a built-in MC68882 floating-point math coprocessor. It is upgradable to enhance performance; adding a cache memory card significantly improves system performance by 20 to 30 percent. Used with monochrome two-page displays, this machine handles complex scenographic drawings with speed and efficiency. For several years, the Macintosh IIci firmly held the middle ground of Apple's machines; that position has been replaced by the Quadra line of Macintoshes. Compared with the IIsi, the IIci is slightly faster, offers more slots for adding expansion boards, and has a math coprocessor. The processor is 25MHz 68030 and, like the IIsi, has inboard color video support. Unlike the IIsi, this machine has three NuBus slots and one cache slot.

5. Quadra 650: This computer was introduced early in 1993 at the same time the Macintosh II line ceased to exist. The Quadra line, in all probability, will last as long as the Macintosh II line it replaced. Both the Quadra 610 and 650 share many of the elements of the Quadra 800, the machine that replaced the Quadra 700. The greatest innovation in the 650 is its new memory architecture that lets the Quadra recognize memory of any capacity in any SIMM slot; one, two, three, or four slots can be filled with any size memory chip. The computer uses the RAM installed no matter what its configuration. In tandem with the new architecture, an additional technology operates: *memory interleaving*. With memory interleaving, speed of operation improves, since SIMMs of the same capacity in neighboring slots communicate in parallel creating, in effect, a single large SIMM. The Quadra 800 also has interleaved RAM capability. What is most remarkable about this machine, however, is that it has a 25MHz 68040 processor (the same as was used in the now-discontinued Quadra 700).

The Quadra 650 has one Processor Direct Slot and three NuBus slots along with the full complement of standard Macintosh ports: two ADB, one SCSI, and two serial ports. The SCSI port is a high-speed port.

AN IMPORTANT WARNING: In the basic configuration of the Centris 650—that is, 4MB of system memory and 80MB hard drive—a variant of the 040 processor named the 68LC040 is used. This processor has the 040's built-in math coprocessor—a necessary adjunct to computer-aided design, modeling, and rendering of graphics—disabled. If a Centris 650 is bought with more RAM or higher capacity hard disks, the regular built-in math processor is in place. With the basic configuration, an additional 25MHz 040 costs approximately $450. It costs little more, therefore, to get a machine with 8MB of RAM and a 230MB hard disk. An internal CD-ROM drive—which adds approximately $300 to the basic cost—is available. Since CD-ROM is going to play an ever-increasing role in graphics and research, the additional cost is a wise investment.

6. Macintosh Quadra 800: The Quadra 800 takes the place of the now-discontinued Quadra 700. It is next to the highest-performance computer offered by Apple. Like the Quadra 950, it uses a 33MHz Motorola 68040 processor, which means it has the math coprocessor and data caches built in. Twice as fast as a Macintosh IIfx—a discontinued machine against which all later Macintosh computer speeds have been rated—this machine

handles large files quickly. The basic configuration of the Quadra 800 is 8MB of RAM on a logic board that holds—by adding 32MB SIMMs—up to 136MB. It is imperative for this machine that the 70-nanosecond chip is used. The memory architecture of the Quadra 650 and the Quadra 800 are identical, so, like the 650, any SIMM size will fit in any SIMM slot. Along with the introduction of the Quadra 800 Apple introduced two new high-speed hard drives: a 500MB and a 1GB, which are both well beyond the needs (or financial abilities) of most scenographers; the standard drive for this machine is 230MB. Like the Quadra 650, the Quadra 800 supports AppleCD 300i CD-ROM drives. This option—which adds approximately $400 to the cost of the computer—comes with a CD onto which System 7.1 is installed. The advantage of having a CD-ROM drive is that, when a main drive fails, a new operating system can be immediately reinstalled from the CD. Although the cost of the Quadra 800 is beyond most scenographers, the investment is a worthwhile one. University theater computer laboratories would do well to have at least one Quadra 800 in residence.

All of the machines listed above are usable for scenographic work. Obviously, the more paid for a workstation, the faster that work is accomplished. Better machines also have better resale values.

A Question of Computer Memory

It is obvious from study of the machines just discussed that memory plays a large part in the usefulness of a computer. It is equally important that new computer users consider the amount of computer memory their machines presently have or are capable of holding. The main reason for this concern is that computer programs are constantly being revised; as upgrades become available, increasing amounts of memory are required to use them. At least 8MB of RAM should be installed in the computer to ensure that graphics and CAD programs run at reasonable speeds. As programs become more powerful, expect greater stores of memory to be required. Most examples for this book were drawn on a Macintosh IIsi with a 25MHz 68030 microprocessor. Also installed is a NuBus board, a 68882 math coprocessor, and 9MB of RAM. While this arrangement rivals the computing power of a Macintosh IIci, if at all financially possible, a machine at the level of the Quadra 650 with 8MB and a 230 disk drive should be purchased. While basic scenographic programs will run on computers with less internal RAM, 4MB has become mandatory for almost all graphics, modeling, and CAD programs. As computer technology develops, expect newer machines to require more memory. The positive side of the picture is that as programs demand more internal memory, the price of memory becomes more affordable. A sound principle is to buy as much memory as the machine supports or the pocketbook allows. If not able to do this at the time of purchase, plan to add memory as soon as possible. As with any other art or technology, it is false economy to buy only the lowest priced equipment or the cheapest programs. It is equally unwise to have powerful machines with inadequate stores of memory.

Monitors

1. Apple Macintosh One-Page (Portrait) Display: This monitor is the best of the one-page displays available, although not the least expensive. It is a solidly built piece of equipment made to work with Apple computers more advanced than the SE. For this reason, it is probably the most compatible. Oddly enough, the two-page display monitor made by Apple is not as good as the one recommended on the next page.

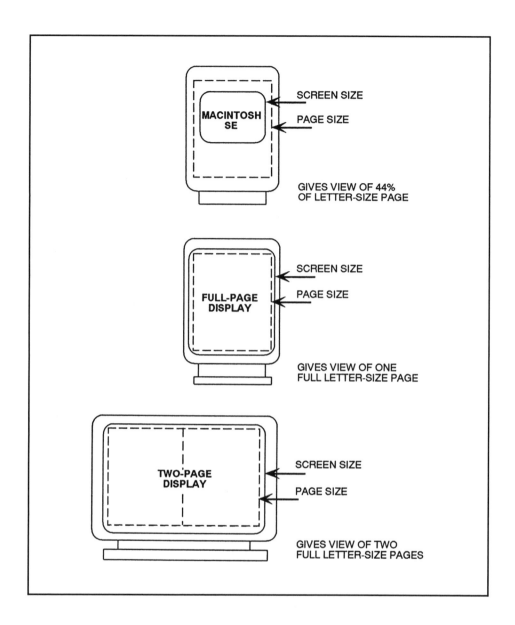

Fig. 7. Macintosh computer screen sizes

2.   Radius Monochrome Two-Page Display: The Macintosh SE has a screen size that only allows one to see a portion of an 8½″ by 11″ page at any one time (with the exception of some graphics programs that will allow a view of the whole page, but only as an reduced image). While this does not cause serious difficulty when using the computer as a word processor, constructing graphics on the SE is another matter; many times effective work requires a view of an image that cannot be contained on the SE's limited screen view. It is possible, however, to obtain monitors that give a larger view of the working area. The two basic screens beyond the 9″ SE screen are the full-page display and the two-page display. Figure 7 gives a diagrammatic view of all three screens. It is

highly recommended that anyone creating graphics on the computer should invest in at least a full-page display monitor at the first opportunity. Prices of these monitors have declined rapidly from the late 1980s. What cost $2,000 in 1988 has fallen below $1,000 at the time of this writing (1993). Nor is there any reason to believe that costs will escalate in the future. Two recommendations are made here. (1) The Radius Two-Page Display dedicated monochrome is adequate for CAD work and most drawing programs; gray scale cards can be purchased for all Apple computers above the Macintosh IIsi. (2) The Mirror Two-Page Display is also a good large monitor that costs less than the Radius Two-Page Display. Either of these are preferable to the basic screen size of an SE, the SE/30, or the Classic; it is simply not possible to work effectively on scenographic drawings with the screen sizes these monitors allow. While two-page displays give larger views of a graphic, the cost of these monitors is considerably higher than the full-page display. To some extent, two-page displays slow down a computer's speed; although not absolutely necessary, accelerator boards are recommended for two-page displays.

3. Apple 13″ RGB Monitor: These monitors are good basic units for color work. While they show a larger area than the SE, SE/30, or Classic, they do not give a full-page view of a drawing. This monitor can, however, be used in tandem with two-page displays. When such a configuration exists, it is possible to select which of the screens—the RGB display or the two-page monochrome display—is the active monitor. In such a case, it is advisable to turn the color of the RGB monitor off using only the black and white option. As with the dedicated monochrome monitor, this color monitor allows differing levels of color control. These levels provide 5 basic ranges of color: black-and-white, 4 colors, 16 colors, 256 colors, and millions of colors.

The kind of monitor and the way the screen resolution is set have a direct bearing on the working speed of the computer. A monitor capable of displaying millions of colors demands more memory and operates at a slower speed than does the same monitor displaying black and white only. Changes to the computer's color possibilities are made through the computer's control panel, as shown in figure 8. A good principle to follow for all drawing on the computer is to match the screen resolution to the work at hand: when solid simple colors are all that are required, keep the monitor set to 16 colors; if drafting or black-and-white line drawings are being made, keep the monitor set to black and white. (Since changes to a monitor's screen resolution do not require the computer to be restarted after a change is made, a good strategy to follow is to make the Control Panel quickly available. This is best done by setting up a QuicKeys 3 macro.)

Although the computer is the heart of any workstation system, only machines with internal screens and internal hard drives are self-sufficient. Most computer artists find very quickly that it is necessary to use other items of equipment in tandem with the basic computer. Most computers, in fact, require other hardware, such as monitors, to be attached. Below are listed several machines, along with some personal recommendations of the author. These recommendations do not preclude the possibility that other scenographers will make different choices. The selection of any item of equipment should, however, be carefully researched before a purchase is made, since hardware ranges from hundreds to thousands of dollars. The major computer magazines such as *MacUser* and *MacWorld*

Auxiliary Hardware for Computers

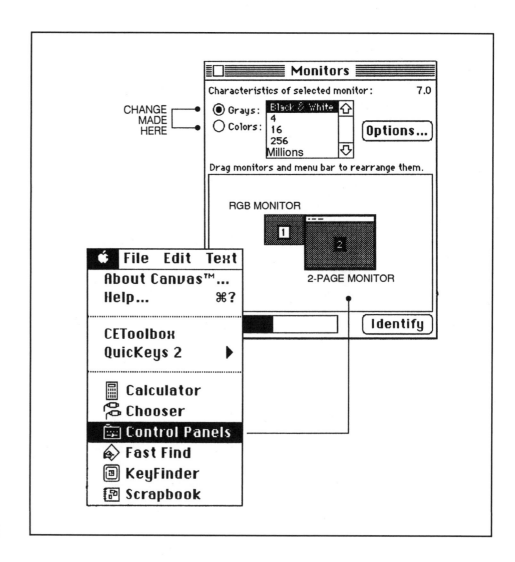

Fig. 8. Monitor control panel

regularly have comparisons of similar machines based on laboratory tests. Similar machines are usually rated for performance and value. These testings are valuable to potential buyers and should be reviewed before purchases are made.

1.   External hard-disk drives: Resident hard drives with large storage capacities cost a great deal. Although these costs have moderated during the past few years and will, in all probability, continue to decrease, really inexpensive large-storage drives are still in the distant future. Since computer graphic files rapidly use up hard-disk space, and it is not possible to store large numbers of files or large graphics on 3.5 disks, it is strongly recommended that the purchase of external hard-disk drives be carefully considered. The best way to store large files is to obtain a hard-disk cartridge drive that allows one to remove disks from the drive and to store them individually. This makes management of large amounts of information easier (an increasing problem as information and files accumulate). External drives also become necessary when color or animation files are

created and stored. While many different companies market hard drives under different names, the basic drives inside the case are made by few manufacturers. Drives also have different speeds. Naturally, the fastest are the best but also the most expensive. Of these, my personal recommendation is Quantum drives. These are rated among the best available although not the most inexpensive.

2. Laser printers: Laser printers that have PostScript or comparable technologies are a necessary adjunct to computer graphics. While dot-matrix machines are much less expensive, they do not print line widths less than a pixel; even though a drawing program may allow the user to assign various narrow widths to a drawing, these machines cannot print them. The cost of laser printers drops yearly, so that the difference between these machines and dot matrix continually becomes narrower. If at all possible, the scenographer should have in the studio a laser printer.

Two 300 DPI printers are recommended—the Qume Crystalprint Publisher (shown in figure 5) or the Apple LaserWriter Pro 600.

3. Dot-matrix printers—an Apple ImageWriter II: In order to obtain a hard copy of the graphics work done on the computer, a printer is necessary. The cost of dot-matrix printers is roughly three to five times less than the cost of a laser printer. These machines cannot take advantage of postscript technology; that is, no line smaller than a pixel can be printed, and draw objects such as circles or curved lines that are not smoothed—the typical jagged appearance of pre-PostScript graphics is unavoidable. For this reason, the scenographer should seriously consider the LaserWriter or a good LaserWriter clone as a wise investment.

4. Ink-jet printers: Apple StyleWriter ink-jet printers and the Apple ImageWriter are roughly similar in price (although the StyleWriter is less expensive initially). Unlike dot-matrix machines, the ink-jet printer shoots ink onto the paper instead of using a ribbon. This gives a higher resolution to any graphic it prints. It is possible, in fact, to obtain results that rival those of LaserWriters. What should be seriously considered, however, is that the cost per page of a StyleWriter is approximately 30 to 40 percent higher than a page printed on the ImageWriter II and even higher than a page printed on a LaserWriter or LaserWriter clone. This machine is a good portable printer for those who do not produce a great volume of work. They are not practicable for those who do. The biggest disadvantage of these machines is that they are are extremely slow compared with LaserWriters or LaserWriter clones. If one must choose between the dot-matrix ImageWriter II and the ink-jet StyleWriter, the latter is preferred. Neither rival the productivity and running costs of the LaserWriter or the LaserWriter clone.

Input Devices

Information is introduced into the computer by various input devices; seven of these are given below. The primary means to place information is through the keyboard; a method that remains the essential to the introduction of text into a document. The mouse and mouselike devices comprise three more categories. Two other categories exist, however, which may or may not use the keyboard. These are pointing devices and scanners.

Most computer workers choose only two main input devices: the keyboard and the mouse (or an alternative trackball). Depending on the compatibility of the device's individual drivers, it is possible to use several at the same time. It is also possible to have a

Fig. 9. Graphics tablet and keyboard

mouse, a trackball, and a graphics tablet on line simultaneously. (In the case of graphics tablets, one must make a selection between the stylus and the cursor; while only one entry point exists, these different devices perform many of the same functions.)

1. Computer keyboard: Two different keyboards are recommended here—(1) the Apple Adjustable Keyboard (shown in figure 9 and discussed more fully below in "Health Considerations in Computer Use" in Computer Graphics Programs) and (2) the DataDesk SwitchBoard Keyboard (not shown). The DataDesk SwitchBoard Keyboard is recommended as an alternative to the regular Apple Extended Keyboard for one major reason: the touch of the keys of the DataDesk machine feels more like that of manual typewriters. This is a personal judgment of the author, who values the tactile qualities of manual keyboards. All keyboards for Macintosh computers are programmable with software utilities programs such as QuicKeys. These programs give users an ability to assign exact functions requiring several combined actions with the mouse or combined keystrokes on the lower board. They also allow for assignment of menu items to function keys or to keystroke combinations. Since the keyboard is the primary access to, and modifier of, the image on the screen, a versatile keyboard is essential to efficient graphics work. The DataDesk Keyboard is lower priced than the Apple Extended Keyboard and considerably lower than the Apple Adjustable Keyboard. Those scenographers with strong concerns for the ergonomic factors of their studios should consider the Apple Adjustable Keyboard instead of a normal keyboard. (See "Health Considerations in Computer Use," below, for possible injuries from keyboard use.)

2. Apple ADB mouse (fig. 10): The Apple ADB mouse is the pointing device used by most computer users. While the original Apple mouse was a rather clumsy affair, the

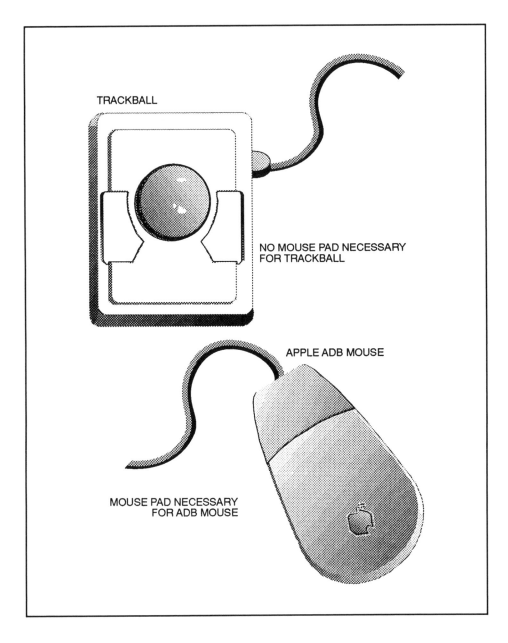

TRACKBALL

NO MOUSE PAD NECESSARY
FOR TRACKBALL

APPLE ADB MOUSE

MOUSE PAD NECESSARY
FOR ADB MOUSE

Fig. 10. Computer input devices

one presently packaged with the MacIntosh is an efficient and effective tool. Once the hand has mastered a few simple movements, its use quickly becomes second nature; other pointing devices, however, take more time to master the movements necessary, and a fairly difficult period of adjustment should be expected; some users never make these adjustments. Sharp divisions exist, for instance, between those who love the trackball and those who abhor it despite several useful functions it gives the user. Only personal experience will settle this matter, although it is my recommendation that time be taken to personally test a device for a period of time before it is rejected entirely. The ADB mouse is composed of independent parts that allow it to be taken apart for service or cleaning.

3. Little Mouse ADB (shown at the lower-right side of figure 9): The Little Mouse ADB operates in exactly the same manner as the regular ADB mouse, with the main difference lying in its construction. Although the Apple ADB mouse has a number of parts—including a ball that rolls within a half shell over any smooth surface—the Little Mouse ADB has no moving parts and uses an optical technology that requires a reflective mirrorlike pad to reflect back the laser beam it projects. This device, although 22 percent smaller than the regular Apple ADB mouse, has a resolution of 300 pixels per inch as opposed to the usual 200 pixels per inch resolution of the standard mouse. For this reason, the Little Mouse ADB is a more accurate tool for computer graphics.

4. ADB trackball (fig. 10): The trackball is nothing more than a mouse turned upside down with the rolling ball enlarged for easier manipulation. Unlike the ADB mouse, only the fingers move, not the whole mouse unit, which remains stationary on the desktop. This means that no mouse pad is necessary, nor is there any reason to have space for the hand and arm to move. While the ADB mouse has one center button for selection, the trackball has two: one for right-handed users and an opposite button for left-handed users. There is an additional button on the opposite side of the trackball unit that serves in two ways: first—and its primary function—to lock a selection (such as keeping a pull-down menu open) or, according to the make of trackball, when simultaneously clicked with the opposite button, to perform some preselected common function such as Save, Cut, Revert. All functions and orientations of the trackball are made possible by changing the up/down positions of DIP switches within the case of the unit. Instructions accompanying the trackball explain the various configurations possible.

5. Wacom SD-510C digital electronic tablet (shown above the Apple Adjustable Keyboard in figure 9): This device has the capabilities of both mouse and cordless electronic pens. An electric stylus acts in a similar way to the mouse but, as in the case of the Wacom stylus, is easier to draw with and control small graphic elements. The electronic pen makes most drawing easier, since it is more nearly like a standard pen or pencil; this allows the drawer a kinesthetic response nearer to that of the artists who have trained their hands to use traditional drawing tools. The Wacom tablet also supports a pressure-sensitive pen for painting programs that allows the drawer to make painted strokes of varying widths. Digital drawing tablets also support four-button cursors. In theory, it is possible to trace images using electronic styli, although there is no real reason to do so if a scanner is available. Even images drawn on thick papers or boards are possible, since the tracing is done by induction; that is, the tip of the stylus penetrates the drawing's surface and communicates with the surface of the tablet below. This form of drawing takes some retraining of both hand and eye because these images are not as easily controlled as tracings done using traditional light tables. The electronic pen does not perform all the functions of the mouse equally well; having both pen and mouse connected to the tablet allows for alternate use as necessary.

Just as the graphics tablet has two input devices—the stylus and the cursor—it is generally used for two basic purposes: to be able to draw or trace more accurately hard images or to enter key points of a hard image onto the computer screen as points that

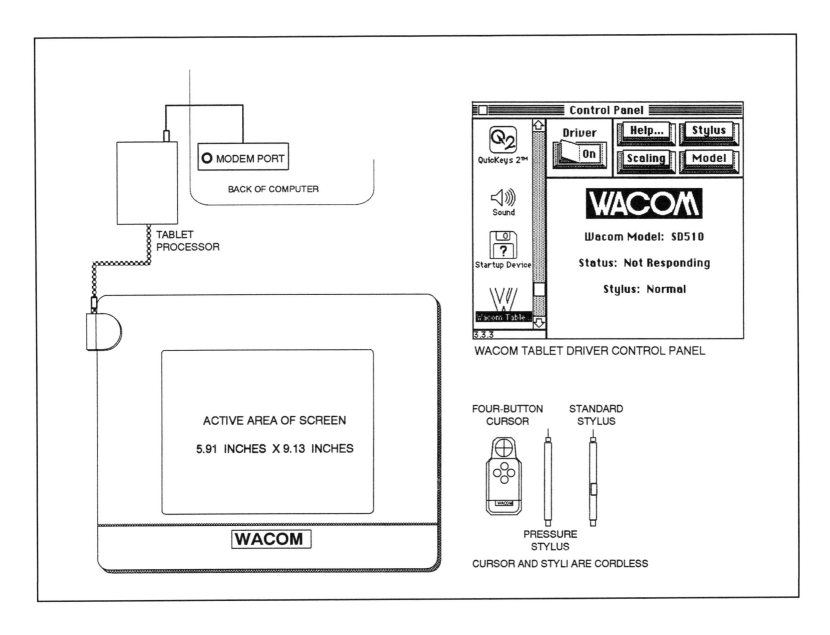

are then connected using an application's other drawing tools. The physical tablet is a flat object approximately one-half inch thick that varies in width and length. The actual active area of a graphics tablet is always less than the overall size of its face; the larger this active area is, the more the tablet costs. Figure 11 is a diagrammatic view showing the main features of the Wacom SD-510C tablet that is seen above the Apple Adjustable Keyboard in figure 9.

Graphics tablets used with high-end CAD and CAM programs are more apt to use another input device called a cursor (shown at the left of the styli in figure 11) than a drawing stylus, mouse, or trackball, since these devices lend themselves to construction

Fig. 11. Diagram of graphics tablet

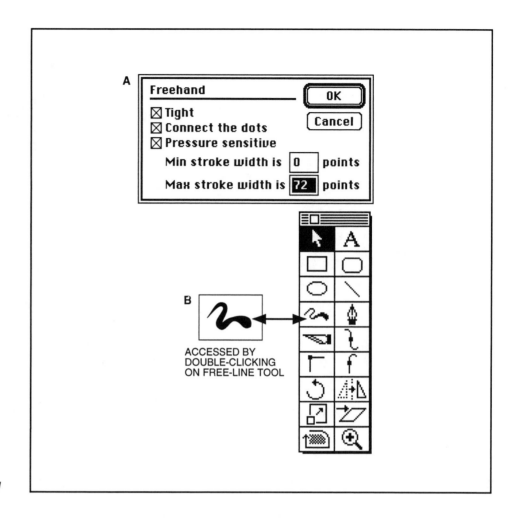

Fig. 12. Pressure-sensitive graphics tool

of technical plans with accurately placed coordinate points. As the publishers of draw and paint programs upgrade their applications, they are increasingly adding pressure-sensitive capabilities to their toolboxes. The first company to create a pressure-sensitive tool for object-oriented drawing was Aldus; FreeHand 4.0 makes it possible for the free-line tool to be converted to a pressure-sensitive tool (fig. 12). For scenographers and costumers, the stylus with its more pen-or pencil-like feel makes it more usable than the mouse or a trackball (fig. 13).

6. ThunderScan hand scanner (fig. 14): This device is a peripheral installed onto the computer through the SCSI port. The width of the images scanned using this device is limited to a 4.2″-wide path. It is possible, however, to "stitch" together separate passes into larger images. The vertical length of any single image depends directly upon the amount of the computer's RAM. The program provides a gauge at the bottom of the image being scanned to let the user monitor how much memory is taken up as the scanner tracks over an image. ThunderScan is accessible in two ways: (1) by opening up its application and (2) by DA selection through the Apple icon at the far left top of the

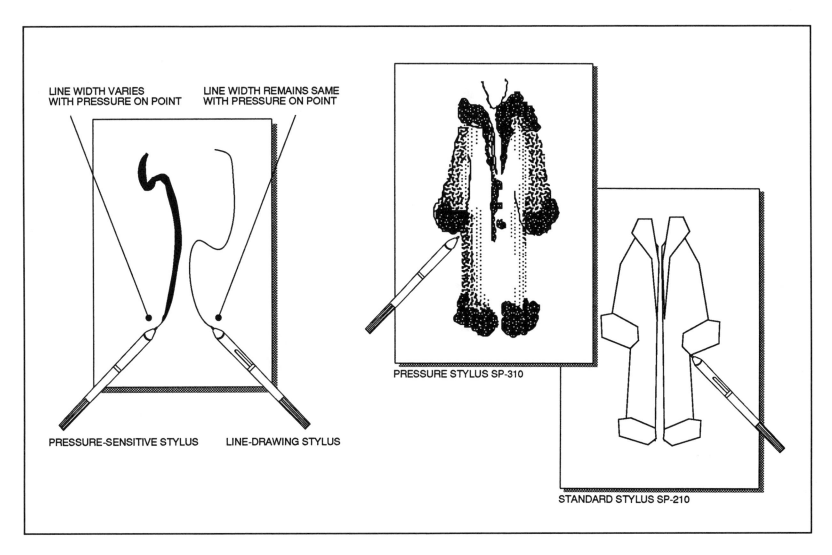

LINE WIDTH VARIES WITH PRESSURE ON POINT

LINE WIDTH REMAINS SAME WITH PRESSURE ON POINT

PRESSURE-SENSITIVE STYLUS   LINE-DRAWING STYLUS

PRESSURE STYLUS SP-310

STANDARD STYLUS SP-210

Fig. 13. Use of pressure-sensitive tool

screen. Manipulation of the image in terms of resolution is directly modified on the scanner itself, but further manipulation of the image is processed through the application. Using an OCR (optical character recognition) program, text is read into the file disk as well. Many of the images included in this book were scanned into the computer using ThunderScan. This device is recommended as an economical alternative to the OneScanner listed below.

7.   Apple OneScanner Flatbed 300 dots per inch scanner: This machine is for black-and-white line art and gray-scale images only. Although only a basic piece of hardware—in many ways not as sophisticated as many other scanners in its price range—what distinguishes this scanner from many others lies not in its construction but in the software that accompanies it: Ofoto, a creation of a company named Light Source that won the 1991 *MacUser* Editor's Choice Award for breakthrough technology of the year. This program has set the standard for scanning technology for the present and in all likelihood

Fig. 14. ThunderScan hand scanner

will influence all similar software in the future. For those scenographers who wish to place found images into computer graphics drawings, this is a highly recommended hardware-software package. (See "Interactive Image Files" in chapter 2 for a further discussion of this subject.)

Upgrading the Computer Scenographics Studio

In the past, it was possible for scenographers to select a range of tools and helpful devices that—with care and maintenance—lasted many years. Unfortunately, this admirable posture has limited application in the world of computer technology; there events and developments happen more quickly than one can comfortably follow. Although rapidly developing technology is fortunate for the future, it presents serious problems for many, especially for those who invest heavily in hardware equipment during any one time frame. In this book, only the broadest of guidelines for building a workable computer graphics studio can be given. Moreover, these recommendations reveal only the *thinking behind* making certain purchases or acquisitions; what is impossible to show is an ultimate configuration of equipment and programs that work for today and for the future as well. As careers progress, it is only natural to expect that working environments must modify. It is likely, therefore, that any system of computers, peripherals, and software needs to be updated periodically. Many items of hardware, however, permit owners to enhance performance of the equipment through changes of internal boards or addition of newer computer chips; programs, of course, are continually upgraded to work better.

Computer Graphics Programs

Individual computer programs are designed to meet specific needs. This is particularly true for graphics programs. Increasingly, graphics programs made by different organizations tend to emulate the best features of their rivals. It is doubtful, however, there will ever be a single all-inclusive program that contains every graphics process. In fact, there are distinct advantages for individual programs to be limited to certain tasks. As the various programs listed below are addressed, reasons are discussed why arbitrary limitations are—and should be—placed on graphics programs. First, let us review the basic kinds of programs appropriate to scenographic work.

Programs for bit-mapped graphics. These programs are used for creating scenographic sketching and rendering on the computer. They have little use in technical specification drawing.

Programs for object-oriented graphics. These programs are used to create high-resolution illustrations. They have limited value for technical drawing. Used in conjunction with bit-mapped programs, object-oriented programs produce images that show how something looks, with no information as to how the object is constructed or how it works.

Programs for technical specification drawings. These programs come under the broad headings of CAD (computer-aided design) and CADD (computer-aided design and drafting). The value of a CAD or CADD program is determined by the number of features it contains to accurately create, size, and dimension working drawings: plans, elevations, sections, and the like. Most CAD or CADD programs are limited to the creation of two-dimensional drawings; a limited number, however, possess three-dimensional capability. These programs generate other kinds of technical-drawing views: perspective projections, orthogonal projections, oblique cabinet projections, and oblique cavalier projections.

Programs for three-dimensional object creation. These programs generate within the memory of the computer mathematically calculated simulations of three-dimensional objects. While these objects are primarily viewed on the monitor screen, they can be printed as paper copies. Although most of the programs under this heading are capable of rendering true perspective projections, some few will also display computer-generated three-dimensional objects as well: orthogonal projections, oblique cabinet projections, or cavalier projections.

Increasingly, the computer is able to produce complex graphic images; its power to simulate the techniques of traditional art materials, to manipulate photographic images, and to create accurate three-dimensional views of complex objects—even mathematical formulas and molecular structures in visual form—equals in some ways, surpasses in others, the abilities of the most sophisticated cameras. Yet all these marvelous capabilities, these keys to unseen worlds, lie hidden in coded strings of letters and numbers magnetically recorded on small disks of plastic material. Artists like myself—trained to use tangible tools and concrete materials—never quite lose the sense of awe engendered by that enigmatic box of chips and wires able to turn obscure codes from magnetic disks into electronic images on a screen. Intangible and inscrutable as these processes are, they result in images that accurately reflect the building of physical objects in our real world of theater.

Scenographers use the computer to produce images for significantly different purposes than do commercial graphic artists, product designers, architects, or engineers. For instance, two of the most influential drawing programs for the Macintosh, Adobe Illustrator 5 and Aldus FreeHand 4.0, are specifically geared to the making of illustrations for publications: books, magazines, and newspapers. Although powerful programs in their own right, they have limited use to the scenographer planning productions for the stage, cinema, or television. Unlike advertising artists who use computers to create images that sell products, or typographical designers concerned with the aesthetic layout of type on the page, the scenographer creates images that are no more than signs along the road to things that only exist in time and space. Although some illustration capability is required for the making of scenographic sketches, most of the scenographer's computer graphics work is technical specification, not illustrative image making. The programs we choose, therefore, reflect the fundamental nature of our work. As the various programs listed below are examined, keep well in mind the main purposes of scenographic work, not the capabilities of the individual applications.

Drawing on the computer demands that artists learn a new kind of drawing environment: a drawing board that remains locked until certain understandings are reached. The most significant feature of this "board"—which hereafter will be called an *interface*—is that it came into being as a direct effort to make the world of computers comprehendable even to young children. The Macintosh interface, moreover, is constructed so that users behave in the electronic world in ways human beings do in their day-to-day external one. On the Macintosh interface screen one functions not only by reading pages as if in a book but also by seeing, touching, and moving objects as they would do in the world where they live. Before examining ways computers aid conceptual processes of scenography, let us examine more closely what is meant by *interface*.

Interface: The Door to Computer Worlds

The dictionary definition of interface is: *a plane or other surface forming a common boundary of two bodies or spaces*. To make full use of any computer program one must understand this plane or other surface the programmer has chosen or imposed upon it. The interface of any program, therefore, determines the way one relates to it. Those new to computers soon learn that questions of a program's interface are not idle speculative ruminations but matters of real concern to any who wish to do productive work. The design of the interface, in point of fact, is the primary factor that determines just how productive one is able to be. The fundamental reason why this book has chosen the Macintosh computer as its platform is that Macintosh interfaces are the most consistent and "user-friendly" of any affordable computer available today. For those who wish to know more about how the interface of computer programs is designed, *The Art of Human-Computer Interface Design*, edited by Brenda Laurel (Reading, MA; Addison-Wesley, 1990), is recommended. This collection of papers and essays on interface design is a readable introduction to the many questions that surround this important subject.

New programs often give users the feeling that they have stumbled upon a mysterious tomb to which the only access to it—the manual—is written in unreadable hieroglyphics. For this reason, those used to Macintosh programs frequently assess the worth of the program in terms of its conformance to other Macintosh interface designs, finding serious fault with a program when it significantly deviates from other Macintosh interfaces.

In *The Elements of Friendly Software Design*, Paul Heckel writes:

> Software designers sometimes design for the novice user and sometimes for the experienced user. But frequently we must design for both. The program should be easy enough for the novice to use, yet versatile enough for the expert. In this light, it is important to realize that every expert was once a novice. Most users' knowledge is dynamic. They learn and change, and their interaction with your program will form an important part of that change. Things that are useful to the novice often bore the experienced user, while those things that are second nature to the experienced user can baffle and confuse the novice.
>
> *One of our problems as designers is that we quickly become experienced users and this causes us to lose our empathy with novices.* (Italics mine.) (Paul Heckel, *The Elements of Friendly Software Design* [Alameda, CA: Sybex, 1991])

Later he says:

> People learn to use computer software that gives its users real power over their problems even if it is difficult to learn. People tend not to use applications that address limited problems and give their users little power even when they're easy to learn and use. This is consistent with our worldly experience. We all acquire skills that are difficult to learn but powerful. Everyone learns to walk, read, and drive a car, and also learns the skills of a professional. These skills are used repeatedly, and once learned, they are taken for granted and the effort expended in learning them is forgotten. So, too, computer spreadsheets and word processors are powerful tools that people take for granted once they learn to use them; yet learning to use one's first spreadsheet or word processor takes considerable time and effort.
>
> The history of the Apple Macintosh also illustrates how power is more important to computer software success than ease of use or ease of learning. . . . *Ease of use and flashing interfaces may kindle computer use, but power fuels it.* (Italics mine.)

Investing in one program instead of another is an important step in setting up a computer studio. Cost, while it certainly is a factor for most artists, is not the only one to be considered. Other factors are:

How does one assess the need for a certain program?

How much should one pay for powerful programs as opposed to cheaper less
    powerful ones?
How much time and effort should be expended in learning a new program?
How much power should we sacrifice for ease of learning?

Underlying all these questions is this: *Does the program significantly improve draw-ings accomplished with it?*

The Macintosh Metaphorical Computer Graphics Interface

We do not realize how much metaphorical imagery is used in our day-to-day lives; it is too ingrained in normal behavior to be seen directly. A cursory examination, however, as to how we conduct everyday life reveals that our primary means of accessing the world lies in the use of metaphorical models. Even the simplest computer program cannot be comprehended directly; the language codes used by programmers are for most of us as inscrutable as the mysterious monolith in Arthur Clark's *2001*. Only through the metaphori-cal imagery of an application's specifically designed interface can we use the information hidden in the program. The interface of all drawing programs and most painting programs is that of an actual worktable around which are placed tools, materials, and devices by which drawings and paintings are made. For CAD programs, the metaphorical image is more of a drafting table that has a light box built into its surface. When a Macintosh drawing or CAD program is launched, the basic screen is composed similarly to what one might find in the draftsman's real-world environment.

A computer definition of *interface* is: *a common boundary between the computer and a user,* that is, the computer screen and the operator facing it. In almost all Macintosh computer programs, metaphor is used so that the user retains reference to the world of common perceptions. The screen, for instance, is called a "desktop," individual items such as word processing documents or graphics are called "files." Files reside in "file folders." "Trash barrels" are used to dispose of unwanted materials. Options are listed in "menus" of related functions. These real-life references keep users oriented to the way offices and studios operate in the world we are most familiar with. The Macintosh graphi-cal interface has become so popular that other computer makers have copied the basic features of this approach to software interface design. Although experienced users of a program come to rely on keyboard input and macro programs such as QuicKeys rather than menu selection, the metaphorical links these helpful clues provide greatly aid in the learning of a new program and help to retain memory how infrequently used programs operate.

Basic Considerations Concerning Computer Graphics Programs

Computer graphics programs fall into two main categories: (1) high-end programs written for powerful computers, printers, and scanning machines and (2) less demanding programs meant for use on smaller computer platforms. Where the division between these two categories lies is not clear. Programs in the first category are, it is not surprising, expensive; these applications run anywhere from $500 to as much as $50,000. Many of these programs are outside the budget limits of the average scenographer. The second category ranges between $50 and $500 in cost and do fall within the possibility of most who need them. These programs are specifically designed for smaller computers that have a memory capacity of 519K or more; this amount of memory is necessary to run these less expensive programs. The computers previously discussed will handle most of a scenographer's computer graphic needs. Most theater graphics do not really require more capabilities than these programs offer. Still, to use the programs recommended in this book assumes that a certain level of computer is available.

The best of the programs recommended share a relatively uniform interface; that is, functions and procedures are similar among programs. But one should also realize that significant differences exist between programs as well; that although one program may have a similar layout of tools and functions as another program, in reality they work quite differently. For this reason, experienced computer graphics users counsel new users against the attempt to learn too many programs too quickly. Many of the illustrations in this book were made using Canvas 3.5, a program by Deneba Systems, Inc. This program was specifically chosen because it supports both paint (bit-mapped) graphics and draw (object-oriented) graphics; making illustrations is more cumbersome with CAD programs, even though they can be used for such work. Canvas 3.5 is, in all probability, the best program available for the Macintosh that spans both basic format types. The program is widely available through computer dealers or—at a distinctly more economical prices—from computer-related mail order houses.

Two considerations should be heeded in selecting a computer program; these are:

1. Cost of programs: Paint and draw programs average $200 to $800. Intermediate programs are available at discount prices for approximately $150. CAD programs are significantly higher; a low-end CAD does not offer much more than some high-end paint/draw programs. High-end CAD programs not only cost thousands of dollars but also require matching hardware to run them. Individual scenographers—as well as those setting up small theater programs—rarely have the financial means or teaching staff to make these high-end programs practicable.

2. Learning accessibility: Visual theater artists need programs that are logically designed so that mastery of the program's required techniques is possible within a reasonable period of training.

Learning curves for computer graphics programs vary greatly from person to person. While some users quickly assimilate abstract principles from written instruction—that is, from reading a program's accompanying manuals—others need tutelage from experienced instructors. All, however, make the most progress from kinesthetic reinforcement of a hands-on approach; that is, learning a program by experiment and unstructured play. It is common that many Macintosh users experiment with new programs before consulting the program's manual. Writers of manuals are well aware that the more adventurous of their users actually prefer to learn new programs through trial and error, not by studious application to the accompanying printed materials. A basic principle of all art training—an axiom as valid today as five thousand years ago—is that an artist's education depends greatly on the interplay of hands, eyes, and brain. Only in the interaction of all three does skill develop or is productivity attained.

All programs have precise restrictions, ground rules that must be obeyed; the programs recommended here are not exceptions. By necessity, each program has procedures incorporated into it that allow no choice except to follow the exact instructions encoded. Testing the limits of a program to find new ways to accomplish tasks the manual's writers did not record (or even envision) is one of the fascinations of computer graphics.

Specific Computer Programs for Scenographic Drawing

In this part of the text, a limited number of graphics programs are recommended for these reasons: (1) to indicate programs that those scenographers new to computer graphics can understand and master and (2) to provide a linked chain of programs that are progressively incorporated into the scenographer's work systems as skill and understanding increase. These programs cover the entire spectrum of experimental work: two-dimensional design, three-dimensional modeling, and technical specification. They are considered by the author best suited to the specific areas of theater art scenographers encounter day to day. First, let us take a closer look at the steps needed to master computer scenographics.

The process of learning computer graphics for the theater breaks down into three phases:

Phase 1—learning the fundamental language of computer graphics, how computer program interface operates, and the rudiments of computer graphics practice. During this phase, direct experimentation with computer graphics programs is the only way to become comfortable in computer world environments; study of written instruction is secondary to kinesthetic experience. For this reason, there is no better introduction to the wide range of computer graphics in general or to paint and draw programs in particular than beginning with Canvas 3.5; its intuitive interface and logical ways of working make the transition from manual graphics to computer graphics much easier than do many other programs.

Phase 2—learning relatively simple three-dimensional programs with interfaces that relate to known stage environments: proscenium arch theaters, open stages, arena configurations. The best introduction to three-dimensional computer environments is Virtus WalkThrough 1.1.3. The interface of this program more nearly approximates the way manual graphics are made. Use of more advanced three-dimensional programs, like MiniCad+ 5.0, should be postponed until Virtus WalkThrough 1.1.3 is mastered. As the scenographer becomes more proficient in creating technically precise objects, both in two-dimensional programs and in Virtus WalkThrough 1.1.3, other three-dimensional programs will be more comprehendible.

Phase 3—learning programs that create drawings with precise technical measurements and a higher degree of technical specification than offered by Canvas 3.5 or similar drawing programs. PowerDraw 5.0 is most probably the highest level a beginning student of computer graphics is likely to attain in the first year of study. Although brief explanations showing some of this program's most important features and possibilities are given in this book, extensive study of this particular program cannot be undertaken until the scenographer is throughly grounded in the basic skills of computer graphics generation. MiniCad+ 5.0 is especially recommended to those with a firm foundation and working knowledge of architectural drafting. Mastery of this program gives the scenographer or the technical director an ability to produce high-level working drawings that can be—without leaving the program—converted into three-dimensional views.

Although this book occasionally provides instruction for the programs recommended, the exercises included do not assume a previous understanding of any program discussed.

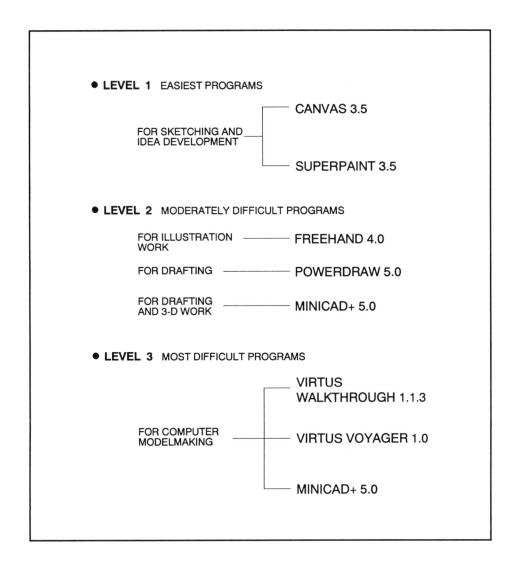

- **LEVEL 1** EASIEST PROGRAMS

FOR SKETCHING AND
IDEA DEVELOPMENT
  - CANVAS 3.5
  - SUPERPAINT 3.5

- **LEVEL 2** MODERATELY DIFFICULT PROGRAMS

FOR ILLUSTRATION WORK ——— FREEHAND 4.0

FOR DRAFTING ——— POWERDRAW 5.0

FOR DRAFTING AND 3-D WORK ——— MINICAD+ 5.0

- **LEVEL 3** MOST DIFFICULT PROGRAMS

FOR COMPUTER MODELMAKING
  - VIRTUS WALKTHROUGH 1.1.3
  - VIRTUS VOYAGER 1.0
  - MINICAD+ 5.0

Fig. 15. Diagram of computer programs

These more particularized explanations are included only as approximate indications of how the program under discussion performs tasks useful to scenographic work.

All the examples demonstrated in this book were obtained using the basic applications shown in figure 15 and the hardware listed above in "Basic Hardware and Equipment." There are, of course, many other programs available that are not discussed in the present text. An encyclopedic listing of all programs usable for scenographic work, however, is neither feasible nor desirable. If one learns the possibilities of the programs included, a solid basis of understanding will be established that will prove useful to the scenographer when more powerful computer systems are developed and newer programs emerge.

Two unavoidable facts exist for all computer graphics users: (1) no single program answers every need, and (2) no matter how proficient one is in manual graphics production,

Graphics Used for Theater Work

new approaches are necessary when computers enter the picture. When scenographers change from traditional ways of drawing to computer graphics, another factor emerges: as programs become more sophisticated, they tend to become more complex and often more difficult to master. As programs are reviewed, keep in mind that our primary concern lies with identifying those applications specifically related to scenographic work, not to graphic work as a whole.

Scenographic drawing falls into several relatively distinct categories. The purposes behind categories are:

1. *To show how something appears:* illustrative images of an object's outer form and surface features as perceived by the retina of the eye or as recorded by the camera lens; factual representations of recognizable objects, portraits, landscapes
2. *To show how something is constructed:* working drawings such as floor plans, elevation drawings, detail drawings
3. *To show how something works or changes during time in relationship to other things or concepts:* maps, charts, graphs, plots, diagrams, schematics

Although each of these categories has specifically written computer programs that serve specific drawing purposes, it is not uncommon for new users to think all graphics produced on the computer are of the same kind. Even for fledgling users, however, differences between graphic possibilities soon becomes apparent. Those who later master the terminology and the techniques associated with computer graphics come to understand that different programs have differing purposes. In so doing, they also learn that some programs are suitable for creating certain kinds of information while other programs are unusable.

Object-oriented applications, for example, give computer drawers the ability to create highly accurate working drawings. Being able to draw objects quickly and accurately—as well as to dimension, position, and calculate their overall areas and relationships one to another—is a requisite of such programs. Bit-mapped programs, on the other hand, are not suitable for working drawings since there is no way to alter bit-mapped drawings accurately. To alter an object-oriented graphic, one simply enters new coordinates or drags the graphic to a new shape or size; this cannot be done to a bit-mapped graphic. Although bit-mapped graphics are usable as parts of working drawings—as later examples in this book demonstrate—they need to be converted into object-oriented formats before incorporation. For true CAD programs, bit-mapped graphics are only marginally allowed. Creating scenographic renderings on the computer—like that shown in figure 16—requires bit map-based programs. Although objects in bit map drawings—such as the center column—seem solid shaded forms, they are, as the magnification view at the right side of figure 16 shows, nothing more than a collection of single pixels; only their small size and arrangement pulls these minute individual blocks into larger perceivable shapes.

Rigid rules governing the interaction of differing kinds of computer programs are not possible. Principles do evolve, however, as experience is gained. As the individual scenographer develops an understanding of computer graphics, these principles become

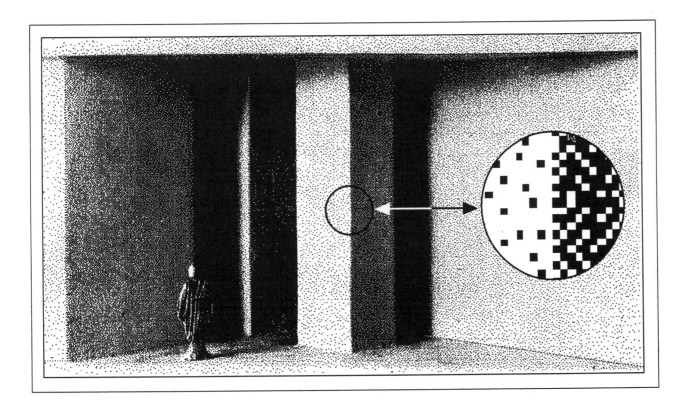

more flexible as they are personalized. The following principles are offered as guidelines for scenographers new to computer graphics:

Fig. 16. Bit-mapped scenographic rendering

1. The specific personal workstation of the artist sets the parameters of the work possible.
2. Conceptual and experimental work is accomplished with programs that have intuitively based interfaces and graphic tools closely approximating real-world experience of the artist. (Canvas 3.5—a dual-format program that allows both object-oriented and bit-mapped graphics supported by pressure-sensitive styli of graphics tablets such as Wacom—is a good example of such a program.)
3. Work requiring precise specification, measurement, and efficient alteration capabilities is accomplished with object-oriented programs. (PowerDraw 5.0, FreeHand 4.0, and, Canvas 3.5 are good examples of such programs.)
4. High-end illustration programs—such as Aldus FreeHand 4.0—should be used only for special projects such as those demonstrated in "PICT Images from Virtus WalkThrough 1.1.3 Model Views" in chapter 4.
5. Scenographic sketching and images simulating real-world atmospheric rendering are accomplished in bit-mapped programs that support anti-aliasing. (Fractal Design Painter 2.0 and Adobe PhotoShop 2.5 are two recommended programs for producing these graphics or for modifying images created in other programs.)

File Formats

Computer programs are being created in an ever-increasing number and written in a bewildering array of file formats. Those who decide to use the computer for creating images have no choice but to learn the main features of each graphic format: how they are produced; how they behave; how they interact with each other. The process is not unlike learning to drive a car with a dozen or so main gear shifts along with a few minor ones thrown in.

Every computer program is written in a specific form of language; not all programs are written in the same language. These differ widely; each has its own type of file format that allows the user to perform certain functions unique to that format. An entire book could be written on these differences; what they are, how they work, and the peculiarities of each, are subjects that frequently exasperate and confuse the graphic artist who thinks in terms of end results, not in the inscrutable possibilities of computer code.

Understanding what a graphic format will do—and, more important still, what it will not do—requires of computer graphics artists a thorough understanding of the possibilities each different program offers or allows. Certain programs do permit the user to convert one format into another.

Fortunately, the ability to change one kind of graphic into another is becoming more standard; the history of graphics program upgrades is a continuing attempt to make formats native to one program readable in others. Perhaps in the future, all graphics programs will automatically convert file formats; for the near term, however, one should expect that the proprietary formats of individual programs will not be recognized by other applications.

Let us examine the predominate kinds of formats that lend themselves to theater graphics and also briefly examine some other formats that may be occasionally used.

Bit-Mapped Graphics

Bit map images are one of two basic kinds of computer graphics. Bit maps can be thought of as images composed of small squares called *pixels*. A mosaic of small colored tiles is a close analogy to graphics in the world of art outside the computer screen. The term *pixel* is derived from a shortening of two words: picture elements. These pixels, as seen on the computer screen, are squares with 1/72″ sides. Like their real-life mosaic tile counterparts, pixels can be combined into graphic images. One of the features of the pixel is that it has square corners. This means that images with rounded contours have a stair-stepped appearance. Bit-mapped art printed at low resolutions is characteristically crude in outline. Images created of pixels are not, however, limited to that basic resolution; it is possible to create bit-mapped images in higher resolutions such as 300 dots per inch and higher. All paint programs are bit-mapped applications. Adobe PhotoShop 2.5 and Fractal Design Painter 2.0 are bit-mapped applications that give sophisticated control over the graphics created or brought into them in the PICT format, which was the first generic graphics file format possible on the Macintosh computer.

Draw or Object-Oriented Graphics

Graphics drawn in an object-oriented format have few attributes of bit-mapped drawings. It is often difficult, however, to discern on the computer screen differences between bit-mapped objects and object-oriented objects (also called *draw* objects), since what appears there are, after all, only electronic approximations of hard-copy printed images. The most basic difference between a bit-mapped images and object-oriented graphics is that the bit map is only a collection of independent pixels arranged in a pattern, whereas graphics created in draw programs are stored as *vectors* or mathematically described objects and paths. Although the object that appears on the screen may seem to be the same kind of image as that composed of bit maps, it is in actuality only a temporary visible manifestation of a set of instructions that the user creates and stores—either temporarily or permanently—on a database within the program. When the object is created, entries are made into this database; when the object is modified, moved, or combined with other objects, this database is updated to reflect the changes. Unlike bit-mapped images, draw objects can be scaled, rotated, cut apart, filled with patterns and colors, all in whatever resolution the user decides or the program allows. There is little impediment to the movement of these objects. These images—unlike bit-mapped images—can be stacked one on top of another without destroying images below.

Not all draw programs are CAD programs, but all CAD programs are draw (object-oriented) programs. As draw programs—such as Canvas 3.5—become more sophisticated, CAD-like features are incorporated in them. True CAD programs, like AutoCad, Claris CAD 2.0, PowerDraw 5.0, and MiniCad+ 5.0, are more *powerful*. But just what does the word *powerful* mean when applied to computer programs? It simply means that the program gives the drawer better, quicker ways to create complex drawings more accurately. This question is addressed by David L. Pellz in the July 1989 issue of *MacUser*. Here are some of his remarks:

> If CAD is such a powerful tool, why don't more people use it? A recent survey found that nearly 80 percent of today's technical professionals still use traditional methods for sketching, drawing, drafting, and design. The typical reasons for resisting CAD are that it is too complicated, too expensive, or too difficult to learn. Potential users lament that they don't have the time to learn a CAD package, that they won't use it enough to justify the investment in training, or that their work is insufficiently conduits to merit it.
>
> With the advent of the packages considered here, these excuses no longer apply. Low-end CAD packages for the Mac justify themselves for relatively demanding applications as well as easy, "casual" use.
>
> CAD is not a new tool—it has been around for more than 20 years. As such, it is a mature and proven technology. What is news, however, is the changing nature of the CAD *user*. The Macintosh brings the power of CAD to the fingertips of mere mortals, even mortals pressed for time. It also makes CAD accessible and affordable. It considerably broadens not only the user base but also the range of applications and market conduits for CAD products.

Since this article was written, many more architects, engineers, designers, and scenographers are using CAD programs. Drawing of every kind is moving from drawing boards to computer screens.

The first hard truth concerning computer graphics is that when a program is bought, the capabilities it provides are temporary in nature. Computer programs are not fixed things; the programmers who wrote them continue to modify them long after the sale to

Recommended Programs for Scenography
Application Versions

you. The time period between these changes varies from a few months to several years. Changes to programs are provided to registered users in two ways: (1) as minor upgrades that carry a decimal number after the main number of the program, e.g., Canvas 2.0, Canvas 2.1, and (2) as major upgrades that are issued as whole numbers, e.g., Canvas 3.0. Minor upgrades are almost invariably given to registered users—a good reason for being a registered user—free. These upgrades are frequently issued to fix minor bugs that did not show up in the testing stage. The numbering of an upgrade, however, has no real logic to it, although only a minor change in magnitude, the upgrade of Photoshop 2.01 to 2.5 represents a significant improvement to the program. Major upgrades cost money. They are only provided cost-free if the program was bought within a limited time frame—usually ninety days—before the issuance of a new version. Major upgrades are offered to older registered users at discounts that vary with the program version owned; the older the version, the higher the upgrade cost.

The graphic examples included in this book were created using the eight basic applications listed below on the hardware discussed earlier in "Basic Hardware and Equipment." Some few other options not frequently used in theater graphics will be given; theater workers who use computer graphics should have a knowledge of their existence, if not a complete familiarity with the workings of these other programs. In addition to the recommended programs, a few other applications will also be discussed below in the section "Recommended Allied Programs."

As we examine the various programs listed, take note how screens in different applications organize the screen in terms of tools and options. (Also note differences.) Much can be learned from an analysis of a program's basic screen; close study not only reveals tools and options available but also provides important insight into the ways a program operates. When learning a new program, give particular attention to the application's native file format; it is a clue as to how graphics created within the program can be used in others.

1. Deneba Canvas 3.5 (or later version): If the scenographer had to choose one program only for computer-generated graphics, Canvas 3.5 would almost certainly be the choice made. Called the "Swiss-Army Knife" of applications, this program, from its inception to its last upgrade, offers more important tools and options than any other written for the Macintosh computer. With the exception of three-dimensional capability, entire productions can be designed and printed using the draw portion of Canvas 3.5 alone. Although not a dedicated CAD program, nor does it have the full set of CAD tools, Canvas 3.5 is highly recommended for the basic stages of scenographic design. This program is especially suited to show movement of scenic elements on interactive floor plans. In this text Canvas 3.5 is used as the primary drawing environment, since it thoroughly demonstrates the possibilities of computers for scenographic purposes. For those new to computer graphics, Canvas 3.5 is recommended as a superior entry-level program.

2. Aldus SuperPaint 3.5 (or later version): This application combines the possibilities of two earlier programs: MacPaint and MacDraw. Although not an expensive application if compared with most programs, SuperPaint 3.5 cannot be recommended for complicated technical drawings. Unlike most other draw and paint programs, SuperPaint 3.5

has only two basic screens with no further possibilities of layers. These dedicated levels—one for bit maps and one for draw objects—are made available by clicking on a key icon at the top of the Toolbox Window. Selecting one window or the other changes the nature of the program—from a object-oriented (draw) program to a bit map (paint) program. Even though this arrangement is rudimentary, it has advantages for those learning the fundamentals of computer graphics. Since the two layers in SuperPaint 3.5 are clearly marked, confusion concerning the type of drawing format being used is lessened. This program is primarily recommended for beginners learning computer graphics basics. SuperPaint 3.5, unfortunately, is also hampered by its general slowness. Still, it has a number of valuable bit map editing tools that are not available in Canvas 3.5.

3.   Aldus IntelliDraw 2.0 (or later version): This is a general object-oriented drawing program meant for a wide range of users. Although it has a number of sophisticated features rivaling the best object-editing features of Canvas 3.5, Adobe Illustrator 5.0, and even those of Aldus FreeHand 4.0—a program from the same company—it has limited use for scenographers. This program, in fact, has many strong similarities to Canvas 3.5; in a few instances it gives options to combine basic shapes into hybrid forms better than those contained in Canvas 3.5. The few features that are useful for scenographic drawing, however, make it advisable to possess the program. One tool in particular—the *symmetrigon tool*—creates certain kinds of objects in ways not found in any of the other programs recommended in this book. The usefulness of this tool will be shown in chapter 3. Aldus IntelliDraw is one of a new breed of applications that use artificial intelligent-like strategies to create, align, link, and automatically update changes to drawn objects. For those who need presentation capabilities or desktop publishing features—such as master-page creation with auto-flow of linked text blocks—this is a good program to have in the studio. As with Canvas 3.5 and Virtus WalkThrough, Aldus IntelliDraw is most useful as a conceptual-development tool and as a program in which to create unusually shaped objects.

4.   PowerDraw 5.0 (or later version): This program, written by Engineered Software of Greensboro, North Carolina, is the most powerful two-dimensional CAD program listed in this text. It is especially recommended to those scenographers who create complex technical specifications to implement their designs. It is, however, the only program suggested that cannot be purchased from discount sources; all versions of PowerDraw must be obtained from an accredited dealer or directly from the company. Educational groups, on the other hand, can obtain multiple copies at significantly lower costs. The main reason for using PowerDraw 5.0 for technical drawing is that it possesses the most complete set of tools for the making of working drawings of any program on the Macintosh platform. Three of PowerDraw 5.0's extensive set of tools are discussed and demonstrated in chapter 3. Although many of the tools and options included are geared to engineering rather than mechanical drafting, the program's ability to construct highly complex drawings is not matched by any other program listed here, including the next recommendation, MiniCad+ 5.0. Although PowerDraw 5.0 allows a scenographer to create isometric and perspective drawings, these are not true automatically created three-dimensional graphics as is possible to make in programs like MiniCad+ 5.0 and Virtus WalkThrough 1.1.3. For technical directors who translate the scenographer's models and sketches into working

drawings—and this practice increases as scenic technology becomes more complex—PowerDraw 5.0 is a superior program.

5. MiniCad+ 5.0 (or later version): Although Canvas 3.5 serves as a complete graphics production tool, there is ample justification to have and master MiniCad+ 5.0. The most important reasons are (1) MiniCad+ 5.0 is a superior CAD program, and (2) it is an integrated two-dimensional and three-dimensional package; that is, once plans are drafted, they can be translated directly into three-dimensional structures without leaving the MiniCad program. Unlike Virtus WalkThrough objects, forms in MiniCad+ 5.0 will merge into hybrid structures. As with PowerDraw 5.0, openings for windows and doors are automatically incorporated into solid wall structures. MiniCad+ 5.0, like Canvas 3.5 and IntelliDraw 2.0, has a capability to merge shapes into new editable outlines as well as options that permit the cutting of basic shapes into odd-outlined forms. For those scenographers who create only basic working drawings or have scenic shops create more detailed specifications, Canvas 3.5 is an adequate application. For those who need to make highly structured two-dimensional technical specifications that need to be turned into real three-dimensional models, MiniCad+ 5.0 is recommended.

6. Adobe Photoshop 2.5 (or later version): Adobe Photoshop 2.5 is presently and likely to remain the best image-editing program available. Through this program, PICT files of computer models can· be rendered into more complex images than is possible using the resources of the original program in which they were created. (See "Rendering PICT Images on the Computer," for further discussion and detailed instructions.) Although Adobe Photoshop 2.5 saves images in its own file format, it is possible to export images edited there into other programs such as Fractal Design Painter 2.0 and in so doing obtain many options not found in Adobe Photoshop 2.5. This program is especially recommended for creating computer scenographic sketches made into slides (the most practical way to create hard-copy color images from computer files).

7. Fractal Design Painter 2.0. (or later version): This application requires computers in the Macintosh II series with a math coprocessor installed. Painter needs at least four megabytes of RAM memory and operates on any system above 6.0.5. System 7, however, is recommended This program is the best Macintosh painting program available for creating or editing computer scenographic sketches. Its drawing tools—pencils, chalks, felt-tip markers, inks, spray guns—are superior to all other paint programs. Used with a pressure-sensitive tablet that supports a cordless stylus, this program closely approximates how artists work using real-life tools and materials. Since printing out files on high-end color printers will not be feasible for years to come, the practice of showing scenographic sketches on the computer itself will become the main way to show color computer scenographic designs.

8. Fractal Design Sketcher 1.0 (or later version): This program is the monochrome companion of Painter. Created especially for gray-scale graphics, Sketcher works on any Macintosh from a Classic II to the Quadra systems, including the PowerBook 140 and 170 Macintosh. Its cost is roughly one-third of Painter. In many ways this program is more suitable for scenographic work than Painter, since much of a scenographer's work is done in black and white or in shades of gray.

1.   Virtus WalkThrough 1.1.3 (or later version) or Virtus Professional: The only software virtual reality program available for the Macintosh, Virtus WalkThrough 1.1.3 is the most intuitive of all three-dimensional modelers available in that it directly emulates the way scenographers work in the world outside the computer. Using the familiar views associated with manual drafting—plans, elevations, and perspectives—accurately scaled computer models not only are possible to assemble but can immediately be viewed from an infinite number of vantage points. For scenographers wishing to construct and test model possibilities before real-world models are started, this program is highly recommended. A full discussion of Virtus WalkThrough 1.1.3 is given in chapter 4.

2.   Virtus Voyager 1.0 (or later version): This program is an extension of Virtus WalkThrough 1.1.3 and cannot be used with versions earlier than 1.1.3. Its sole purpose is to make independent files of computer models for viewers who do not have the original program. A Voyager document, in other words, is a self-running file using a simplified interface that allows viewers with minimal previous experience in three-dimensional computer graphics to explore computer models. Since the disk containing a Voyager model has as part of its basic format a Help File, the scenographer who creates the model need not be in the same location as the viewer to demonstrate how a proposed setting appears. Virtus Voyager is fully explained in chapter 4.

1.   Aldus FreeHand 4.0 (or later version): This program is one of the two major illustration programs available on the Macintosh platform. Like its counterpart—Adobe Illustrator 5—it is primarily used by by graphic artists needing a high degree of control over line widths, object shapes, and object-fills; technical illustrators, cartographers, technical illustrators, and the like, are those who FreeHand 4.0 best serves. Because it lacks almost all CAD features, it is not recommended for working drawings or technical specification that must be dimensioned. No computer graphics workstation, however, should be without this program, since it is useful in creating computer scenographic drawings.

2.   Capture 4.0 (or later version): This useful utility program gives computer graphic artists the ability to make bit-mapped images of anything appearing on the computer screen. Every image in this book that shows dialog boxes or other screen information items were made using Capture 4.0. Figure 17 shows the basic screen for the program along with the customizing options available for capturing screen images. An interesting feature of Capture 4.0 is that it makes a bit-mapped image of any object at differing magnifications; that is, if an image is being viewed at 200 percent, the Capture image will also be 200 percent of the original. When it is pasted into a document from the clipboard—the default and recommended setting for temporarily holding the image—it retains its larger size. If Capture images are saved as PICT, TIFF, or MacPaint files, they can be turned into high-resolution graphics using Streamline 3.0 listed below. These, in turn, can be incorporated into programs that use PostScript images such as FreeHand 4.0 or Adobe Illustrator 5. All this sounds confusing in print; the process becomes more evident in practice.

3.   Streamline 3.0 (or later version): Streamline 3.0 is a utility program that converts bit-mapped images into scalable PostScript outline graphics. Able to read several of the

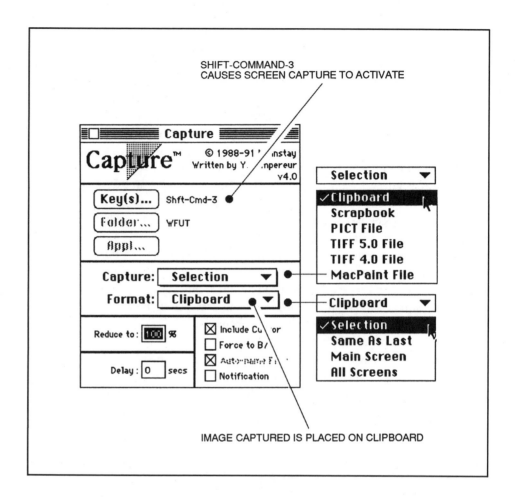

Fig. 17. Capture 4.0 screen

more important file formats—TIFF, MacPaint, and PICT in particular—this utility is particularly useful for creating working-drawing profile drawings. Use of the program is demonstrated in chapter 3. Streamline 3.0 is used to convert bit-mapped images into high-resolution scenographic renderings.

4. QuicKeys 3.0 (or later version): This utility program is an essential program for any serious computer user. It is the first addition that should be added to the basic setup of the computer. Those installing it soon find that they cannot do without the many automatic shortcuts it allows. QuicKeys 3.0 is most useful on extended keyboards. These keyboards have—in addition to the standard key layout—a row of fifteen function keys above. One of the most remarkable features in this program is its ability to use the same keys for different functions in different applications; this flexibility allows users to create a specific set of shortcuts for that application alone. Even if one occasionally forgets the keystroke pattern for a particular program, typing the *Option-Command-Return* keys brings up the full menu as a visual screen. The number of functions possible using this utility are too numerous to list here.

5. Norton Utilities for the Macintosh 2.0 (or later version): Norton Utilities, pub-

lished by Symantec Corporation, is a collection of applications that provides necessary computer housekeeping duties such as defragmenting hard disks (an essential operation that should be performed periodically in order to keep the computer running effectively), repairing lost boot blocks, or recovering lost or damaged files. Included in this set are several alternatives to utilities shipped with the basic Macintosh operating system; Keyfinder is, for instance, a better version of Key Caps. Norton Utilities is highly recommended.

There are a number of public-domain programs (also known as *shareware*) that are extremely helpful in making computers more efficient work environments. Many of these single-function programs are modest in intention and performance; most require little hard-disk space. Nevertheless, what they do is to make individual workstations more effective, less stressful places for those who spend long hours at computer tasks. While there are hundreds of shareware programs floating about the various networks, only two are recommended here, since they are particularly suitable for CAD and other types of graphics work where the scenographer may have several windows of complex drawings open at the same time. A word of caution is useful, however: seek out and install only those programs that are absolutely necessary; loading the computer with scores of INITs and CDEVs is the surest way to experience trouble. No one would think of ordering every item on the menu of a restaurant no matter how good its reputation. Cramming a computer with too many INITs or CDEVs leads to electronic indigestion; the more installed, the greater the possibility for program conflicts or system crashes. It is wise to install as few INITs and CDEVs on the system file as possible, using an INIT manager— such as Extensions Manager 1.5, a shareware program created by Ricardo Batista—to control those present. The following applications are also helpful shareware programs.

1. DiskDup+ 2.21 (fig. 18): This shareware program, written by Roger D. Bates and issued by Softdisk Publishing in 1993, permits the copying of 400K, 800K or 1440K Macintosh disks on any Macintosh computer with 1 megabyte or more memory. The value of this program lies in its ability to copy disks to other disks or files from the resident hard disk onto floppy disks without having to constantly switch disks in the copying process. Since the normal copying program integral to the Macintosh handles only 32K of information at a time, it is advantageous to have an independent program that reads greater amounts of information at the same time. When the reading limit of 32K is reached in the standard copy program, it calls for the disk being written to be inserted; after writing out its 32K of information, it is then ready to read another 32K, and so on. DiskDup+ 2.21, on the other hand, uses available RAM to read the contents of the entire original disk before it ejects it and calls for the copy disk. It then writes the information temporarily stored to the new copy. DiskDup+ 2.21 will also initialize a disk if an uninitialized disk is used. It even saves the user the task of assigning the copied disk its proper new name. If the program is used for more than evaluation, the author requests that a small registration fee be sent to P.O. Box 14, Beaverton, Oregon 97075.

2. WindowShade 1.2 (fig. 18): Frequently, when working on a specific drawing, it is necessary to have other file windows open. As the current active window is modified, the other inactive but still-visible windows often need to redraw their contents in response

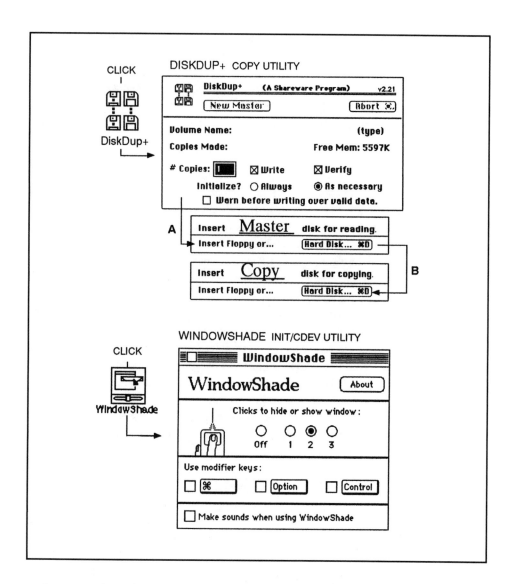

Fig. 18. Utility program screens

to changes made on the active window. To prevent the time-consuming redraws, inactive windows are collapsed. The inactive window does not, however, collapse entirely; a sizable portion of the window remains. WindowShade 1.2, created by Rob Johnston, is a control panel device specifically designed to shrink open windows to their title bars. It is an essential utility for those who need to keep several windows open at the same time. To use WindowShade 1.2, double-click the mouse on the title bar of a selected window. The window then collapses to its smallest dimension—the title bar. To open the window to its full size, double-click again on the title bar. (Some applications—such as Claris CAD 2.0—have this feature built into the program, but only for some of its menu windows; without WindowShade 1.2, however, such features do not extend to other programs.) When windows have been collapsed to their title bars by WindowShade 1.2, they are still immediately available; redraw, however, is prevented, thus saving a great deal of time. WindowShade 1.2 should *not* be installed concurrently with any other programs performing the same function (such as ZoomBar 1.7, another window-shrinking utility). If both programs are present in the control panel—the place where these INITs live— conflicts occur. Customization of WindowShade 1.2 is set in the Control Panel. This particular public-domain shareware program has no user fee attached; other shareware programs often do and should be paid, even though they are distributed on the honor system. If you like and use such programs, make sure to send in the always modest fees asked by their creators. WindowShade 1.2 is System 7.0 compatible.

Organizational Programs

Most of the work scenographers do on computers is graphically oriented; images and technical specification form the larger part of design work. There are occasions, however, when other kinds of information must be created or used: organizational charts, diagrammatic representations of work procedures, timetables, calendars. Many word processing programs have some ability to format information in chart or table form. When more detailed charts or diagrams are needed, specifically designed programs must be employed. Of the many available, only two are given here.

The first program—ACTA—creates written outlines of projects in linear form. Outlines of projects function as skeletons do for organisms; they determine subsequent growth and eventual form. (This book, for example, began as an ACTA outline.) While still in outline form, ACTA makes it possible not only to rearrange information easily but to keep elements of an outline in logical order; that is, as ideas or emphases change, the program automatically attaches appropriate numbering or labels to new entries as it deletes old numbers and labels of entries removed or reordered. After the outline is complete and edited, it can be imported into word processing programs for expansion.

The second program—Inspiration 4.0—is an application that creates *mind maps,* a form of outlining done with graphic symbols arrayed in patterns that show complex relationships not easily presented in linear form. Although Inspiration is basically meant for conceptual exploration, charts and diagrams are easily constructed or rapidly altered as necessary. Figure 19 is a diagram using Inspiration to show how creative research for scenographic design projects is structured. An added advantage to this program is that traditional written outlines of the visual diagram are immediately available with a keystroke command.

Electronic Materials Management

In *Collier's Rules for Desktop Design and Typography*—a small book highly recommend to any serious computer graphics artist—David Collier makes these astute observations:

> When computers first made it into the office a myth grew up that one day there would be a thing called the paperless office, work would be a tidy organised place with no scraps of paper to litter desks and get lost. Even now quite sophisticated computer users hold the most extraordinary beliefs about the power of the PC; that electronic documents, unlike paper ones, cannot get lost, that Apple Macintoshes are easy to use, and so on.
>
> In the real world computers are just as messy as any other form of document

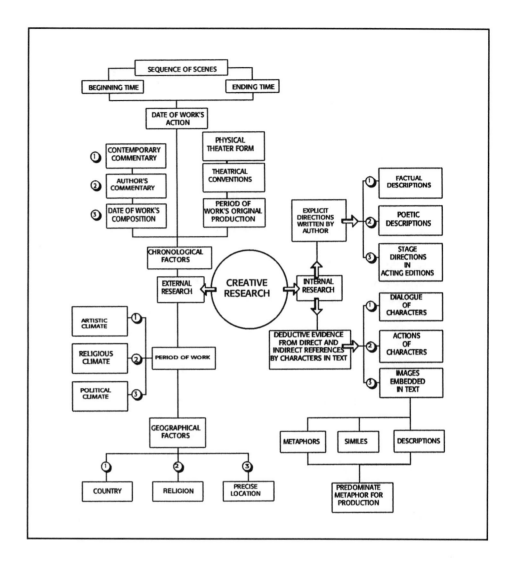

Fig. 19. Inspiration 4.0 diagram

production and need just as much organisation, if not more. If you lose a transparency or the copy for a feature in a paper-based studio, you can at least turn the place upside down till you find it. On the computer, unless you're well-prepared, it could be gone for ever. (David Collier, *Collier's Rules for Desktop Design and Typography* [New York: Addison-Wesley, 1991])

These remarks apply equally well to those computer studios where graphics files are the main output; any scenographer that uses the computer in the design process knows well the frustration of not being able to locate important drawings in the labyrinth of nested files. With each new project the problem of finding lost files or setting up new file categories that are uniquely named (the key to any automatic system of location) are compounded. And it becomes increasingly more difficult to make sure that backup files are made of the latest version of any drawing or document that has been recently altered. As

Collier also points out: "While it's amazing that computers can store so much information in their memories it's less amazing when the memory falls over and loses the document you're working on. This is a particular problem for designers who tend to work with large files, as computers use lots of memory to store complicated visual information. *The main remedy here is to check that there are no viruses affecting your computer and to save your work regularly so that any losses are minimised*" (italics mine).

As with a physical graphics studio, the electronic studio must be kept in scrupulous order. This refers not only to the physical environment of the workstation—that, of course, demands conscientious maintenance of the general area with particular care given to expensive equipment—but to the documents created on the computer and to the way these files are stored. Just as tools and materials in the physical studio often get misplaced, unless great care is taken, similar occurrences happen in the electronic studio. This is especially true for hard-disk users—and any extensive use of computer graphics virtually demands that either an internal or external hard disk be a part of the workstation—where it is all too easy to temporarily (and sometimes permanently) lose a file or a folder in a deeply nested level of the hierarchy system. This loss commonly happens in two ways: (1) by being lost because of a power failure or by being accidentally erased or (2) by being placed in embedded folders, misnamed, or named so ambiguously that even the person who created the file has forgotten what it was called. Frequent saving, of course, is the most important step for minimizing lost. Just as important, however, is careful consideration of electronic storage. Fortunately the Macintosh computer provides users logical ways to store work using a program called the Hierarchical File System or HFS. Figure 20 is a diagrammatic drawing showing how the basic system works. Although a basically simple system in concept, it can in practice be difficult to master.

All computer users should be throughly familiar not only with the ways files are stored but also with the ways to locate them. For all operating systems prior to System 7.0, one of the most important of the disk accessories (those small applications that reside under the Apple menu) available to Macintosh users is the *Find File*. This useful option allows one to search for a file buried deep in some level not apparent from reading desktop directories. By typing the name of the file desired (or even an approximation of how it is named) in the dialog box to the right of line *Search For*, and then by clicking on the *running-man* icon, a search is initiated. When the file is found it is displayed in the box immediately below the *Search For* box. When the button in this box is clicked, the information telling where the wanted file is displayed below; other items of information, including related files, are also displayed here. A superior version of the *Find File* accessory called *Fast Find* is included in Norton Utilities. *Fast Find* works in similar ways to the *Find File* accessory.These steps are included in figure 21. System 7.0 has, however, improved the abilities of the original *Find File* (not shown). It is, in fact, no longer a desk accessory and has been incorporated into the Finder itself. In order to find a file when an application is open one must return to the Finder. This is no problem, since System 7.0 has built into it a permanently operational Multifinder.

A useful method for keeping track of materials on computer hard disks (or on 3.5 disks) is to print out copies of a folder's files. The *Print Directory* option shown in figure 21*A* prints a hard copy of all files or folders visible in an active window. In case of a

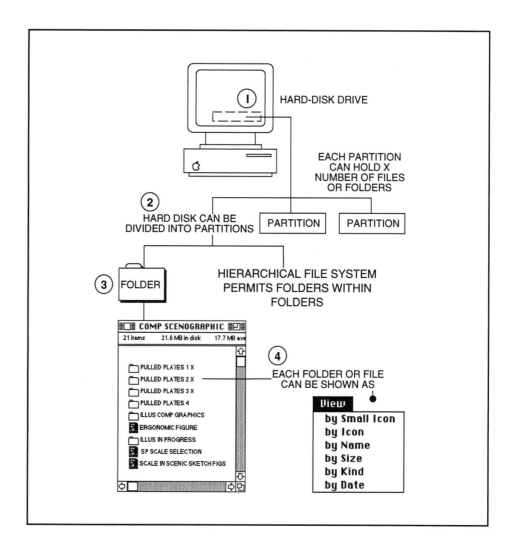

1 HARD-DISK DRIVE

EACH PARTITION
CAN HOLD X
NUMBER OF FILES
OR FOLDERS

2 HARD DISK CAN BE
DIVIDED INTO PARTITIONS

PARTITION   PARTITION

3 FOLDER

HIERARCHICAL FILE SYSTEM
PERMITS FOLDERS WITHIN
FOLDERS

COMP SCENOGRAPHIC
21 items   21.6 MB in disk   17.7 MB av

PULLED PLATES 1 X
PULLED PLATES 2 X
PULLED PLATES 3 X
PULLED PLATES 4
ILLUS COMP GRAPHICS
ERGONOMIC FIGURE
ILLUS IN PROGRESS
SP SCALE SELECTION
SCALE IN SCENIC SKETCH FIGS

4
EACH FOLDER OR FILE
CAN BE SHOWN AS

View
by Small Icon
by Icon
by Name
by Size
by Kind
by Date

Fig. 20. Hierarchical file diagram

disk crash, these directories become essential. Not only do they aid in finding what materials were lost, but these directories also prove useful as guides when setting up a new hard disk. Frequently backing up files on external disks, as well as keeping hard-copy records of completed work, is a fundamental habit to form.

Health Considerations in Computer Use

As use of computers increases, hidden dangers emerge. A growing number of studies on computers in the workplace clearly show this use is not risk-free. Many issues raised by those who perceive possible harm from computer workstations are controversial. No long-term observations exist, since warning flags did not exist before the end of the 1980s when computers began to replace typewriters.

Graphic designers who work on manual drafting boards or perform other graphic chores such as painting or modeling have long been aware that prolonged work periods create problems: general fatigue, eye strain, muscle tension, neck strain, headaches, even nausea are common complaints for many scenographers working, as they frequently must,

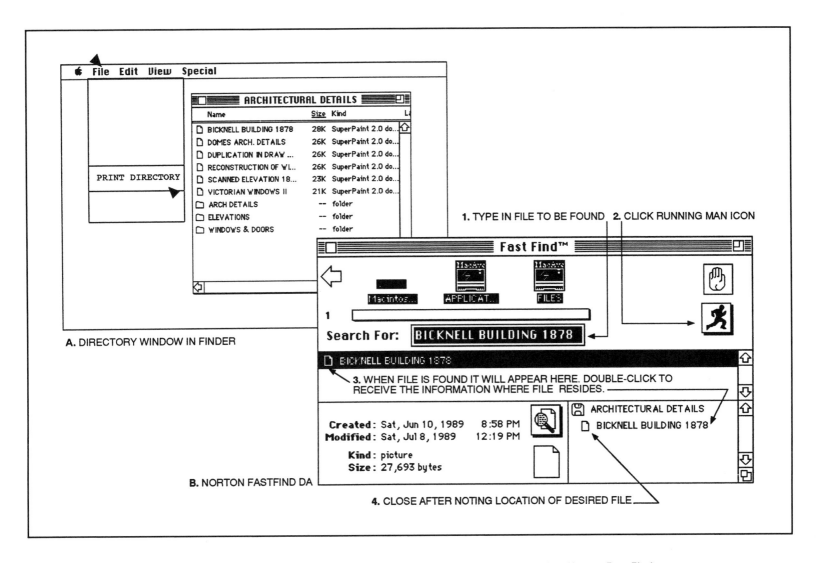

A. DIRECTORY WINDOW IN FINDER

B. NORTON FASTFIND DA

1. TYPE IN FILE TO BE FOUND   2. CLICK RUNNING MAN ICON

3. WHEN FILE IS FOUND IT WILL APPEAR HERE. DOUBLE-CLICK TO RECEIVE THE INFORMATION WHERE FILE RESIDES.

4. CLOSE AFTER NOTING LOCATION OF DESIRED FILE

Fig. 21. Norton Fast Find screen

against tight deadlines. Not to realize these problems courts immediate distress, possibly long-term physical disability. Those scenographers considering establishing a computer workstation in their studio or those now using computers are well advised to seek the best information concerning computer safety currently available. At the present time few full-length studies exist on the dangers of computer use, although new information surfaces daily. One book is available now: Dr. Ronald Harwin and Colin Haynes's *Healthy Computing: Risks and Remedies Every Computer-User Needs to Know* (New York: AMA-COM, 1991) provides a good introduction to this important subject. As for continuing findings, a good source of information concerning computer use is available in publications like *MacUser* and *MacWorld*, two popular monthly magazines devoted to emerging Macintosh technology. Computer-related health problems can be minimized by following these suggestions:

1. *Maintain a distance of approximately two feet between yourself and the computer*

screen. Radiation drops quickly after that distance. Although we know little about the dangers of electromagnetic fields in relation to forms of cancer, precaution is advised. If using more than one computer at the same time, maintain at least a two arms-length distance between your body and other machines; television sets and laser printers also emit some radiation. Monochrome monitors (dedicated black and white screens) give off less radiation than color monitors. When using a color monitor, turn off the color (this is done in the control panel) when possible; that is, if you are drafting or working on black and white illustrations, it is not necessary to have color available. Turning off the color of the computer not only speeds the operation of the computer but also lowers radiation emissions.

2. *Carefully plan the lighting of all computer studio areas*. The first step in planning the lighting of a studio is to seek out personal incompatibilities with differing kinds of light sources. This is done by having regular eye tests to determine if any problems exist among various forms of light: incandescent, florescent, halogen, color-corrected light. Care should also be taken to minimize glare on the screen; this is one of the major sources of eye fatigue and headache. Positioning of task lighting is critical to the maintenance of a glare-free screen. Antiglare screens—although frequently expensive—and hooded glare devices are available from almost any computer supply store or from mail-order companies. Simple adjustment to the monitor's tilted position prevents some glare problems.

3. *Carefully plan the ergonomic design of the physical computer workstation*. The chair in which one sits should be as carefully chosen for the individual who uses it as a good pair of shoes or a properly fitted pair of glasses. The height of the keyboard and the position of the mouse and mouse pad should be calculated by the individual user for the maximum freedom of movement. Figure 22 shows a diagram that calls attention to the major points one must consider in making the individual workstation ergonomically sound.

4. *Do not work too long at any one time*. Preventing many computer-related problems is possible simply by not working long periods without a break. Computer use is in a real sense *addictive*. It is possible, in fact, for a computer user after intense periods of work to experience conditions similar to an alcoholic hangover with attendant nauseous headaches and feelings of anxiety. In extreme instances, workers who repeat similar movements with the mouse or on the keyboard over long stretches of time encounter a disability known as *carpal tunnel syndrome* (CTS). Belonging to a category of injuries called cumulative trauma disorders, this serious condition grew to epidemic proportions during the late 1980s. Even though awareness of the problem has caused preventative steps to be introduced in offices where workers are most in danger, these and other repetitive stress injuries (RSI) are sure to increase. In extreme cases, major surgical operations were required. Most scenographers are not in as much danger from the hazards of CTS or RSI, since they do not work in the same way or spend as much time on the computer as will most office workers. Still, in my own experience, soreness of the wrist area occurs after working on projects for too long. In 1993 Apple introduced a new product—called the Apple Adjustable Keyboard—that deserves attention from concerned users (see figure 9). The Apple Adjustable Keyboard is a radical departure from the ordinary one in common use. It is designed in such a way that the keyboard separates in

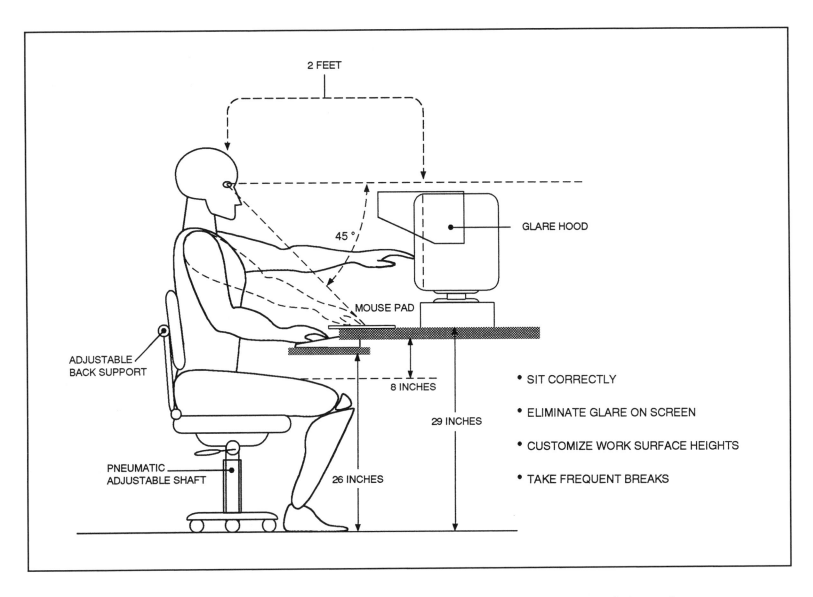

the middle allowing the right-hand and left-hand keys to angle away from one another from 0° to 30°. This split-angle design puts the keys into positions more natural to the hands than does the traditional keyboard. Theoretically physical stress is reduced making it possible to work for longer periods before discomfort appears or injury occurs. Position of the wrists and hands, however, is only one of the factors that relates to the possibility of injury; even the striking force of typing contributes to hand and wrist injury.

Fig. 22. Ergonomic factors diagram

2 The Computer as a Design Research Tool

Although computers calculate immeasurably faster than any human brain, they do not really amplify human intelligence. Nor do they make artists more creative. It is important, then, for those who use computers to understand what they can do and—equally important—to find what their limitations are.

Frederick Brooks, one of the guiding spirits of the University of North Carolina Virtual Reality Research Center, lists two areas where the human mind is superior to the possibilities of today's most powerful computer: *visual and aural pattern recognition* and *evaluation of information from an overall sense of context*. Where the computer is superior to the human mind lies in areas that require the processing of "massive amounts of data and remembering things without forgetting." Is this reason enough to justify the expense of a computer component in the scenographic studio, not to mention the time it takes to learn an entirely new approach to graphic design? Are there benefits to scenographers that lie beyond storage of information? These are questions we need to address.

As all creative theater workers know, planning productions is essentially a mutable activity; a process during which chance and random discovery play important roles. Computers are not ordinarily thought of as facilitators of creative interplay. It is precisely because they are not so considered that the subject is broached in this text; here we will explore some ways computers prove useful in scenographic design; to show how they are beneficial during the earliest creative stages of design. Here is a brief passage from Howard Rheingold's *Excursions to the Far Side of the Mind* that bears on on our present subject:

> New communication technologies and new knowledge about how the human mind functions are changing the traditional attitude that visual expression is reserved only for the "talented." And the pace of change seems to be quickening because of the continuing development of graphics-based personal computers. The psychological and technological tools for augmenting human intellect we have today are but the

earliest generations in a rapidly evolving technology; judging from the computer systems now on the drawing boards, the tools themselves soon will *show* people how to use them.

Most importantly, *the new revolution is not just about new tools*. It's about a whole new way of using tools. Like all revolutions, it's about a new way of seeing.

Those old prejudices about talent and visual expression have been jogged out of their tracks by several recent discoveries. One eye-opener was the discovery that visual thinking influences our reasoning processes: experiments by perceptual psychologist revealed that our perceptions, particularly our visual perceptions, structure the way we think about the world. Another area of discovery emerged from the design of new ways for people to use computers, a field in which the development of a graphic vocabulary plays a key role. At the creative end of the consciousness spectrum, the use of imagery for communicating abstractions the way artists and designers do seems to involve a specific set of mental skills. Western educators in kindergartens and graduate schools are beginning to develop methods for training these skills.

. . . The one aspect that connects such wildly disparate endeavors as medical self-care, psychological and spiritual growth, peak athletic performance, artistic and scientific creativity is *the power of images to program and reprogram one's unconscious belief systems*. (Howard Rheingold, *Excursions to the Far Side of the Mind*. [New York: William Morrow, 1989])

With these words in mind, let us more fully explore how computers aid scenographers during the conceptual stages of design projects. We begin with an assessment of what computers can do and—equally important—what they cannot.

Many graphic artists and scenographers unfamiliar with computer technologies hold that computers take the "art" out of art; that electronically generated images do not have that personal touch real-life materials give to graphic art. Moreover, the very nature of the intervening screen—along with the input devices necessary to record images—stands between an artist's imagination and accomplishment. Computer art, in short, not only lacks the grit and texture of everyday reality but actually impedes the artist's vision. Such fears are not easily put aside for those who until now have worked without computers.

Even the most skeptical of these artists are often pleasantly surprised at the opportunities afforded by the graphic potentialities of the computer. Many artists are convinced of the computer's possibilities when they discover that it is possible, using graphics tablets and cordless styli, to draw in exactly the same manner as on paper. It is also possible to turn these freely created sketches into high-resolution images that rival their real-world counterparts. But what about that kind of drawing the scenographer does in the preliminary stages of a project? How can the computer help there? Does the computer have a role in those earliest phases? The answer is *yes*; but in order to use the computer in this capacity artists must be willing to change old and familiar ways of working.

The biggest myth concerning computers is that they save time; they do not. If

Advantages and Limits of Computer Graphics

anything, as much time or more is spent on projects than if they were manually undertaken. Why, then, use a computer? The reasons why scenographic designers and technicians should master computer-aided design are many and persuasive. The most basic of these reasons are that computers give artists an ability to:

Produce graphic images with high degrees of accuracy.
Correct mistakes easily.
Alter concepts and designs quickly.
Duplicate materials.
Share design information interactively.
Share design information electronically.
Store vast amounts of information easily in small spaces.

Of all these reasons, the option to change concepts and designs quickly is easily the most crucial to productive collaboration. The capability of two or more persons sitting before a single computer—or through networking using different computers—to share information, significantly accelerates design communication processes. A simple example using Canvas 3.5 illustrates the advantage of computer-aided drawing over manual drafting.

Let us assume that we have opened Canvas 3.5 and have, after selecting the rectangle tool, drawn a rectangle like that shown in figure 23. The same image—or a similar one—can be drawn manually on a regular drawing board. This drawing would take approximately the same time as the computer image. Speed of drawing is not the only advantage, however; the computer-drawn rectangle has advantages not available with the manually drawn one, such as these:

1. Objects can not only be measured precisely in seconds but can have this information attached to the image automatically.

2. In addition—using options basic to Canvas 3.5—sizes, areas, and perimeters of objects can be calculated and assigned to the image using the pop-out dialog box contained in the information bar at the bottom of the window those shown in figure 23.

3. Objects can be converted into file formats other than those in which they are created. For instance, an object created in the Canvas's proprietary file format can be saved and exported as a PICT image making it readable in a program such as FreeHand 4.0.

Since the earliest uses of images to communicate ideas, drawing and writing have diverged. Images still, however, retain their power to transmit ideas. Has the computer really changed this situation? Will all graphic image making in the future be relegated to electronic devices? Probably not. It is not only improbable that use of the hand to draw and write will not disappear, but that there will be an increasingly greater integration of hand and machine as computers become "smarter" in recognizing hand-made marks and drawings. Learning to draw "by hand," therefore, is still necessary training for graphic artists. Ability to draw effectively on the computer, moreover, is enhanced significantly by learning to draw with pencil, pen, and ink.

The basic layout of the screens for all Macintosh computer graphics programs are

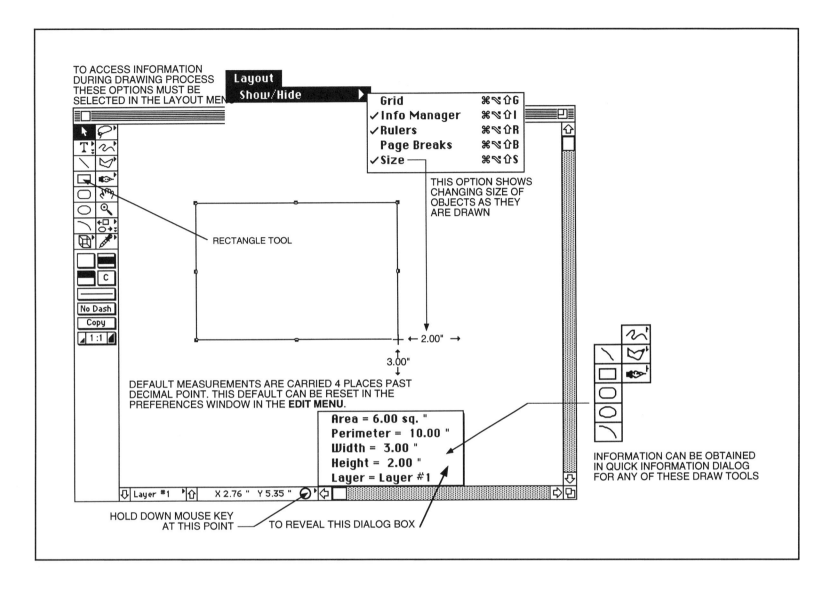

TO ACCESS INFORMATION
DURING DRAWING PROCESS
THESE OPTIONS MUST BE
SELECTED IN THE LAYOUT MENU

Layout
Show/Hide

Grid   ⌘⌥⇧G
✓ Info Manager   ⌘⌥⇧I
✓ Rulers   ⌘⌥⇧R
Page Breaks   ⌘⌥⇧B
✓ Size ———   ⌘⌥⇧S

THIS OPTION SHOWS
CHANGING SIZE OF
OBJECTS AS THEY
ARE DRAWN

RECTANGLE TOOL

← 2.00" →

3.00"

DEFAULT MEASUREMENTS ARE CARRIED 4 PLACES PAST
DECIMAL POINT. THIS DEFAULT CAN BE RESET IN THE
PREFERENCES WINDOW IN THE **EDIT MENU**.

Area = 6.00 sq. "
Perimeter = 10.00 "
Width = 3.00 "
Height = 2.00 "
Layer = Layer #1

INFORMATION CAN BE OBTAINED
IN QUICK INFORMATION DIALOG
FOR ANY OF THESE DRAW TOOLS

Layer #1   X 2.76 "   Y 5.35 "

HOLD DOWN MOUSE KEY
AT THIS POINT ———   TO REVEAL THIS DIALOG BOX

roughly similar to that shown in figure 24; the Canvas 3.5 program's basic screen—the program used in figure 24—generally approximates the layout of tools and materials found in the scenographer's real-world studio. Note particularly the strong similarities of working areas to tool storage. Macintosh screens are often said to be *intuitive* in layout; that is, artists are able to relate kinesthetically learned drawing relationships to the computer's drawing environment.

It becomes quickly evident to anyone using a computer that a strong element of play pervades the entire field. The meaning of *play* intended here is familiar to all creative people despite differences in craft or art, age or level of proficiency. A strong undercurrent

Fig. 23. Computer graphics screen

The Role of Play in Computer Graphics

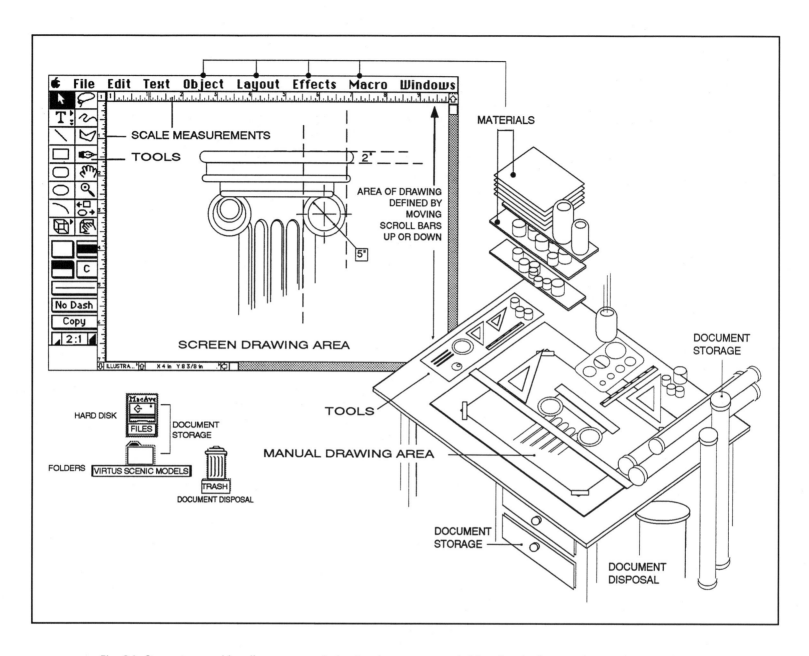

File Edit Text Object Layout Effects Macro Windows

SCALE MEASUREMENTS

TOOLS

2"

AREA OF DRAWING
DEFINED BY
MOVING
SCROLL BARS
UP OR DOWN

5"

SCREEN DRAWING AREA

MATERIALS

MacAve
FILES

HARD DISK

DOCUMENT
STORAGE

FOLDERS   VIRTUS SCENIC MODELS

TRASH

DOCUMENT DISPOSAL

TOOLS

MANUAL DRAWING AREA

DOCUMENT
STORAGE

DOCUMENT
STORAGE

DOCUMENT
DISPOSAL

Fig. 24. Computer graphics diagram

of play has been, most probably, the single most important part of the arts from their inception; it is possible, one might say, to postulate that *any* art is the spirit of play made manifest in thought, sound, or material. Paul Rand, the noted graphic designer, gives credence to this with the following perceptive observation:

A problem with defined limits, implied or stated disciplines which are, in turn, conducive to *the instinct of play*, will most likely yield an interested student and, very often, a meaningful and novel solution.

Of the two powerful instincts which exist in all human beings and which can be used in teaching, says Gilbert Highet, one is the *love of play*." The best Renaissance teachers, instead of beating their pupils, spurred them on by a number of appeals to the play-principle. They made Games out of the chore of learning difficult subjects—Montaigne's father, for instance, started him in Greek by writing the letters and easiest words on playing cards and inventing a game to play with them." (Gilbert Highet, *The Art of Teaching* [New York: Random House, 1989])

This "love of play" that Rand alludes to must certainly be taken into account when we attempt even the most elementary understanding of the creative process. Creative play is, then, not a temporary respite from theatrical problem solving but a seriously considered means of facilitating it. The question is, then, to what extent do computers aid theater artists in this important phase of work?

Electronic images are not really images at all; they are simply a series of small black squares temporarily captured on an electronic screen. The lines, shapes, and patterns we perceive there are nothing more than the effect of an electric impulse displayed in one of two modes: ON or OFF; a "drawing" done by computer exists only as a transitory passage of electric impulses, and, like all electric impulses, they are fleetingly temporary. Unlike the more permanent mark of a pencil on a piece of paper, an electronically created image disappears as a source of power is turned off. It is possible, however, to capture these fleeting images as facsimiles on another machine—a printer—and in doing so obtain a more permanent record. It is this possibility—the ability *to record light images in ink on paper*—that gives the graphic artist a radically new tool; a tool unlike any that preceded it. While the technology of this new tool is presently limited in scope, even now theater artists will find computer-generated graphics of great use.

Drawing has been an important part of theatrical production for the past four hundred years; figure 25 is a chart that shows the relationship of graphic work to actual theatrical practice during this period. Although it is evident that emphases have changed radically during this period, no single trend or development has had the significance of that now in progress: the introduction of the computer into the drawing studio.

Few would question the proposition that scenographic artists need to be technically proficient in a number of visual systems. But after that general agreement, there is considerably less understanding as to what these systems involve and what purpose they serve. Often there is a confusion as to what skills are necessary for professional competence. Still, most instructors and students of theatrical design would agree that two broad areas of drawing are necessary in any course of study: (1) the ability to represent three-dimensional objects on two-dimensional surfaces, and (2) the ability to make scaled drawings showing how three-dimensional structures are to be achieved on stage. After that there is less agreement as to what is necessary.

It is safe to say, therefore, that basic assumptions concerning the nature of drawing are not only being questioned in today's theater but are in many instances being redefined. Some of those questions raised call into doubt traditional practice: *Is it necessary for students to learn the intricacies of perspective rendering when many designs are presented in model form? Is it necessary to learn manual drafting technique when computer graphics*

REQUIRED SKILL	HISTORICAL EMPHASIS (1656-1860-90)	MODERN EMPHASIS (1900-PRESENT)
1. ILLUSORY DRAWING BASED ON PERSPECTIVE SKILLS	ALMOST TOTAL	STEADILY DECREASING IMPORTANCE
2. ABILITY TO FASHION THREE-DIMENSIONAL CONCEPTS IN SCENIC MODEL FORM	LITTLE TO NONEXISTENT	STEADILY INCREASING EMPHASIS SINCE 1920s
3. ABILITY TO COORDINATE ALL ELEMENTS OF VISUAL PRODUCTION: COSTUME, LIGHTING, PROPERTIES, ETC.	ALMOST NONEXISTENT UNTIL MIDDLE 1990s	ALMOST TOTAL
4. MAKING OR SUPERVISION OF WORKING DRAWINGS AND SPECIFICATIONS	LITTLE (FLAT PAINTING EASY TO DUPLICATE BY SCENIC PAINTERS OF THE TIME)	STEADILY INCREASING EMPHASIS UP TO 1920s WITH DECREASING EMPHASIS TAKING PLACE IN TODAY'S PRACTICE AS PROFESSIONAL SCENIC SHOPS ASSUME RESPONSIBILITY FOR SCENIC DRAWING SPECIFICATIONS
5. INTEGRATION OF SCENIC CONCEPTS WITH OVERALL MEANINGS OF TEXT	LITTLE OR NONEXISTENT	INCREASINGLY IMPORTANT
6. USE OF MODERN TECHNOLOGY AS PART OF ARTISTIC PROCESS: FILM, TELEVISION, COMPUTER TECHNOLOGY, ETC.	NONEXISTENT	STEADILY INCREASING EMPHASIS

Fig. 25. Chart of scenographic emphasis

programs can be used to produce more precise drawings than any draftsman can on manual drawing boards? And why learn figure drawing—or any other formal drawing technique, for that matter—when cameras or computer-scanned images produce detailed likenesses in a fraction of the time it takes to make manual renderings? These questions are not easy to answer.

Still, a good case might still be made for old-fashioned kinesthetically experienced drawing instruction. It could also be adequately defended that in the act of drawing, the mind is trained in ways that cannot be duplicated by any other method, certainly not by keystrokes using the most sophisticated computer graphics program. In his book, *Solitude,*

Anthony Storr makes this statement: "The act of drawing sharpens the perceptions of the draughtsman; an idea passionately advanced by Ruskin, who believed *that it was only by trying to capture the external world in form and colour that the artist learns to apprehend it*" (italics mine).

Although drawing with the computer is the subject of this book, there is much to be said for the direct encounter of the eye, the mind, and the hand. What we address here, then, is how various scenographic drawing possibilities are enhanced through computer use, while not to suggest that manual drawing has outlived it usefulness. Quite often many scenographic processes are best served with pen or pencil.

The very nature of computer technology demands that work patterns be logical if work is to be productive. Can any artist be spontaneously creative using a complex machine? Although all designers know that any artistic process needs periods of unstructured gestation, there comes a point in every project when its various strands and pieces must be given a specific form and direction. It is at this point the computer becomes helpful. But the advantages of a computer are not without cost; they must be gained by study and practice.

Since each program is written to conform to basic ways of processing and storing information, it is to the advantage of the user to know the way that program "thinks." This is a time-consuming task. The main ways by which we come to understand the program's structure are not only to carefully study the visual interface, where tools and functions are displayed by icons or in menus, but also to know the less obvious methods of performing a task or a function. These are generally contained in the pattern of keystrokes that provide quick alternates to the clicking of an icon or the pulling down of a menu to select a desired function. Using macro programs such as QuicKeys or taking advantage of the internal libraries-making functions many programs provide also promotes the speed and productivity of a program's user. Although all designers have individual work procedures carried over from manual ways of working, it is to the advantage of those using computers in their graphic work to rethink previous patterns of work, discovering the new patterns to accomplish tasks devised by the application's programmers. Freely drawing ideas on the computer screen, of course, is not—and maybe never will be—as easy a task as using pencil and paper. Sketching is possible on the screen only with electronic styli on graphics tablets. This kind of drawing is only productive on tablets like the high-resolution Wacom that uses styli without constricting power cords. A growing number of programs are now supporting pressure-sensitive painting. Notable among these are Fractal Design Painter 2.0, Adobe Photoshop 2.5, and Aldus FreeHand 4.0, which also supports the pressure-sensitive stylus of the Wacom tablet. The way one creates an image using traditional tools and materials (fig. 26*A*) is significantly different from the ways an image is created using a computer's drawing environment (fig. 26*B*). Even from this crude diagram it is easy to see that new kinesthetic skills must be developed.

For exploring basic visual concepts Canvas 3.5, SuperPaint 3.5, and FreeHand 4.0 are recommended. These programs permit different kinds of graphic formats to be present in a single file; bit-mapped images, for instance, can be combined with high-resolution

Working on the Computer

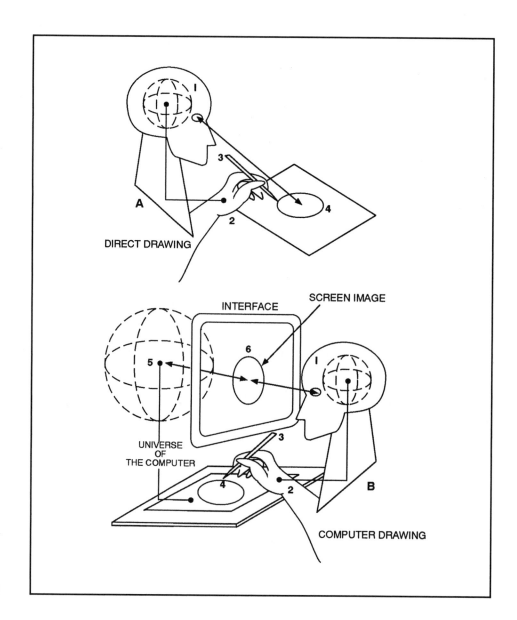

Fig. 26. Computer drawing diagram

objects to form a hybrid image. Scanned images saved in permanent library files can be introduced into either of these programs and modified with the program's tools. Although I use Canvas 3.5 as my primary experimental program, the bit map editing tools of SuperPaint 3.5 are more extensive and serviceable. After scanning an image into the computer, the first stop is SuperPaint 3.5 for preliminary editing. Since both programs support bit-mapped and object-oriented images, the scenographer is given a great deal of freedom to experiment with shapes and forms in various arrangements. Figure 27 shows a bit-mapped drawing composed of images scanned from different sources, with some editing in SuperPaint 3.5, but finished in Canvas 3.5. Some of the tools used are shown in figure 28. At best, working with bit-mapped graphics is a time-consuming process.

Bit-mapped renderings derived from high-resolution PICT images using programs such as Virtus WalkThrough 1.1.3 and Photoshop 2.5 (fig. 29) are discussed in chapter 4.

Fig. 27. Bit map scenographic drawing

Designing a production using the computer is not really all that different from the way designers have always worked. The goals are identical. Just as they always have, most scenographers begin the search for design concepts by analyzing the text and assembling visual images that best externalize it for others to see. This analysis of the text helps the scenographer to weed out those images that promote concepts from those

Interactive Image Files: Libraries and Templates

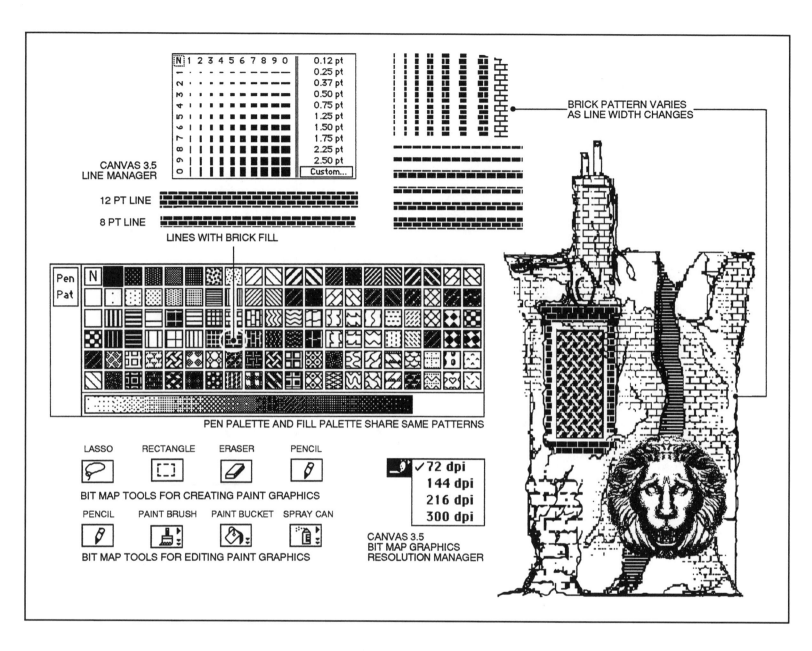

Fig. 28. Bit map tools and palettes

that do not. During this period, the need to find imagery that promotes both the playwright's conceptions and the director's ideas is the scenographer's primary concern. Just showing these materials, however, rarely produces a coherent picture of the eventual design onstage. The exploratory process for that final image almost always is accompanied by quick sketches and diagrammatic drawings. In the past these images were as quickly discarded as they were made; few designers keep them long. Even the most powerful computer using the most appropriate software does not alleviate the usefulness of this gathering-sifting-drawing process. Can the computer contribute to the conceptualizing process? Is

it possible, perhaps, to communicate more clearly intents through a machine? Yes indeed.

Most graphic artists grow up in a world where drawn images are fixed things; static objects constructed in nonreversible steps. In most cases changes to a finished image are difficult. Few artists trained in traditional art schools deny that computers provide graphic artists new ways to gather and use graphic information. But what is not as well understood is that this information is not static, that it is, rather, capable of limitless change and interaction and will remain fluid as long as it resides within the computer's memory banks.

Most scenographers assemble image files and libraries of useful information. These materials are usually kept in file cabinets or other containers where the information is accessible. This practice most likely will continue even after computers are introduced into the working studio. Image sources may remain the same; how they are handled is decidedly different. Scissors and photocopying may be useful for manipulating physical graphic images, but the computer necessitates new ways of gathering, manipulating, and storing images. Moreover, once gathered and modified, using these images requires a certain amount of education and skill. Let us now take a brief look at the procedures required to turn found images into computer-stored files.

For computer graphics the scanner is the main way images from the external world come into the computer's world. Scanners are used in three primary ways. These are:

1. Image duplicator—as a direct copying device for images that have immediate application. Images from various sources can be combined, altered, or rescaled to create a single image or can be combined into a set of images (collage). Most theater graphics

Fig. 29. Photoshop 2.5 scenographic drawing: Hamlet—act 5, scene 1

Scanners and Scanning Technique

artists will find this function the most useful to their work.

2. Research archiver—as a means of copying images onto the computer screen, which can then be saved and stored in the computer's hard disk or on 3.5 disks. This allows one to create files of archival materials (called *clip art* in computer jargon), which may have no immediate use but can be retrieved at a later time. Once these images have been saved and stored, they can be retrieved and altered by use of bit map tools into images that suit individual needs.

3. Template maker—to introduce into the computer an image that can be used as a *template*; that is, to make a preliminary pattern from which a more complete drawing can be made. An image can be introduced onto one layer (all the draw or paint programs used in this book have layer capabilities) while the image being created resides on a layer above the original. By autotrace functions—or even by use of drawing tools—refined images can be created much as one might use a light box and translucent papers in the manual graphics studio.

Scanners give computer graphics designers the possibility to create catalogs of images taken from original image resources: furniture, set properties, architectural details, once scanned or drawn, can be assembled into files, each of which can contain a number of individual items. When needed at a later time these images can be copied from the file and integrated into drawings such as floor plans, elevations, axonometric grids, or sketch concepts. Images of every kind can be placed into a computer file. Systematically assembling image files before actual need occurs saves hours of drawing.

Scanners are as useful to artists with advanced drawing skills as to those less advanced. The greatest benefit scanners bestow on artists, however, is the opportunity to assemble catalogues of images from many sources: furniture, set properties, and architectural details can be assembled into computer files. Unlike their physical counterparts, the images from computer files can be duplicated, scaled to different sizes, and altered to fit the specific needs of sketch concepts, scenographic drawings, paper model parts, painting outlines, working specifications, and so on. In a short preface to *Ideas on Design*, Peter Mayle provides a telling reason why scenographers should take full advantage of the image-gathering possibilities of scanner technology:

> If good designers have anything in common, it is that they all seem to be equipped with a subconscious sponge, capable of absorbing a wide and unrelated range of stimuli to be tucked away at the back of the mind for future use. A builder's yard or a factory are as likely to provide a fruitful scrap of inspiration as a book on Islamic calligraphy or a visit to the Louvre. But how did that scrap become part of a design solution? Logic? Intuition? Lateral rationalisation? Maybe thinking by jumping is as close a description as we can get, particularly since designers spend most of their workings lives hopping back and forth between different contexts and dimensions and periods of time. (Peter Mayle, *Ideas on Design* [Winchester, MA: Faber and Faber, 1989])

Scanner Resolution and Creating Picture Objects

Scanners vary in the ability to capture image materials. At the lower end of the spectrum, machines such as the Thunderscan hand scanner and the Mirror VS300 overhead scanner provide relatively low-resolution capability; both, however, can read images from the most basic bit map image of 72 DPI to 300 DPI. The Typist—another hand-held scanner—differs from these in that it is primarily an *optical character recognition* machine (which means that it has the capability to scan editable type into word processing programs) but is also able to process graphic images.

A level higher than these machines are a number of 600 DPI flatbed scanners. These can be obtained for either gray-scale images or for color images. Greater images sizes are also more possible with flat bed scanners. While these machines cost between two to four times more than dedicated 300 DPI machines, they are able to scan images at significantly higher resolutions. Since the basic unit of any bit-mapped image is always a pixel, this means that the higher the resolution an image is scanned, the bigger will be the on-screen image and the larger will be the saved file. This is the main reason why many choose to scan images at lower resolutions. There are some ways that the crudeness of the dot pattern of a 72 DPI image can be made into sharper images. Once an image has been scanned into the computer and edited to the desired appearance,it can be altered into a file format that will keep the image's basic resolution no matter what size it is scaled. The trick is to convert the bit map image into a *picture object*. In Canvas 3.5 it is possible to make this conversion in the Object Information dialog box (fig. 30). After a bit map image is selected, the dialog box is opened either through the Object Menu or—preferably—through the keyboard shortcut of Command-I. When the screen appears, go to the upper-left top corner and click in the window that shows the small paintbrush icon (a symbol for paint/bit map objects). A pop-out box will open showing a number options. The only only possible for bit map images is the icon at the lower-right side of the box: the picture-object icon. When this is clicked with the mouse, the bit map is instantaneously transformed into a picture object, a PICT format. The resulting image no longer has the characteristics of a bit map image; that is, the only way it can be altered is to resize it (by dragging on its box outlines when selected) or to scale through the Scale dialog box. Nor can this new form of graphic be rotated, flipped, stretched, or benefit from any other kind of change other graphic formats enjoy. The great advantage of converting the bit map into a picture object is, however, that when it is scaled, it keeps the resolution it started with. That is, if it is rescaled to 50 percent or 25 percent, the image will become increasingly more clear. If a bit map image, on the other hand, were scaled to these lower percents, it would become increasingly more indistinct. In the picture object, all pixels remain and are progressively reduced in size. The bit map image loses pixels as it diminishes in size and for that reason becomes more muddy and confused.

For the making of library items that will be used as collage elements—such as our curtain file example—the creation of picture objects is advised. If one wishes to alter an image in any way other than size or scale, the library item should be kept as a bit map and converted only after it has been introduced into a drawing and changed as desired. Many of the images in this book are bit maps converted into picture objects.

Capturing images on scanners is not always the simple process that scanner manufacturing companies would have the buyer believe. Obtaining a good scan and saving the resulting image in the most efficient usable way take thought and skill. Each image presents a unique set of problems; every scanning process requires planning. The steps

Steps in Scanning Images

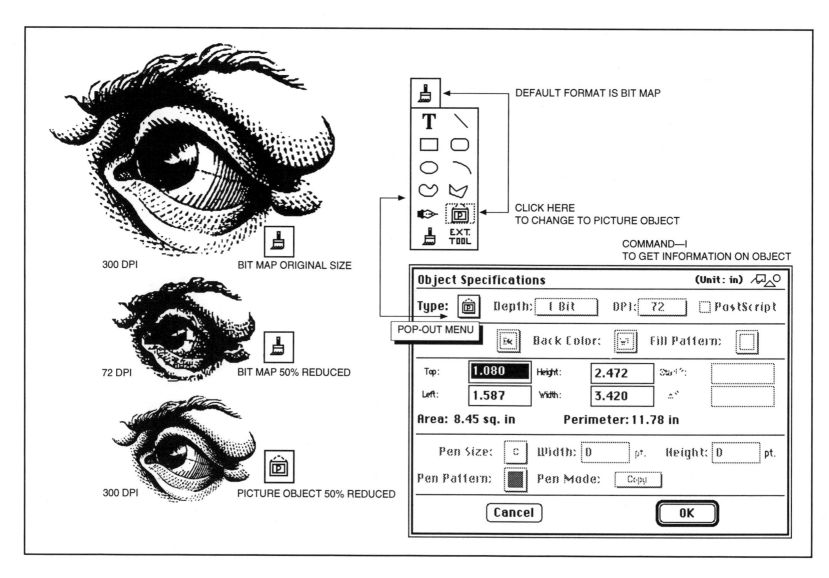

Fig. 30. Picture objects diagram

and principles given below are those one can expect to face when scanning an image into the computer (a diagrammatic view of the process is shown in figure 31).

1. *Select image*. Images with strong contrasts and outlines scan best. Images that contain superfluous elements such as smudges or blurred edges should be avoided, since these extraneous elements are scanned into the file along with the desired parts. Cleaning the image pixel by pixel after it is scanned into the computer file is a tedious business and to be avoided when possible.

2. *Turn on scanner*. Scanners are usually the last link in the chain of peripheral. Always turn the scanner on *first* if it is connected to the computer SCSI port; then turn on the rest of the computer setup. Most scanners need a warm-up period during which diagnostic routines are performed. SCSI peripherals need to be up and running before the computer is started.

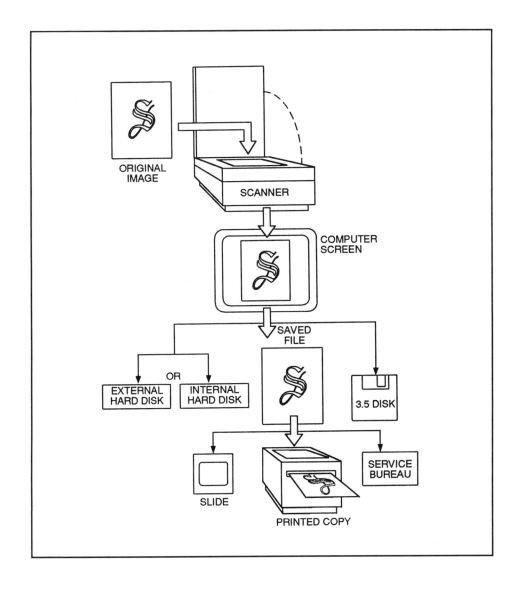

ORIGINAL
IMAGE

SCANNER

COMPUTER
SCREEN

SAVED
FILE

OR

EXTERNAL
HARD DISK

INTERNAL
HARD DISK

3.5 DISK

SLIDE

PRINTED COPY

SERVICE
BUREAU

Fig. 31. Progress of scanned image diagram

3.   *Preview image.* Ofoto, the software that is used with the OneScanner recommended, gives the ability to see a low-resolution preview of images before the actual scanning process begins. This preview allows the user to make decisions concerning resolution size, cropping, and resizing of image.

4.   *Set scanned image parameters.* Ofoto will select optimum image parameters if not specifically changed to different settings. For specific image requirements, these default settings can be changed. Resolution and cropped image size are set during step 4. It is also necessary during this step to determine the image's file format. For most scenographic work, PICT format is preferable. Most images scenographers use are converted into contours for working drawings or for outlines for scenographic sketches. Initially scanned images used for these purposes—which are bit-mapped images—must

be converted into high-resolution graphics using conversion options in programs like Adobe Streamline 3.0, a dedicated high-resolution image conversion program.

5. *Scan image*. The time the image takes to scan depends on the size of the image and the resolution selected; large images scanned in high resolution take longer than smaller images in lower resolution. The scanned image first appears in the resident scanning program; in this case, Ofoto. At this stage, the image can be inspected for completeness and accuracy of scan. Unsatisfactory scans can be scanned again with different settings until a satisfactory image results.

6. Although some manipulation of the image is possible in the resident program, it is preferable to save the image in an appropriate file format that the target program— the program where the image is to be used—understands. Scanned images can also be saved in various locations such as internal hard drives, external hard drives, floppy disks, or optical hard drives. The image can also be printed immediately.

Computer-Image Libraries

Figure 32 shows a file of curtains scanned from the catalog issued by the renowned furniture maker Thomas Chippendale in 1753. Using SuperPaint 3.5, each image was edited with bit map drawing tools like those shown in figure 28. Although SuperPaint 3.5 has limits as a drawing program (Canvas 3.5 is the better program for basic drawing), its bit map editing tools are more extensive and more effective than those in Canvas 3.5. Systematically assembling image libraries like that shown in figure 32 prior to actual need saves many hours of searching when comparable images are required. Stored as bit map graphics these images can be further manipulated as needed. Transformed into PICT files (or picture objects in Canvas 3.5), these images can be rendered in any size— although no longer capable of being manipulated as bit-mapped images. But what is the advantage of these library image files; and how are they used?

Three distinct types of stored files (or libraries) are used In the scenographic drawing shown in figure 34-4:

1. Template files: In this example a perspective grid box saved as a template file is opened as a new file (fig. 33-1). Templates are special types of files that always open as a new unsaved document; as such they should be immediately saved with the name of the drawing being constructed. (Template file construction is more fully discussed and demonstrated in chapter 3.)

2. Library files: These files—like that shown in figure 32—consist of previously drawn images or scanned bit-mapped graphics saved as a uniquely named collection: *Curtains 3*, for instance. When building a large number of library files, great care should be given to the names attached. Great frustration occurs when searching for a file that has been ambiguously titled. To use a library file, it must first be located and then opened. The library now becomes the active window, the perspective, the inactive window. After a selection is made, it is copied to the clipboard using the keystroke Command-C. The library file is then closed. When the drawing under construction is once again the active window, the selections made from the library file are pasted into the new drawing using the Command-V keystroke that pastes the image or images into the drawing. These images can be, as noted before, of different formats. In the example shown in figure 34-4, the perspective grid box is an object-oriented image, whereas the lion mask and curtain unit

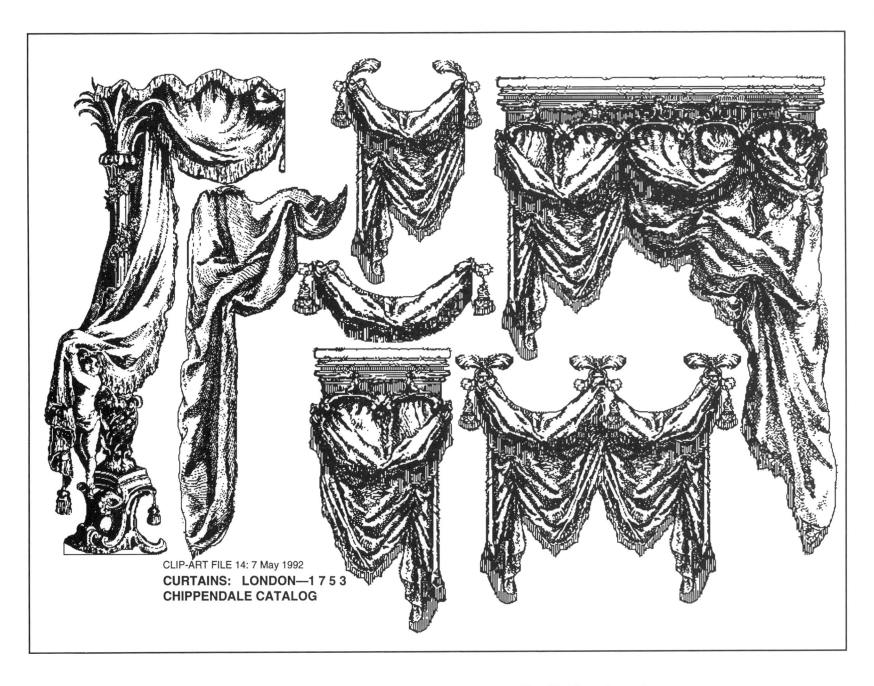

CLIP-ART FILE 14: 7 May 1992
**CURTAINS: LONDON—1 7 5 3
CHIPPENDALE CATALOG**

are bit-mapped graphics saved as PICT images; PICT images can be resized and reshaped but not otherwise edited. Using programs with layer possibilities, drawings can be precisely structured; this allows an image like the perspective box to be placed on the bottom layer with other elements on layers above; these can be shown or hidden as needed. "Turned-off" layers are temporarily invisible; as such they will not print as do visible layers.

3.   Macro files: Macros are files containing a limited number of previously drawn

Fig. 32. Library image file

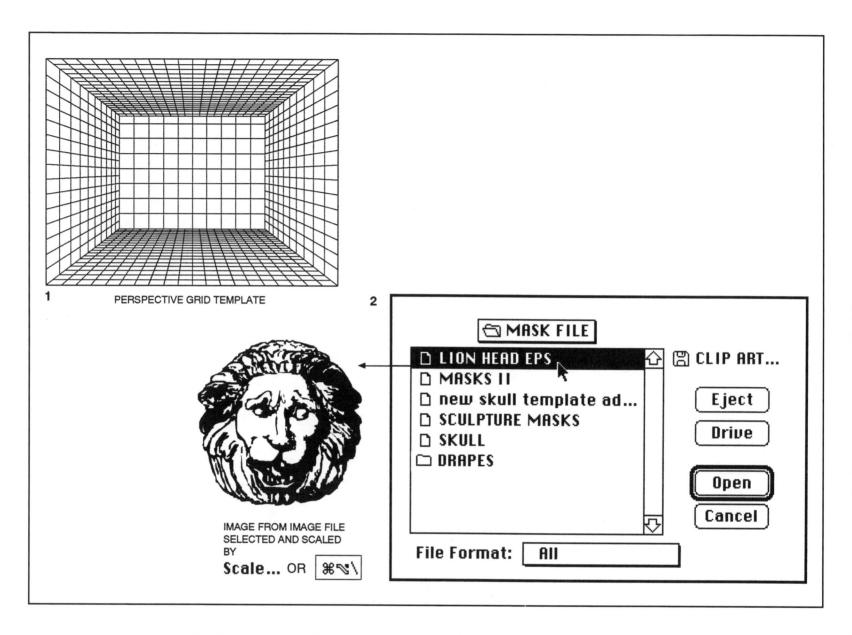

1 PERSPECTIVE GRID TEMPLATE

2

🗁 MASK FILE

📄 LION HEAD EPS
📄 MASKS II
📄 new skull template ad...
📄 SCULPTURE MASKS
📄 SKULL
📁 DRAPES

💾 CLIP ART...

Eject

Drive

Open

Cancel

File Format: All

IMAGE FROM IMAGE FILE
SELECTED AND SCALED
BY
Scale... OR ⌘↘\

Fig. 33. Library image files

objects saved as a named set. A macro set usually contains commonly used objects. These sets are another form of library; in some programs, in fact, these sets are called *libraries*, not *macros*. There can be any number of macro sets available, but only one set is available at any one time; individual sets must be "loaded" into the drawing being constructed. In the example shown in figure 34-3, a macro set containing commonly used scenic elements is accessed from the *Macro* heading in the Canvas 3.5 menu bar. Not only can previously created sets of macros be loaded using this menu option but new sets can be created at any time.

Scenographers are not the only workers to benefit from library and macro files.

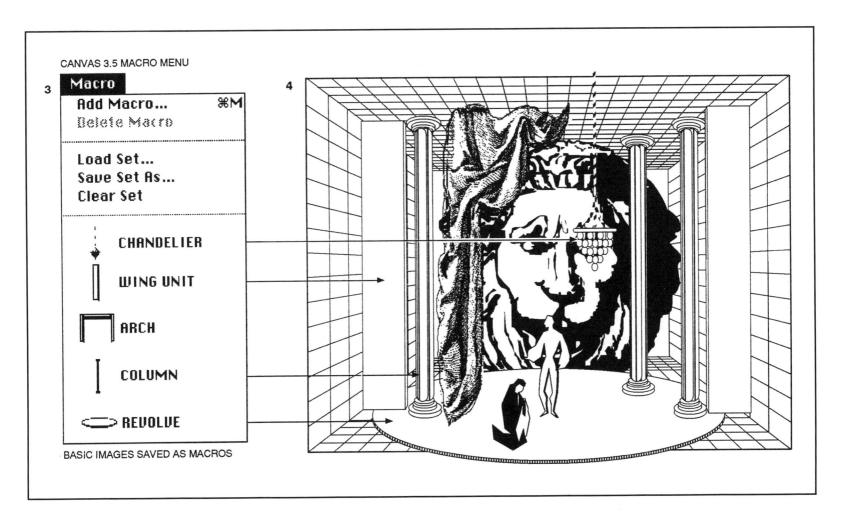

Within the figure:

CANVAS 3.5 MACRO MENU

3

Macro

Add Macro... ⌘M
Delete Macro

Load Set...
Save Set As...
Clear Set

CHANDELIER

WING UNIT

ARCH

COLUMN

REVOLVE

BASIC IMAGES SAVED AS MACROS

4

Fig. 34. Macro image window diagram

Directors are able to construct floor plans from basic template files to which furniture and other scenic elements may be added. Costume designers especially benefit from computer image library files in that basic figure forms saved as libraries or macros take much less time to create than do manually drawn outlines. Not only can templates of figure outlines be stored, the basic form can have editable patterns and textures incorporated. It is possible to create sketches with both bit-mapped graphics and with object-oriented graphics. Figure 35 shows two different kinds of bit-mapped elements: a skull taken from a personal (as opposed to a purchased) clip-art collection and a scanned pencil and paper drawing both edited using SuperPaint 3.5 bit map tools. During the editing process the two were merged into the single image shown in figure 36: an idea for a design for the Ghost of Christmas Future in Charles Dickens's *Christmas Carol*. Editing of bit maps is considerably easier if a graphics tablet is used; programs that support pressure-sensitive features of a tablet enhance a drawer's ability to control images to a much greater degree than is possible with other input devices (fig. 13). Figure 37, on the other hand, shows an object-oriented costume template along with an object-oriented clip-art library image.

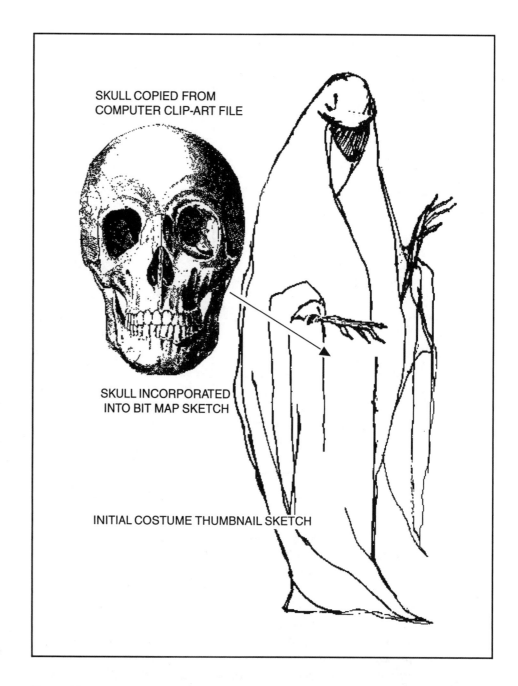

SKULL COPIED FROM
COMPUTER CLIP-ART FILE

SKULL INCORPORATED
INTO BIT MAP SKETCH

INITIAL COSTUME THUMBNAIL SKETCH

Fig. 35. Bit-mapped costume images

Figure 38 shows how the separate images might be combined. Of all the programs recommended, FreeHand 4.0 is best suited to accomplish the procedures shown in figures 35 to 38. A feature of FreeHand 4.0 is an option to place images—either bit-mapped or object-oriented—into a selected outline form. Regardless of the profile shape of the placed image, the outline cuts off all parts that extend beyond the outline's shape. After the interior image is pasted into the outline, it is bonded to the outline; if the outline is scaled

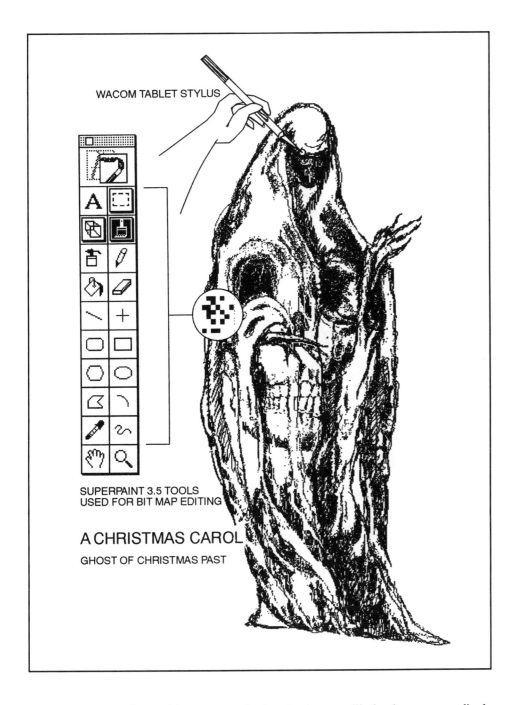

WACOM TABLET STYLUS

SUPERPAINT 3.5 TOOLS
USED FOR BIT MAP EDITING

A CHRISTMAS CAROL

GHOST OF CHRISTMAS PAST

Fig. 36. Bit-mapped costume drawing

to another size or distorted in any way, the interior image will also be correspondingly scaled and distorted. These interior images can, however, be removed using FreeHand 4.0's *Cut Contents Menu* option.

Although bit-mapped images are the easiest to create and modify, they have limited use in computer scenographic or costume design; working drawings especially are object-

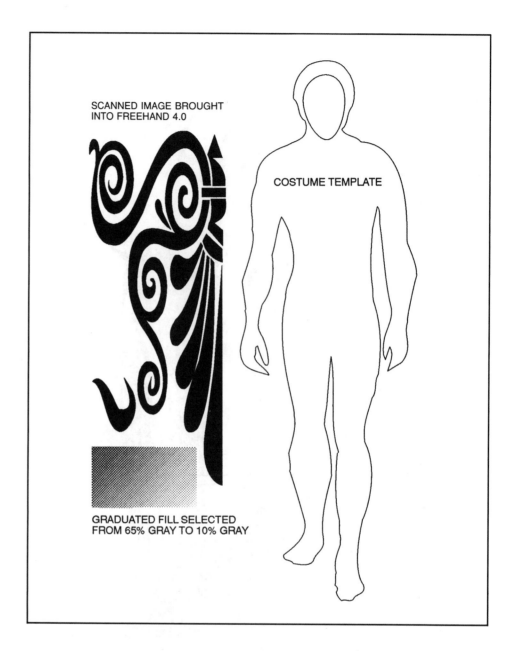

SCANNED IMAGE BROUGHT
INTO FREEHAND 4.0

COSTUME TEMPLATE

GRADUATED FILL SELECTED
FROM 65% GRAY TO 10% GRAY

Fig. 37. Object-oriented costume images

oriented in nature. If not too complex—that is, if the pixel patterns are not too diffuse and irregular—bit-mapped images are convertible into high-resolution object-oriented images. Figure 39 shows a costume pencil sketch scanned into the computer using a program called Ofoto. The resolution of the scan is determined through the dialog box shown to the right of the main image window. Ofoto gives the option to manually set the resolution of the image or to have the program itself figure what is the best option for scanning. In most cases, the program gives a better final image than that selected by manual selection. Saved as a PICT file, the sketch was then converted from a bit-

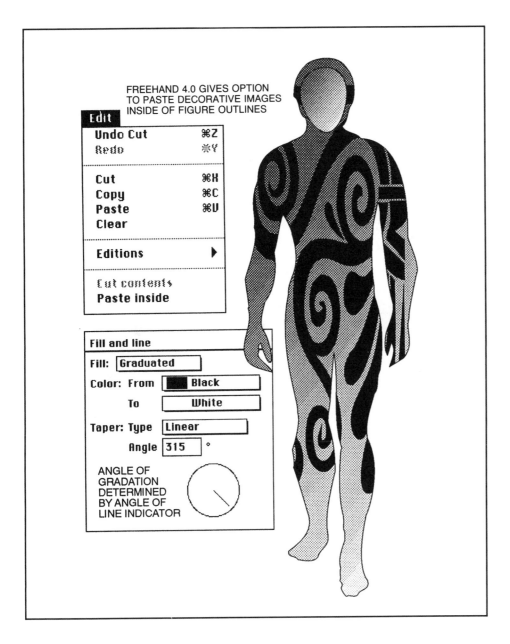

FREEHAND 4.0 GIVES OPTION
TO PASTE DECORATIVE IMAGES
INSIDE OF FIGURE OUTLINES

Edit

Undo Cut ⌘Z
Redo ⌘Y

Cut ⌘H
Copy ⌘C
Paste ⌘U
Clear

Editions ▶

Cut contents
Paste inside

Fill and line

Fill: Graduated

Color: From ▇ Black
To White

Taper: Type Linear
Angle 315 °

ANGLE OF
GRADATION
DETERMINED
BY ANGLE OF
LINE INDICATOR

Fig. 38. Object-oriented costume drawing

mapped graphic into a high-resolution object-oriented image using Adobe Streamline 3.0, a program whose fundamental purpose is to make such conversions, since a high-resolution costume can be modified in numerous ways.

A distinct reason for using object-oriented images is that they are not only quickly scaled to any size but can be distorted to new shapes in much less time than it takes to draw them anew. Although bit-mapped images are relatively quickly scanned, adjusting the resulting outlines for scenographic sketches or for working drawings requires signifi-

Commercial Clip-Art Image Libraries

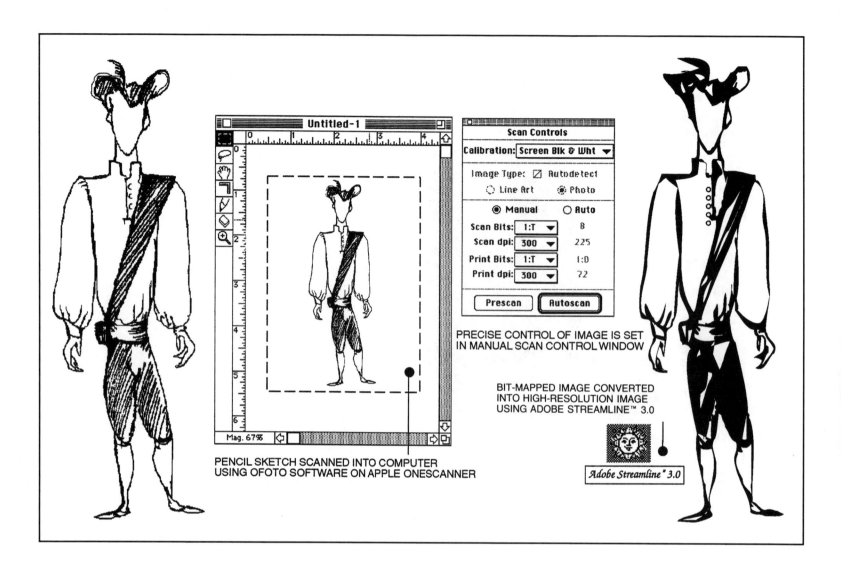

Inside the figure:

Untitled-1

0 | 1 | 2 | 3 | 4

Mag. 67%

PENCIL SKETCH SCANNED INTO COMPUTER
USING OFOTO SOFTWARE ON APPLE ONESCANNER

Scan Controls

Calibration: Screen Blk & Wht ▼

Image Type: ☑ Autodetect
○ Line Art   ◉ Photo

◉ Manual   ○ Auto

Scan Bits: 1:T ▼   8
Scan dpi: 300 ▼   225
Print Bits: 1:T ▼   1:0
Print dpi: 300 ▼   72

Prescan   Autoscan

PRECISE CONTROL OF IMAGE IS SET
IN MANUAL SCAN CONTROL WINDOW

BIT-MAPPED IMAGE CONVERTED
INTO HIGH-RESOLUTION IMAGE
USING ADOBE STREAMLINE™ 3.0

Adobe Streamline® 3.0

Fig. 39. Scanned costume image diagram

cantly more computer graphics skill from the scenographer. Inasmuch as these images almost always involve manipulation of Bézier curves, they take significantly more time to create than do bit-mapped images. For this main reason, those building permanent libraries of computer image files should seriously consider additions to their own library files good commercially made collections of high-resolution clip art. If one considers the many hours it takes to convert scanned images into high-resolution files, the cost of these collections does not seem that unreasonable. It is important, however, to find those commercial collections worth the costs involved. Although most commercial collections are geared to the publishing needs of desktop users—for advertisements, brochures, newsletters, and the like—some few are employable for scenographic drawing purposes. These collections are especially valuable to scenographers whose computer drawings must provide details of complicated elements: decorative outlines for scrollwork, complex

Fig. 40. Clip-art library images

patterns for moldings, or irregularly profiled three-dimensional forms. Having a library of predrawn high-resolution images composed of individual elements capable of being taken apart, adjusted, and placed into new configurations reduces drafting time. Many of the commercially drawn images are, in fact, composed of multiple elements that can be ungrouped and edited into new shapes and configurations. Figure 40 shows three files (*A*, *B*, and *C*) from a collection of 300 images from the commercial company 3G Graphics, Inc. Called Images with Impact 2, this package follows an earlier one named Images with Impact 1. If both packages are purchased, the scenographer has no less than 500 high-resolution image files available. Although not all these images are appropriate to

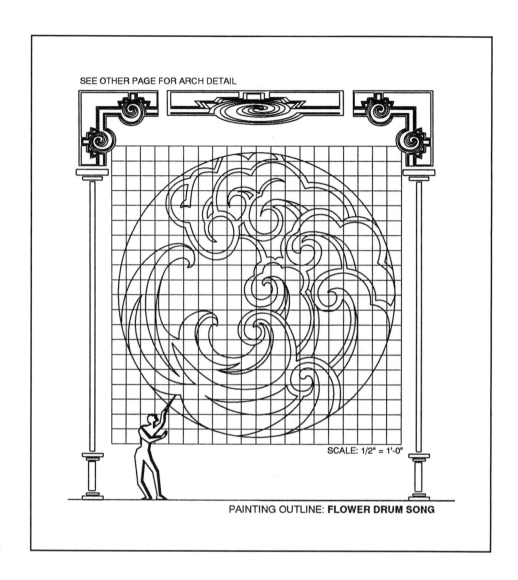

Fig. 41. Clip-art images in working drawings

scenographic drawing, a significant number are. Figure 41 shows two of the images from figure 40 being used as a basis for a drop-painting outline in the 1950s musical *The Flower Drum Song*, a production that requires the scenographer to use classical Chinese images in the design of the scenery. Figure 42 shows another drop-painting outline taken from images in the same collection. The assembly of both drawings required only minutes; scanning and adjusting similar images would have taken at least an hour. If drawn using only a computer drawing program's basic tools, the task would have taken several hours. (Another working drawing based on the package is shown in the section "Building Shapes and Forms on the Computer Drawing Board" in chapter 3.) Considering the hundreds of hours it took to create the images in these collections, their relatively inexpensive cost recommends a careful look by busy scenographers. Using these images as bases, scenographers can quickly create hybrid images that would take many hours to accomplish. As

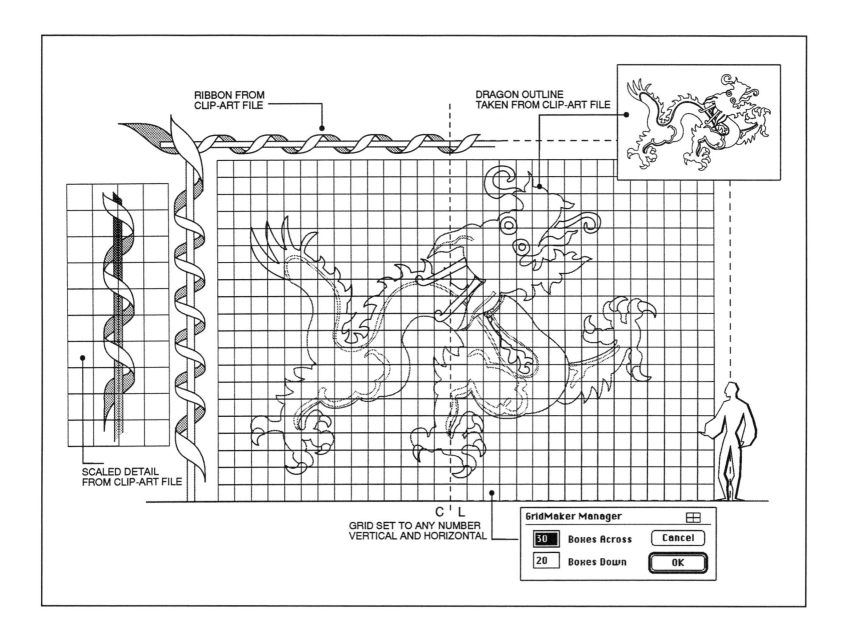

RIBBON FROM
CLIP-ART FILE

DRAGON OUTLINE
TAKEN FROM CLIP-ART FILE

SCALED DETAIL
FROM CLIP-ART FILE

C L
GRID SET TO ANY NUMBER
VERTICAL AND HORIZONTAL

GridMaker Manager

30 | Boxes Across | Cancel
20 | Boxes Down | OK

with all computer purchases, these collections should not be bought directly from the company but from discount computer catalogs all of which have sections devoted to clip-art collections.

Of special interest to scenographers is *The Macmillan Visual Dictionary*, edited by Jean-Claude Corbeil and Ariane Archambault, published by Macmillan Publishing Company (New York, 1992). This extraordinary reference book contains 3,500 computer-generated color illustrations annotated with 25,000 terms covering 600 subjects. This book is a unique research resource.

Fig. 42. Clip-art images in working drawings

Text Ornaments as Image Resource

Another good source of images for both scenographic sketches and for working-drawing details is available by converting text ornaments into object-oriented images. Text ornaments are small images used by printers to relieve the starkness of a page of type. These small details are frequently placed at the head of a chapter; frequently a text ornament is used to separate units of text within large book units such as chapters. In computer jargon these small graphics are often called *dingbats* and are considered as text elements of word processing programs. A text ornament is accessed just as any other typeface option; that is, by selection through a specific ornament set in the font menu. Specific ornament images are then produced by typing letters on the keyboard. Individual letters and numbers produce certain images; by use of the Option key or the Space key—or a combination of both—other ornaments are available. Since it is unreasonable that anyone memorize the entire set of images that correspond to various letters, numbers, symbols, and keystroke combinations, font manufacturers, such as Adobe, provide printed character sets showing how letter, number, symbol, and keystroke combinations match various images. As with letters, numbers, and symbols, these ornaments can be made into almost any point size, although almost always there is a limit placed by individual word processing applications. Figure 43 shows several of these ornaments (point size and key equivalent are not shown).

Text ornaments are not, however, usable to the scenographer as text. In order to use these images in sketches or working drawings, it is necessary to convert them into object-oriented forms with editable outlines in a drawing program file format such as PICT or EPS. To accomplish this, a graphics program with *font outline conversion* is necessary. After the conversion it is possible to change the object's shape, orientation, and line weight and fill in numerous combinations. Increasingly, draw programs provide text conversion options: Canvas 3.5, FreeHand 4.0, Adobe Illustrator 5.0, are a few of the major programs allowing fonts and ornaments to be changed from text to manipulatable graphics. Figure 44-3 shows the menu command used in Canvas 3.5. Also shown there is the text ornament before and after its conversion to a Bézier object. After conversion all the text-editing properties are gone, but it can now be used as the basis for a working drawing. The steps for making a text ornament conversion are as follows:

1. Open a drawing program that supports text and text ornament conversions (fig. 44-1).

2. Go to the Text (or Font) Menu in the menu bar at the top of the window (or by using the keystroke combination Command-T, which calls up a text dialog box) and select the ornaments file (in this case, *Woodtype Ornaments 2*), where the image to be converted resides (fig. 44-2).

3. Type out the keystroke that contains the image to be converted. (A HELPFUL HINT: Since it is difficult for anyone to keep in mind what key represents what figure, a preliminary process is advisable; that is, to have previously printed out a complete copy of the figures contained in the ornaments file along with the precise keystroke required to produce them.) The text ornament can now be converted to the outlines of an object-oriented image (fig. 44-3).

4. Converted image can now be scaled (fig. 44-4) to any size by dragging on the

Fig. 43. Printer ornaments as graphic elements

bounding box handles or can be scaled to an exact size by use of the program's Scale dialog box.

    5. If the converted figure has more than one element to its makeup—as is the case in figure 44-5—it is still a grouped object. To further manipulate the individual elements, or to add elements, ungrouping the figure into discrete parts is necessary. After this is done, each part may be modified by selection of vertex points or Bézier curve handles.

    6. The finished image—grouped once again into a single unit, as shown in figure 44-6—is now usable as a scaled working-drawing element. Other text ornaments—such as those shown in figure 44-2—can also be converted to graphic images and incorporated into a single working drawing.

    Figure 45 is a computer scenographic drawing based on the text conversion of the

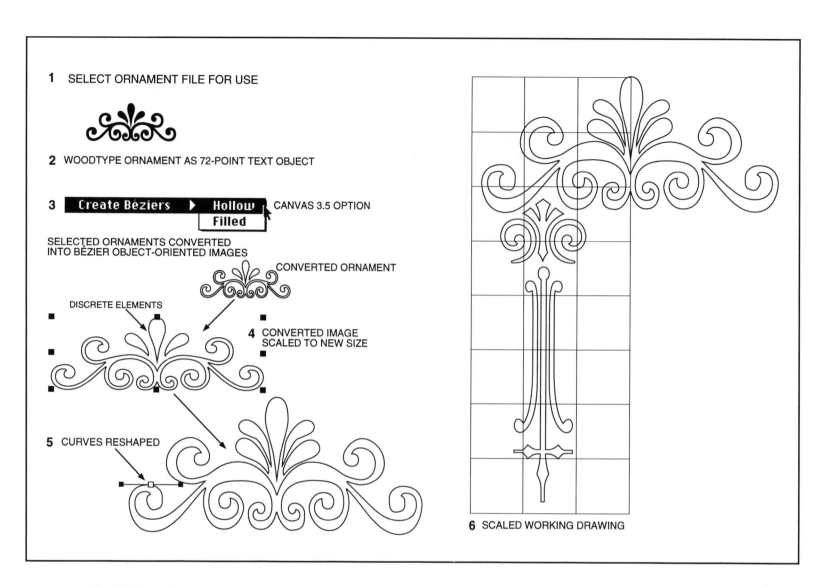

1   SELECT ORNAMENT FILE FOR USE

2   WOODTYPE ORNAMENT AS 72-POINT TEXT OBJECT

3   **Create Béziers** ▶ **Hollow**   CANVAS 3.5 OPTION
                       Filled

SELECTED ORNAMENTS CONVERTED
INTO BÉZIER OBJECT-ORIENTED IMAGES

CONVERTED ORNAMENT

DISCRETE ELEMENTS

4   CONVERTED IMAGE
    SCALED TO NEW SIZE

5   CURVES RESHAPED

6   SCALED WORKING DRAWING

*Fig. 44. Converting printer ornaments into
graphic elements*

Reshaping of Research Materials

figure shown in figure 44. As one can readily see, finding and using images from odd places—as has been demonstrated in this example—point up once again the versatility and convenience of computer drawing.

In many instances a found image is introduced into the computer in a scale unsuitable for the purpose intended. That is, in order to use the image, it must be changed into another size—sometimes changed into another shape—before being incorporated into a drawing. Changing the size of an image manually is at best a time-consuming tedious business. On the computer, changing sizes and scales of images is a matter of seconds. The number of scaling options available in almost all draw and paint programs—and especially in CAD applications—is one of the most important reasons for any scenographer to own a computer.

If either an overhead or an opaque image projector is available (a device that allows one to project opaque images onto a surface such as illustration board), tracing projected images can be made directly on the new surface without resorting to grids. This technique is especially useful when a small-scaled image must be made into a relatively larger one.

Another possibility is to place the image on an office copying machine having the capability to resize images. Most of the machines that have this capability will reduce or enlarge an image in several preset percents. A laser printer will also allow the enlargement or reduction of an image that can then be printed out on a hard copy. The percent of

Fig. 45. Scenographic design from printer ornament graphic elements

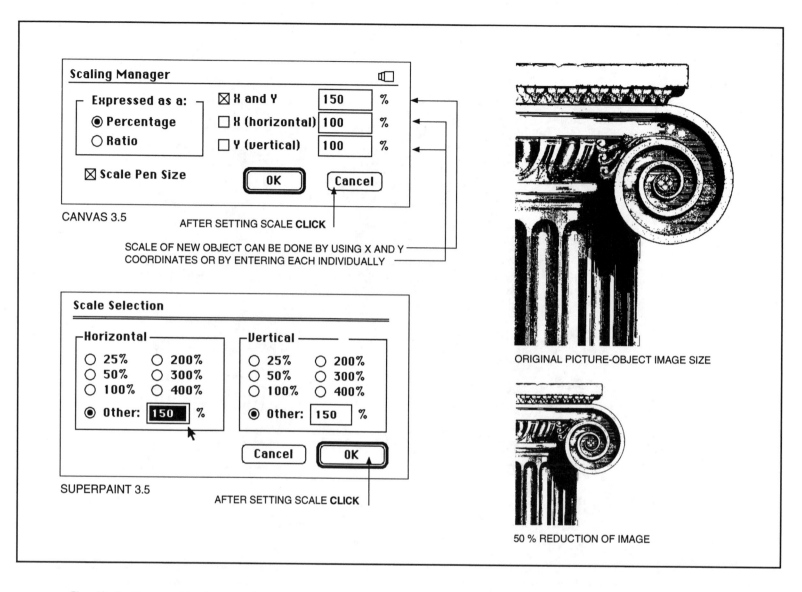

Fig. 46. Scaling graphic elements diagram

enlargement or reduction is entered into the computer by the keyboard, which does not have a set percent ratio as do many of the office copiers.

The primary way of resizing of an image is through a process called *Scale Selection* or sometimes simply *Scale*. These options reside in specific menus according to the program being used. It is also possible to resize an image in some paint programs through the selection process alone. Figure 46 shows how this is accomplished. The process is relatively simple, and most programs allow this in both the paint and draw layer.

Depending on the file format of the image, its nature is altered as it is scaled. When a bit map image, for instance, is changed to a smaller version of itself, its features are compressed and becomes a cruder image than it was in its former size. This is because the same number of pixels will not fit into the smaller space causing some to be lost.

This makes the resulting image less precise. It is possible, however, to change the file format of a bit map image so that it maintains its resolution (i.e., its sharpness) as it is reduced or enlarged. Canvas 3.5 accomplishes this by changing the nature of the image from one format (a bit map image) to another (a PICT image). Figure 30, shown above, demonstrates how this process works in Canvas 3.5, a program with superior scaling options and procedures.

Images such as those we have examined in this section do take time to construct. There are, however, several advantages that accrue from their making. These are:

1. Images are interactive; that is, they can be modified quickly in any way the scenographer or director chooses: objects can be added, moved, or deleted. Fill patterns can be changed and gradients altered to simulate lighting change.

2. Images can be manipulated quickly; that is, objects can be independently altered in proportion in size, proportion, or position.

3. Images can be printed as hard copies, as transparencies, or as slides. As a transparency or as a slide, it is possible to project onto the back wall of the theater images of a sketch. This gives a reasonably accurate view how the setting appears to audiences.

Although it is possible to create all graphics necessary for a production on the computer and to print them out without ever using a traditional drawing board, it is more than likely scenographers will continue to use previously learned skills and techniques for making manual graphics. It is not advisable, moreover, to keep these two worlds mutually exclusive; one of the main reasons to master computer graphics technique is to incorporate possibilities computers bestow on other forms of art production and in so doing extend the potentialities of the artist's world. Computer-generated graphics are usable for producing graphics that involve other forms of technology such as office photocopiers, projectors of various kinds, and 35-mm slide makers. As new technologies emerge and are developed, new ways to combine these with time-honored graphic practices will become apparent.

In all later parts of the book we will return to the questions raised in this section. In chapter 4 techniques for capturing images from computer models are discussed in detail.

There is little question that the computer is an important development in scenography art. As an adjunct to the conceptual processes of design the computer is only limited by the mind that uses it. One thing is certain: for those students training today for tomorrow's theater, the computer will be their primary tool not only for technical specification but for design conceptualization as well. Only the most intractable of scenographers will continue to deny a place in their studios.

3 The Computer Drawing Board

In his journal of 1885, Henry David Thoreau made this entry: *Men have become the tools of their tools*. Although it is doubtful he was prophesying computers or their users, the statement has resonance for scenographers who, until only recently, had little choice in matters of tools and materials for their work. Now there are alternatives to established ways of drawing and painting; computers, scanners, electronic drawing tablets, and a host of specialized programs are available to any scenographer willing to spend money on equipment and invest time in mastering the programs that employ them. Many scenographers, however, retain that instinctive distrust of machines Thoreau intimated more than a century ago. The question they pose is this: *What advantage does computer-graphics technology provide to theater artists that repays the time and cost needed to master this radical departure from time-honored ways of working?*

The concern is valid. Scenographers contemplating significant changes to the ways they work must be certain that advantages exist. Further, they must be convinced that these advantages enhance previously learned skills and understandings. A difficult task for many potential computer users is to assess the claims made by those now converted to computer use. At the heart of these concerns lies the most important questions of all: *Will computer technology really make my work easier and will it improve the quality of the work I accomplish?* Perhaps we should review the nature of the work we want the computer to assist us with.

In *The Stage Is Set*, Lee Simonson, clearly delineates the main differences between the work of typical graphic artists and that of scenographers. He reminds us:

> When scenic projects are carried out they are in the literal sense of the word translated, carried over from one medium to another. In this process lie all the unavoidable technical problems of stage-craft which have preoccupied the designers of every epoch in the theatre's history. The technical problem in its fundamentals is always the same: How are the form, colour, texture, atmosphere, and light of a design to be preserved when enlarged and erected in a theatre? A scenic drawing is no more than an intention; it is no better than the methods eventually used to embody

it. Paper, as the Germans say, is patient. A swirl of the brush can create atmospheric distance in a water-colour, the sense of physical liberation that a landscape gives when one walks in it. But the space evoked by a water-colour wash or perspective drawing is the very quality most easily lost when the design is translated to a board floor that meets a canvas back-drop or a plaster wall. Space was never more convincingly evoked than by the perspective scenic drawings of the nineteenth century, which caricatured their intentions when executed. Any number of designs that as drawings seem to express the spirit of a play, once in the theatre, are transformed into something as grotesque as a donkey trying to make love to a fairy queen.

. . . Every stroke of the designer's pencil or of his brush must be enlarged at least twenty-four times on the stage. And the scene-designer's art consists not in being able to record his intentions as skillfully as the painter of easel pictures, but in being able to make a picture that, once it is enlarged, retains its original values of texture, colour and form. Mathematical enlargement by itself is of no use because in every square inch of a drawing colour, form, and texture are inextricably combined. They can be translated to the stage only by being disintegrated and then recombined. (Lee Simonson, *The Stage Is Set* [1911; reprint, Salem, NH: Ayer, 1975])

Simonson clearly shows us how the scenographer's work differs from other graphic artists. Of course, he cannot tell us directly—since I am sure he did not envision it—if the computer assists the work he considers necessary to stage design. That determination we must make for ourselves. Let us now look more closely into the ways drawing is realized on the computer.

Computer Drawing

Chief among the questions posed by artists new to computer graphics: *Just how much does computer drawing differ from that done by hand?* Another question one could ask: *How are the goals implicit in Simsonson's remarks addressed by the capabilities of the computer?* The answers lie—as they do with any new approach or technology—within the empirical experience of those who ask them. Perhaps the best way for us to address them here is to review some of the things computer graphics programs do. A partial list might include the computer's ability to :

Create specifically shaped objects using generic tools.
Create specifically shaped objects accurately by dialog box input.
Precisely size or scale objects by keyboard input.
Automatically scale objects or groups of objects to exact percents.
Determine sizes and perimeters or calculate total areas of objects automatically.
Dimension objects accurately by command.
Create symmetrical objects that automatically mirror profiles as they are drawn.
Create symmetrical variations of a circular object's perimeter in equally spaced
    increments (such as a cogs on a gear or the spokes of a snowflake outline).

Create and align objects using specialized artificial intelligence features.

Automatically recalculate dimensions to drawings.

Change an object's nature from one basic type to another basic type by dialog box or by keyboard command.

Customize an object's line width, color, and pattern.

Merge two or more objects into single objects.

Cut holes into objects or cutting objects into separate pieces.

Slice objects or lines into two or more parts using other lines or other objects as a cutting tool.

Convert scanned bit-mapped images into high-resolution object images; adapt commercial clip-art images to working drawing details.

Permit parts of a single drawing to be placed on independent layers of a computer document.

Duplicate drawings of any size to any number (depending on the computer's storage capacity).

Produce copies of drawings in any number on a variety of printers.

Impressive as this list is, still other features and capabilities exist for scenographers using computer graphics in their work.

Scenographers must keep in mind that the work they do is part of a process completed by others. The images scenographers make—as Simonson reminds us—are meant to provide others with information that furthers this process. The images created by scenographers are basically utilitarian in nature, having little worth as strikingly original artifacts. Frequently the images a scenographer makes do not survive the project for which they are created. For this reason the very mutability of the computer's output is suited to the practice of scenography. With its ability to quickly create, duplicate, alter, store, and delete graphic information, the computer is a perfect tool for the scenographer's purposes.

There are especially good reasons for using computers in technical drawing. Some of the advantages are:

1. *Ability to create complex technical specification*. Creating and modifying working drawings on computers are quicker, more accurate processes than are possible with manual graphics drawing.

2. *Ability to create multilayered drawings*. All four of the basic drawing programs used in this book—Canvas 3.5, FreeHand 4.0, PowerDraw 5.0, and MiniCad+ 5.0—allow individual drawings—or individual elements of a drawing—to be created on separate layers. Moreover, these layers can be displayed all at once or selectively hidden from view. All visible drawings print out as a single drawing regardless of the layer they occupy; hidden layers do not print. The ability to hide layers gives the scenographer an opportunity to show—and print out when necessary—a production's different settings. Figure 47 is a diagram showing (*A*) how a drawing with four layers appears on the computer screen, and (*B*) how the drawing is structured in the computer's memory. Canvas 3.5—the program used to demonstrate layer capability in figure 48—has an unlimited number of layers (subject to the amount of memory available). A layer is directly analogous to a sheet of glass or acetate and is entirely transparent when first

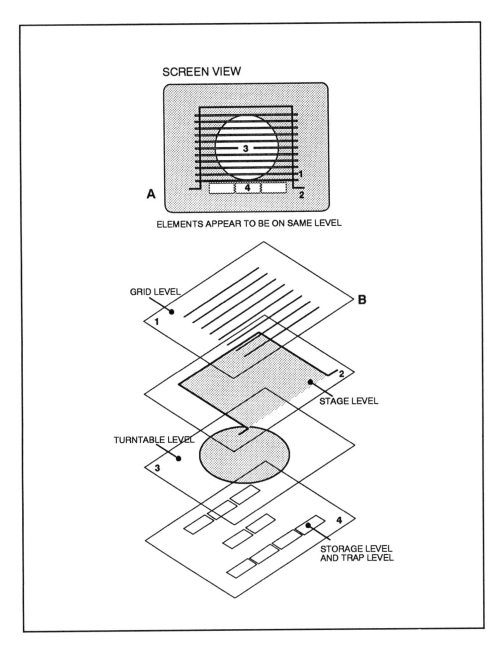

SCREEN VIEW

A

ELEMENTS APPEAR TO BE ON SAME LEVEL

GRID LEVEL
B

STAGE LEVEL

TURNTABLE LEVEL

STORAGE LEVEL
AND TRAP LEVEL

Fig. 47. Diagram of computer theater layers

created. After a layer is defined—and all programs that support layers have dialog boxes where they are made and controlled—it is given a name so that its identification as a separate entity from other layers is possible. Although many drawings only require a single layer, more complex drawings—such as the floor plan templates that are examined later—need the capability to separate a composite drawing into separate elements. All layers can be independently controlled; that is, any layer can be made visible, invisible, grayed (to show subordination to the main drawing), or changed in order of stacking.

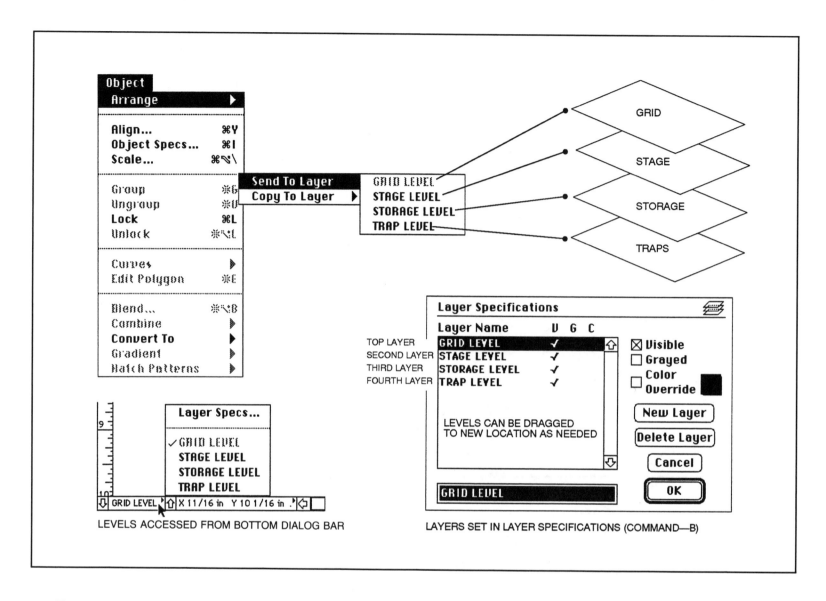

Fig. 48. Canvas 3.5 layer specifications diagram

3. *Ability to change drawings during interactive discussions.* Changes to original drawings can be made without redrawing the entire project. It is possible for all concerned with the information the drawings display—directors or technical staff, for instance—to actively participate in making necessary changes.

4. *Ability to show scenic unit changes during a performance.* Using computer commands, it is possible to indicate exactly how scenic units move, rotate, pivot, or shift on- and offstage during the run of a production. Potential conflicts during these scenic changes can be studied and modified before actual scenic units are built or brought to the physical theater. A single drawing with multiple layers can contain every scenic change of a multiscene production. Entire settings can be stored intact on individual layers; settings not being examined can be rendered invisible by "turning off" the layer

in a dialog menu. Nonprinting storage areas can be used as offstage storage areas as in actual theater facilities.

5. *Ability to create composite task-specific drawings from templates*. Libraries of master drawings can be made and stored as repeatable templates. These drawings can be set to specific drawing size in specific scales with selected line weights, information blocks, and so on. Unlike manually drawn graphics, templates relieve scenographers from the repetitive work of drawing in a stage's permanent features—walls, proscenium opening, permanent equipment or features of the theater—each time a new floor plan is begun. In a template, these features are already present and in place when a template file is opened. Templates are possible for every type of scenographic drawing required. Template libraries of objects—such as furniture, windows, doors, turntables, platforms, columns, posts—can be imported into any other template drawing.

In the following sections the advantages listed above are discussed and demonstrated in greater detail. At this point it would be wise to review the various kinds of scenographic drawings scenographers produce.

Scenographers convey their concepts to others in four basic types of graphic work: diagrammatic drawings, illustrative drawings, perspective drawings, and working drawings. While variations and permutations may exist within these basic types, the purpose of each category is fundamentally different. All four are, however, necessary to the practice of scenography, nor is it possible to bridge the gaps between concept, craft, and realization on the stage of any scenographic project without resorting to all these forms. Let us briefly define each of these categories more specifically showing how each kind of drawing fits into the scenographer's overall work pattern:

1. *Diagrammatic drawings*. These drawings do not necessarily show how a design will appear onstage (i.e., a pictorial image seen from a particular seat in the auditorium) or how to build its constituent parts. They are, rather, intended *to show the process of ideas from conceptual hypotheses to physical form*, from an idea in the mind of the scenographer to an artifact that can be perceived by others. A single diagram may include, moreover, such diverse forms of information as the flow of traffic of scenery and movement of performers and, at the same time, indicate how that information relates to the text's content and the playwright's purpose. As Keith Albarn points out in his book *Diagram* (London: Thames and Hudson, 1977), "The diagram is evidence of an idea being structured—not *the idea* but a model of it, intended to clarify characteristics of features of that idea. It is a form of communication which increases the pace of development, or allows an idea to function and develop for the thinker which offering the possibility of transfer of an idea or triggering of notions; finally, through appropriate structuring, it may generate different notions and stages of mind in the viewer."

Diagrammatic drawings are often nothing more than crude line drawings; they graphically show concepts or—more likely—relationship of an idea's progress to the consequences it produces. Figure 49*A* is a diagram showing how the scenographer for a production of *Hamlet* relates some of the key elements of the text's plot to levels of reality. This diagram is the link between the intangible concepts of the author's words and the embodiment of those words on stage in terms of actions and physical objects in

Scenographic Drawings

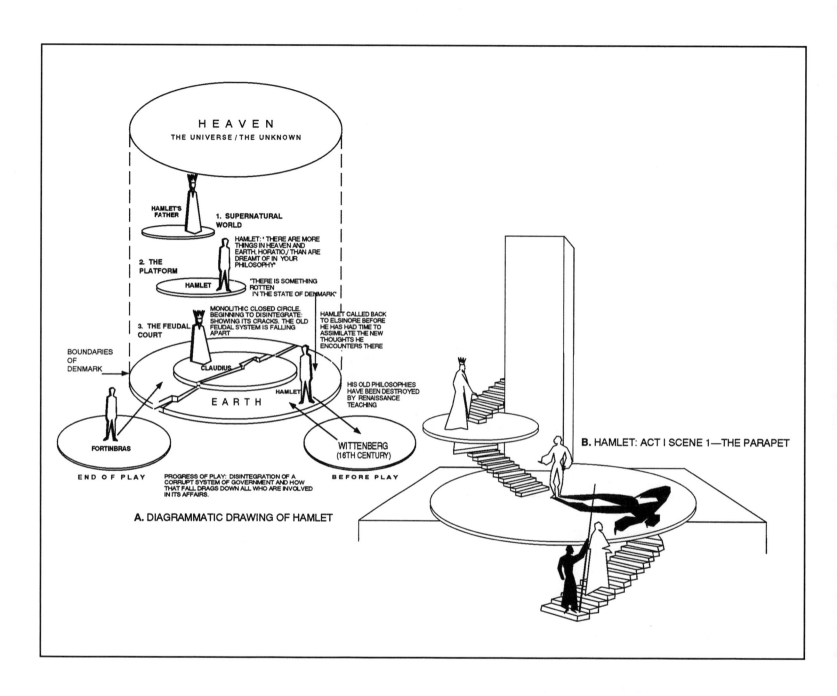

Fig. 49. Diagram as scenographic concept

space. Although diagrams are not intended as pictures of settings, they point the way to production on the stage and, in this particular case, have a direct affect on the physical form of the setting. The abstract levels reflected in the diagram have provided vital visual clues that are echoed in the drawing for the setting shown in figure 49*B*. The ability of diagrammatic drawings to show complicated relationships graphically is especially useful in the first stage of planning these productions. They are also useful when planning complex productions such as musicals, operas, or multiscene projects. Flow charts demonstrating how scenes dramatically relate to one another or how scenic units are managed during a run of a production can be shown better in programs specifically written to handle such information. Although mainstream drawing programs are usable for graphical diagrams and charts, specialized applications—such as Inspiration by Ceres Software—present this information better (see figure 19). An advantage of applications like Inspiration is that not only are intricately plotted diagrams quickly produced, they are easily amended or reorganized. As extensions of exploratory processes, most diagrammatic drawings rapidly lose value, since they are only steps in a progress; in the past the wastebasket was the usual end of a diagrammatic drawing. With computers, however, thinking processes that informed initial stages of projects can be saved along with other production files. Since graphical designers think primarily in visual terms, finding computer programs that amplify and extend natural predispositions to diagram will benefit those who frequently need to analyze dramatic texts for stage production.

2. *Illustrative drawings*. These drawings, unlike those just discussed, do attempt to give an idea of how a stage structure will appear from a particular point of view. While diagrammatic drawings are primarily made to show concepts or spatial patterns, illustrative drawings are intended more to persuade others to accept the visual aspects of a design. (In fact, when we speak of a setting's "design" we usually mean only those elements that appeal directly to the spectator's aesthetic eye—form, color, texture, effect of light and shadow—not those that more directly relate to a performer's movement or how the form of the setting relates to the text's underlying themes.) The illustrative drawing of the past included graphic approaches constructed from a wide spectrum of materials. Although the standard technique for professional American scenographers was for many years a rather restrictive watercolor-dye approach (and was more or less mandated by the union examination requirements of the New York United Scenic Artists Local 829 that gave and supervised the test), scenic drawings of present-day scenographers use a wide range of materials and techniques. Many forego entirely illustrative drawings and only complete models and working specifications. One of the distinct advantages of creating such drawings on the computer is that the scenographer can not only draw and paint an illustrative sketch in true perspective but can change its form and color electronically to reflect changes in design. Virtus WalkThrough—a virtual reality program—also has the ability to capture any perspective viewpoint as a PICT file, which can be opened in many draw or bit-mapped programs for further graphic manipulation. For the near future, however, printing out full-color drawings is not economically feasible for the average scenographer. It is possible, however, to have any color drawing printed onto a slide allowing the scenographer to show fully rendered drawings using 35-mm projection equipment. This same process can be used to create painted drop or painted detail slides which, in turn, are employable by scenic artists in the painting studio.

3. *Perspective drawing on the computer*. The sixteenth-century historian Giorgio Vasari reports that Paolo Uccello was intrigued with perspective drawing so much that "[his] wife . . . told people that Paolo used to stay up all night in his study, trying to work out the vanishing points of his perspective, and that when she called him to come to bed he would say: 'Oh, what a lovely thing this perspective is!' . . . And indeed, if

perspective was dear to Uccello it also proved, thanks to his works, attractive and rewarding to those who have used it since."

Scenographers who make perspective sketches—and the number is less today than in former years due to the complexity of production demands and the use of scenographic models to show intention—still find that even relatively simple designs require hours of precise drawing to ensure that outlines of objects are accurately represented. In my own case, I would as soon fall down a flight of stairs as have the task of drawing them in perspective. Fortunately, computer technology comes to the aid of those like myself who draw perspective views as part of the scenographic planning process but do not wholeheartedly share Uccello's predilection.

In this book perspective drawing on the computer is examined in two ways: (1) as an extension of manually constructed perspective drawing using principles and techniques learned in perspective classes, as shown in figures 50—53, and (2) as end products of computer programs that automatically calculate three-dimensional objects from two-dimensional plans and elevations. A number of these kinds of drawings are demonstrated in chapter 4.

Even with sophisticated drawing programs, constructing perspective templates on the computer is a time-consuming task. The advantage for making such templates, however, is that they can be used repeatedly as electronic sketch pads or storyboards. If the template is located on a separate layer below a blank document window, the guidelines of the template operate in the same way as one would with a paper copy but with the advantage that it can be turned off when no longer needed, leaving only the drawing on the top layer showing. Following the principles demonstrated here, grids with differing heights, widths, and depths are possible. These grids do not have to be square, as is the one demonstrated in figures 51 and 52. Drawing perspective grids that reflect the dimensions of specific theaters—like that shown in figure 52—is especially beneficial to students who have perspective drawing skills but are new to computer graphics procedures. Although no substitute for true three-dimensional programs, these grids are useful as template drawings. An added advantage of perspective grids stored as a template format is that it gives scenographers an endless supply of blank perspective pages. Although the drawings made with these templates are not corrected automatically—as they would be in true three-dimensional programs—they do provide quick ways to test out three-dimensional ideas. Figure 53 shows a setting created on a computer-constructed perspective template using clip-art library elements. The ability to selectively hide layers facilitates constructing perspective drawings; that is, layers that contain the decorative elements of the drawing can be studied without the template's guidelines obscuring the view. Many drawing programs with layer capabilities have specific keyboard commands built into the running of the program for this purpose. In Canvas 3.5, for instance, the keyboard shortcut to render invisible all layers other than the active one is *Command-4*. To see the template again, the Canvas keyboard shortcut *Command-5* makes all layers reappear.

Figure 54 was constructed using the perspective chart shown in figure 52. Although the chart still exists below the main drawing, it is invisible; this drawing was then printed showing only the scenographic design. Key to the making of this sketch is the ability Canvas 3.5 gives to treat selected elements in ways that simulate perspective views; the

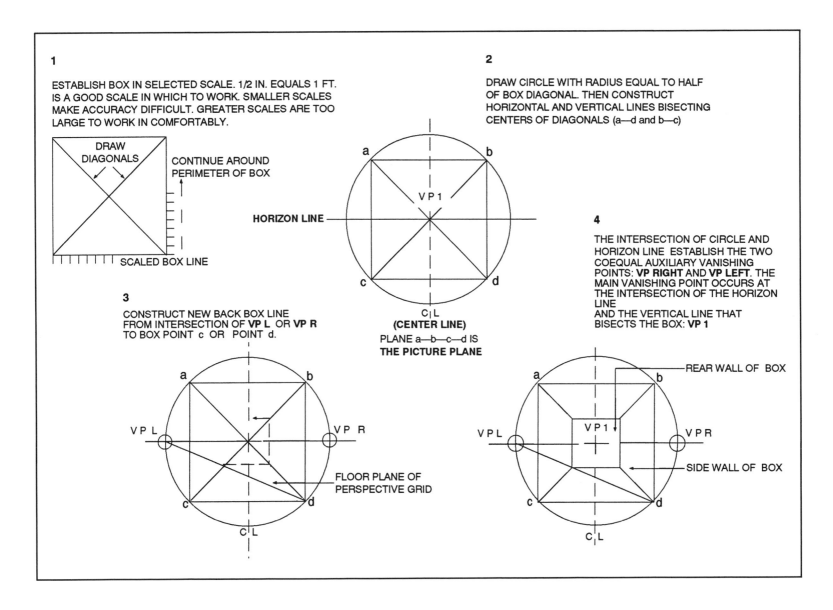

1

ESTABLISH BOX IN SELECTED SCALE. 1/2 IN. EQUALS 1 FT. IS A GOOD SCALE IN WHICH TO WORK. SMALLER SCALES MAKE ACCURACY DIFFICULT. GREATER SCALES ARE TOO LARGE TO WORK IN COMFORTABLY.

DRAW DIAGONALS

CONTINUE AROUND PERIMETER OF BOX

SCALED BOX LINE

2

DRAW CIRCLE WITH RADIUS EQUAL TO HALF OF BOX DIAGONAL. THEN CONSTRUCT HORIZONTAL AND VERTICAL LINES BISECTING CENTERS OF DIAGONALS (a—d and b—c)

VP 1

HORIZON LINE

C L
(CENTER LINE)
PLANE a—b—c—d IS
THE PICTURE PLANE

3

CONSTRUCT NEW BACK BOX LINE FROM INTERSECTION OF **VP L** OR **VP R** TO BOX POINT c OR POINT d.

VP L

VP R

FLOOR PLANE OF PERSPECTIVE GRID

C L

4

THE INTERSECTION OF CIRCLE AND HORIZON LINE ESTABLISH THE TWO COEQUAL AUXILIARY VANISHING POINTS: **VP RIGHT** AND **VP LEFT**. THE MAIN VANISHING POINT OCCURS AT THE INTERSECTION OF THE HORIZON LINE AND THE VERTICAL LINE THAT BISECTS THE BOX: **VP 1**

VP L

VP1

VP R

REAR WALL OF BOX

SIDE WALL OF BOX

C L

boarded decks used in the design were created using the program's perspective options. Although possible to draw boards line by line, this task would demand an inordinate amount of time. Figure 55 demonstrates how such decks are made.

4. *Working drawings.* No matter how aesthetically satisfying a scenographic rendering is, the ideas and dreams engendered by it must be put into tangible instructions for scenic shop artisans. With few exceptions, these instructions are submitted as drawings rendered in standard scales that show exact shape, size, and appearance of scenic elements the scenographer wants reproduced on the stage. Although there are differing ways of specifying this information, all have similar goals: an accurate, visual representation of the sizes and shapes of scenic units with complete instructions for their construction and

Fig. 50. Steps in perspective grid construction

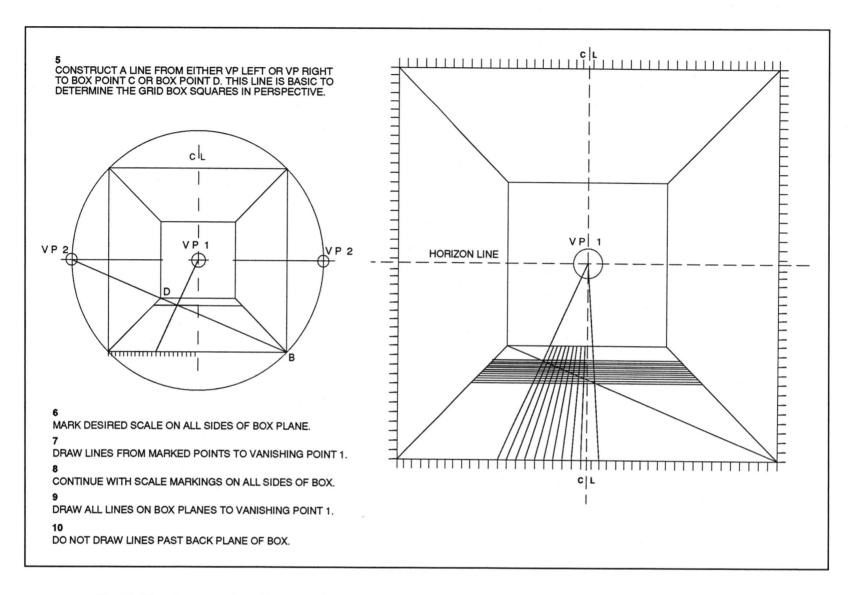

5
CONSTRUCT A LINE FROM EITHER VP LEFT OR VP RIGHT
TO BOX POINT C OR BOX POINT D. THIS LINE IS BASIC TO
DETERMINE THE GRID BOX SQUARES IN PERSPECTIVE.

6
MARK DESIRED SCALE ON ALL SIDES OF BOX PLANE.

7
DRAW LINES FROM MARKED POINTS TO VANISHING POINT 1.

8
CONTINUE WITH SCALE MARKINGS ON ALL SIDES OF BOX.

9
DRAW ALL LINES ON BOX PLANES TO VANISHING POINT 1.

10
DO NOT DRAW LINES PAST BACK PLANE OF BOX.

Fig. 51. Steps in perspective grid construction

Types of Working Drawings

finish. Let us examine more closely what is involved in making these drawings before seeing how computers are used in their making.

The basis of drawing has not changed since the Renaissance. In a notebook section that gives advice to painters and drawers, Leonardo eloquently sums up the basis for all graphic representation. He says:

> The first principle of the science of painting is the point; second is the line; third is the surface; fourth is the body which is enclosed by these surfaces. . . . Point is said to be that which cannot be divided into any part. Line is said to be made by moving the point along. Therefore line will be divisible in its length, but its breadth will be completely indivisible. Surface is said to be like extending the

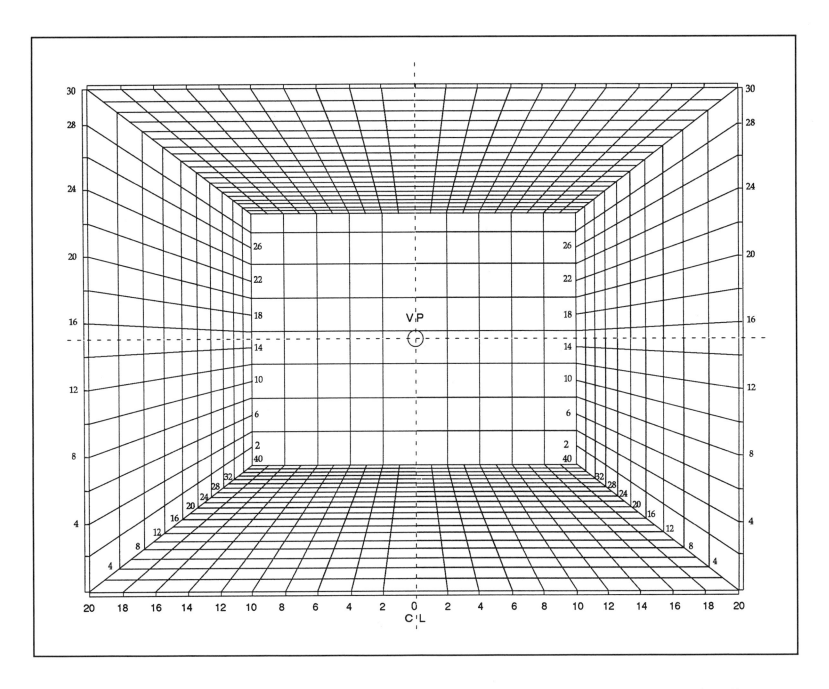

Fig. 52. Computer-made perspective grid

line into breadth, so that it will be possible to divide it in length and breadth. But it also has no depth. But body I affirm as arising when length and breadth acquire depth and are divisible. Body I call that which is covered by surfaces, the appearance of which becomes visible with light.

Here we have an uncanny anticipation of the way computers store in memory the

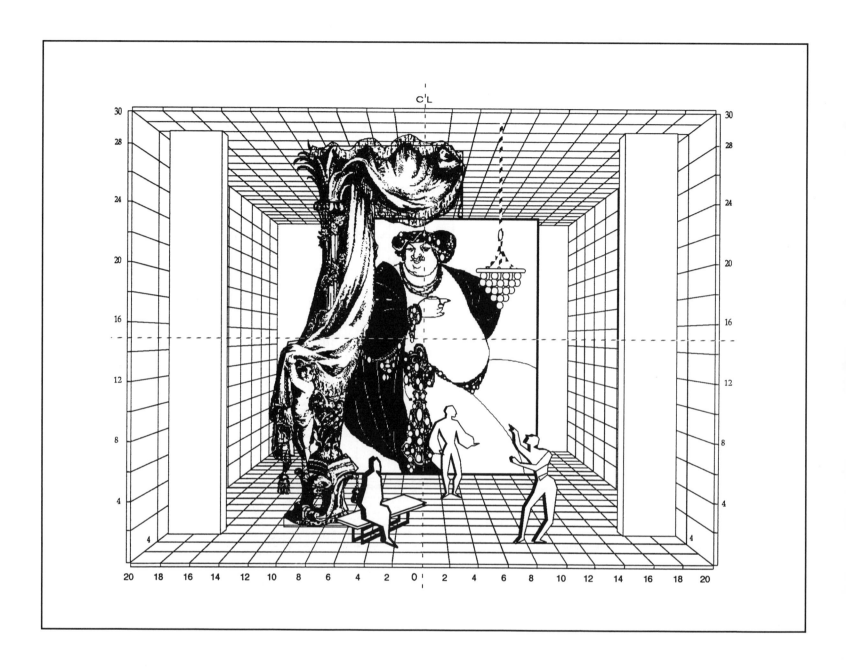

Fig. 53. Scenographic concept from library elements

numerically encoded geometric models our drawing programs produce on the monitor screen. Leonardo's explanation serves equally well for his time and for the computer composed of zero-dimensional points, one-dimensional lines, and two-dimensional surfaces. These combine into three-dimensional solids.

While there are many different kinds of working drawings, all are basically either *plans* of an object (seen from above) or *elevations* (seen from directly in front of, or from the side of, an object). Few working drawings attempt to give an illusion of three-

NIGHT OF THE IGUANA

DARWIN REID PAYNE 1992

dimensionality, although axonometric drawings give a better image of an object's physical form than do either plans or elevations. Most productions need a variety of working drawings to ensure that the production will accurately reflect the scenographer's concepts as presented in either the sketches or in the models. Working drawings fall into these major categories:

Fig. 54. Scenographic perspective drawing:
Night of the Iguana

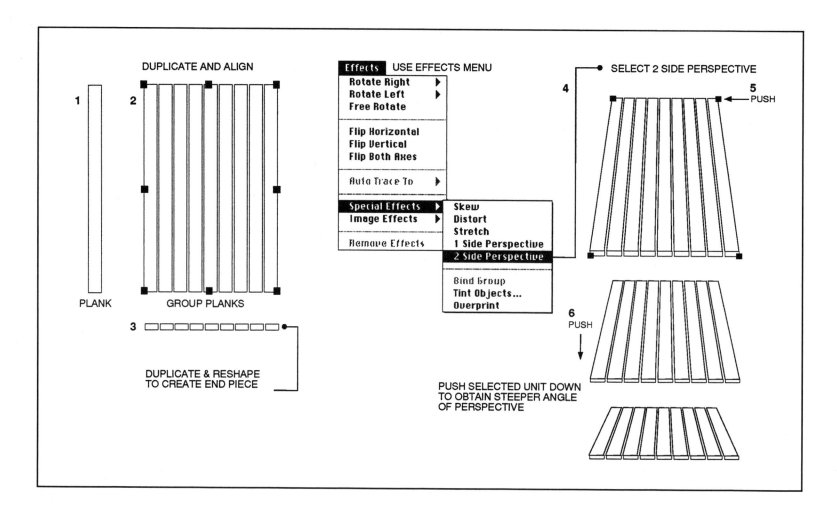

Fig. 55. Making plank units in Canvas 3.5

1. Floor plans
2. Lighting plots
3. Elevations (front and side)
4. Flat schedules (front view of all flat units to be constructed)
5. Rear elevations (not made as much as in the past—information these drawings give are frequently incorporated in the front view flat schedules)
6. Platform schedules (either a plan view of all individual units or an isometric projection view of all individual units)
7. Detail construction drawings (all drawings contained in 3, 4, or 5 broken down into smaller units and accompanied by more complex instructions)
8. Paint schedules (basically a flat schedule that includes precise colors, painted patterns, and painted details)
9. Backdrop specifications (a scale drawing of the backdrop to be duplicated, generally marked into grid patterns or cover with a transparent material on which the grid pattern is drawn)

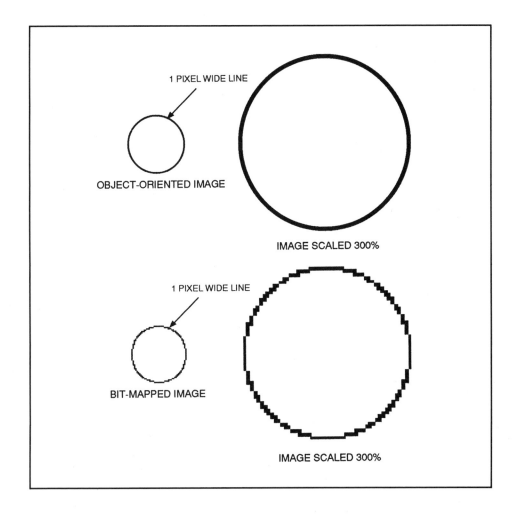

1 PIXEL WIDE LINE

OBJECT-ORIENTED IMAGE

IMAGE SCALED 300%

1 PIXEL WIDE LINE

BIT-MAPPED IMAGE

IMAGE SCALED 300%

Fig. 56. Object-oriented and bit-mapped graphics

10. Rigging schedules (a plan showing only hanging pieces of scenery, the number of the line sets they require, and the position they occupy on the batten)

For those needing to review the basic principles of scenographic technical specification, *Drafting for the Theatre*, by Dennis Dorn and Mark Shanda (Carbondale: Southern Illinois University Press, 1992), is recommended.

Drawing Objects on the Computer Screen

There are two basic kinds of computer graphics images: object-oriented images and bit-mapped images. Both types are shown in figure 56. Computer graphics objects consist of basic parts: bounding lines and interior fills. Computer graphics lines can be specified in various widths (sometimes called *weights*) calculated in *point* sizes, a term that derives from printer's measurements for type; in drawing programs the smaller the point size, the thinner the line thickness. The thinnest line capable of being printed is frequently called *hairline*. Computer graphics lines can also be given characteristics other than solid black; they can be displayed as dashes (or interrupted lines), as variable percents of black (or grays), as color in color-supported applications, or as patterns. (See figure 28 for lines other than solid black.) Interior fills—like lines—have a wide range of possibilities; an object can be transparent or opaque, can have patterned, graduated, or PostScript fills. (See figure 28 for examples of object-fill patterns.)

With object-oriented graphics (also called *vector graphics*), the basic elements of an object can independently be assigned. That is, objects can consist solely of a boundary line with no fill or pattern; fills can be altered with no damage to the outline shape. Lines of object-oriented graphics are entirely editable as to size, color, and pattern. Object fills can also be edited from one color or pattern to another color or pattern through selection of a new fill color or pattern.

Bit-mapped graphics have the same basic parts as object-oriented graphics—line and fill—and can initially be assigned line size, color, and pattern and fill color and pattern. Bit-mapped graphics, however, are not edited in the same way—or with the same ease— as object-oriented graphics. Bit-mapped graphics can only be altered using tools that turn the individual pixels ON or OFF: pencil, paint brush, eraser, marque, and lasso are the primary tools used for editing bit-mapped graphics (see figure 28). Bit map tools cannot be used to edit object-oriented graphics. Drawings done on computers begin with simple shapes created in a relatively few basic ways. These are:

1. *By selecting an object tool (line, rectangle, circle, arc, oval, rounded rectangle, polygon), clicking on a starting point (fig. 57A) with the input device—either mouse or stylus—and dragging the object down and across the screen page.* When the mouse button or stylus is released, the figure is complete (fig. 57B). In some programs, the size of the object being drawn is monitored in the scale that has been set by the drawer. This information is displayed in an information bar or palette; these bars usually occur at the top or bottom of the screen; sometimes the information is displayed in a box. In almost all cases, as the object's size changes, the information detailing its size is updated. In most programs the default scale is 1" = 1". This default can be changed to any desired new measure, after which the monitoring information will reflect the new scale. In Canvas 3.5, an option exists to show the size of the object directly attached to the figure (fig. 57C).

2. *By use of key combinations to modify the basic way of drawing.* In the way of drawing discussed above, the object began at a corner point and progressed in a diagonal manner. There are times, however, when the drawer needs to create the figure from a central point outward. This option is available in most object-oriented and bit-mapped programs. To draw from the center out, the drawer selects a tool, holds down the Shift and Option keys simultaneously while dragging the screen cursor away from the center starting point to the place that the object is to terminate (see circle at bottom of figure 57). These keystrokes are common to many drawing programs but not all; CAD programs usually dedicate special tools for drawing objects in exact ways. Using other key combinations—such as the Shift key and an object tool—a drawn object is restrained to certain shapes. For instance, in most programs when the polygon tool is selected and the Shift key is held down while drawing, the resulting object will always be a square; not held down, the polygon tool can be made to draw rectangles of varying heights and widths. It is also possible with CAD programs to draw objects by key input alone.

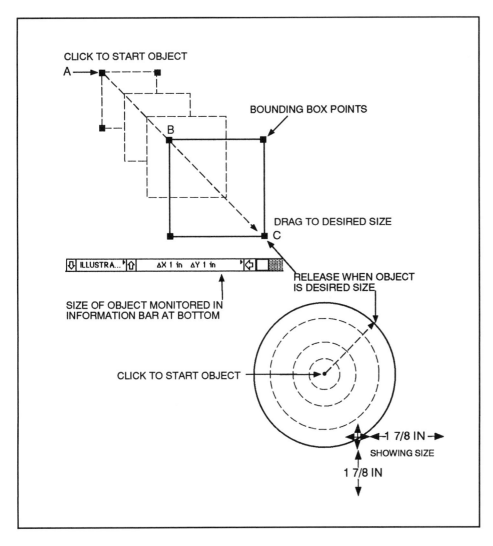

Fig. 57. Drawing object-oriented graphics

3. *By use of specialized tools: polygons—which consist of multistraight-sided lines at varying angles—and Bézier curves—which are compound irregular curved lines (fig. 58).* In this method of drawing, individual points are progressively placed by clicking the input device. When the last point of the figure is double-clicked on the starting point, the figure closes and the basic outline of the object is determined. The individual points for polygon objects are called *vertices*; this simply means they are the outermost points of a polygon figure. Another feature of polygon drawing is that, using keyboard strokes or menu options, new vertices can be added to a figure to create new sides. Vertices can also be eliminated to create a simpler object form by highlighting individual points and using the key *Delete* or *Backspace*. When Bézier vertices (more properly called *controlling points*) are selected, additional points are added. Bézier curves can be thought of as an infinite assortment of French curves, since through their use any compound curve is possible.

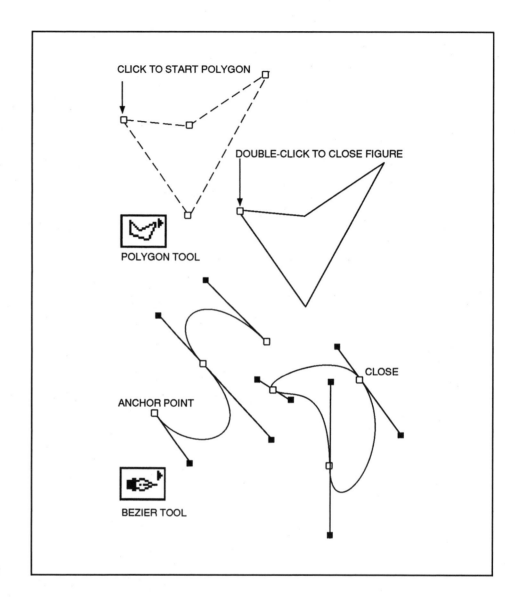

CLICK TO START POLYGON

DOUBLE-CLICK TO CLOSE FIGURE

POLYGON TOOL

CLOSE

ANCHOR POINT

BEZIER TOOL

Fig. 58. Drawing polygon and Bézier objects

4. *By use of dialog boxes to determine size and attributes of objects (fig. 59).* Each program uses a different graphic schematic for creating shapes from numerical input. Some dialog boxes—such as those in MiniCad+ 5.0—give access to the dialog box simply by double-clicking on a shape icon—such as a rectangle, square, oval, or circle—in the Toolbox. When the screen for that particular shape appears, the size of the figure is determined by typing in the dimensions desired. These dialog boxes are also used to accurately position figures on document pages. PowerDraw 5.0 operates in a similar way to MiniCad+ 5.0 to provide access to customizing dialog boxes but requires the Option key to be held down when selecting the tool icon. (PowerDraw 5.0 has standardized many of its functions to use this same key; in doing so it allows the drawing tools to modify the drawing in numerous ways without having to remember a large number of

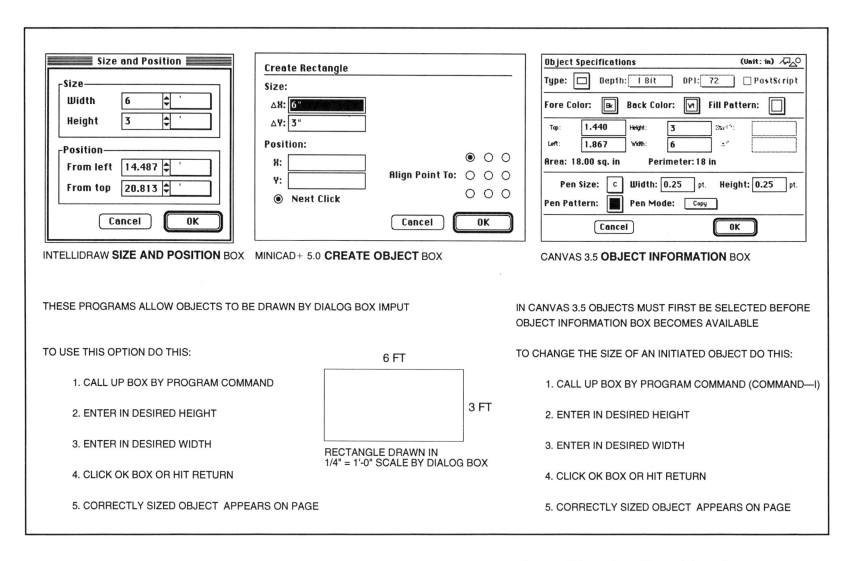

INTELLIDRAW **SIZE AND POSITION** BOX   MINICAD+ 5.0 **CREATE OBJECT** BOX

CANVAS 3.5 **OBJECT INFORMATION** BOX

THESE PROGRAMS ALLOW OBJECTS TO BE DRAWN BY DIALOG BOX IMPUT

TO USE THIS OPTION DO THIS:

    1. CALL UP BOX BY PROGRAM COMMAND

    2. ENTER IN DESIRED HEIGHT

    3. ENTER IN DESIRED WIDTH

    4. CLICK OK BOX OR HIT RETURN

    5. CORRECTLY SIZED OBJECT APPEARS ON PAGE

6 FT

3 FT

RECTANGLE DRAWN IN
1/4" = 1'-0" SCALE BY DIALOG BOX

IN CANVAS 3.5 OBJECTS MUST FIRST BE SELECTED BEFORE OBJECT INFORMATION BOX BECOMES AVAILABLE

TO CHANGE THE SIZE OF AN INITIATED OBJECT DO THIS:

    1. CALL UP BOX BY PROGRAM COMMAND (COMMAND—I)

    2. ENTER IN DESIRED HEIGHT

    3. ENTER IN DESIRED WIDTH

    4. CLICK OK BOX OR HIT RETURN

    5. CORRECTLY SIZED OBJECT APPEARS ON PAGE

Fig. 59. Object-oriented image information dialog boxes

keystroke combinations.) Even though shapes can be created by selection of a tool and dragging the shape to a desired size, use of dialog boxes and numerical input is by far the most accurate way to draw. This method of drawing is especially suited to page-layout programs, where precise placement of text and objects is crucial. These procedures are also features of CADD (computer-aided design and drafting) and CAE (computer-aided engineering) programs. The placing of objects on the page by the dialog box is not frequently used by drawers who use the drawing space in experimental ways. The general way most scenographers draw is (1) select a tool option like a line, circle, oval, rectangle, square, or arc, (2) drag the shape to a general size, and (3) use dialog boxes to apply precise dimensions. Objects can also be scaled to different sizes by precise percents or by ratios.

    5. *By use of highly specialized tools to create objects or to place objects in ways not easily accomplished with general tools or standard actions.* There are occasions when

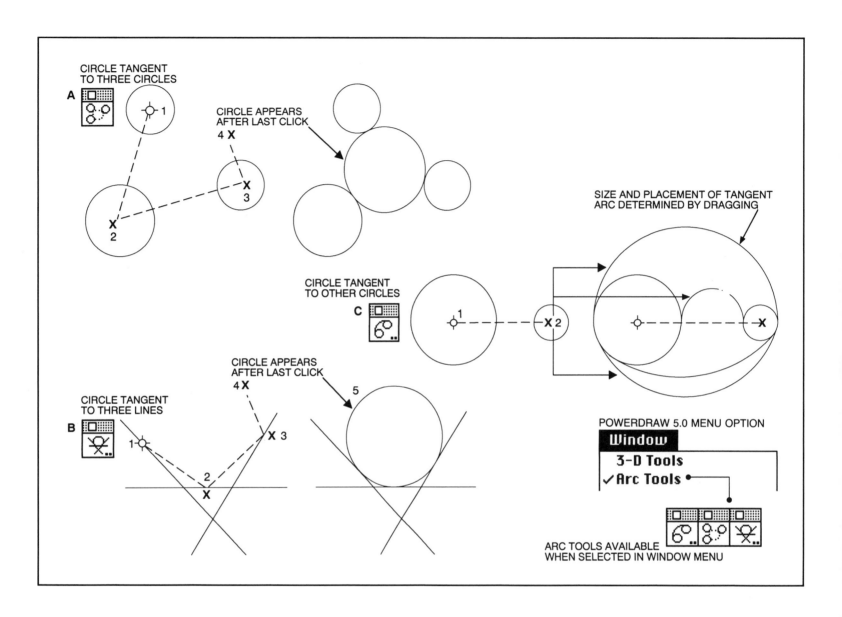

Fig. 60. PowerDraw 5.0 arc tools

the drawer needs to create objects that are dependent on the position of other objects or are not easily constructed using basic tools. The difference between general drawing programs like FreeHand 4.0 or Canvas 3.5 and CAD programs like MiniCad+ 5.0 and PowerDraw 5.0 can be measured in the number of these specialized tools available to the drawer. For example, if a drawing contains three circles like those shown in figure 60A, it would take some little time and considerable maneuvering to create a fourth circle that is exactly tangent to the first three. PowerDraw 5.0, however, has a set of tools that deals specifically with circles and their tangent arcs. By use of a specific tool in this set (fig. 60B), an accurate circle can be created that is precisely tangent to these lines by dragging the cursor to the first one (fig. 60-1), then to the second (fig. 60-2), and finally

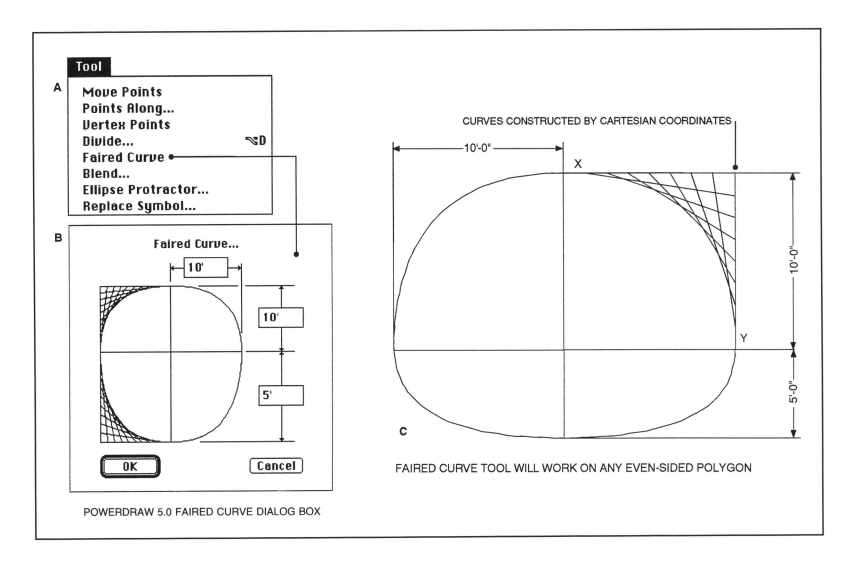

POWERDRAW 5.0 FAIRED CURVE DIALOG BOX

Fig. 61. PowerDraw 5.0 faired curve tool

clicking on the third (fig. 60-3). When this action is complete (fig. 60-4), the circle shown in figure 60-5 appears. This program also has other particularized tools that perform functions extremely difficult to achieve in other drawing applications. Take, for instance, the need to create objects with curves based on the intersections of lines in a Cartesian graph (called a *faired curve* in PowerDraw 5.0). Construction of these curves is possible in Canvas 3.5 as well as in other drawing programs; but it requires a number of steps—as well as a grasp of geometrical drawing technique—to do so. Figure 61, on the other hand, shows the PowerDraw 5.0 tool that creates these curves on any even-numbered polygon with two or more sides simply by selection of the polygon when the tool is active.

Another tool in this program automatically places into a drawing accurately calculated radial lines in degrees that match the perspective of the ellipse being drawn (fig. 62). To

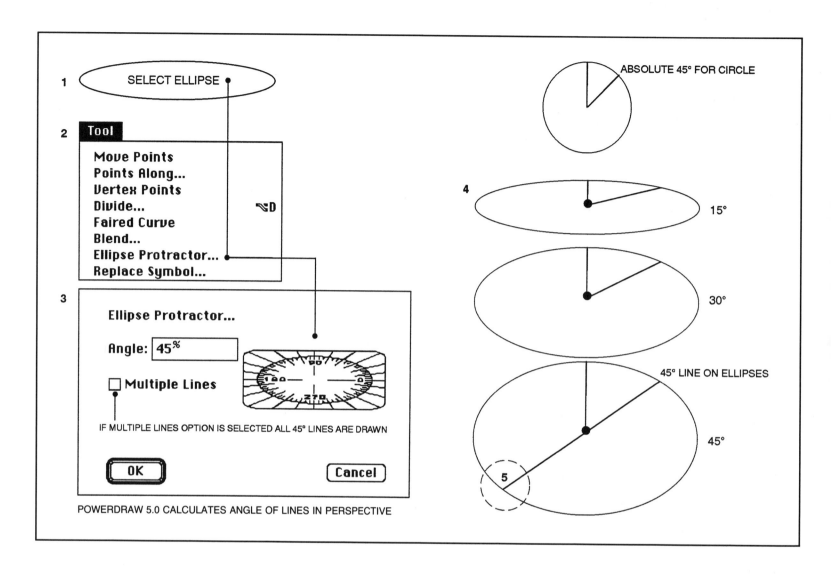

Fig. 62. PowerDraw 5.0 ellipse protractor tool

find a precise angle declination for an ellipse (which is nothing more than a circle seen in perspective), these steps are followed using PowerDraw's *ellipse protractor tool*: (1) draw an ellipse and leave it selected, (2) go to the Tool Menu and select *ellipse protractor*, (3) enter into angle box the degree of the line wanted (note that the Tools Window image shows the way the degrees read from 0° to 365°; also note that when *Multiple Lines* box is selected, the line extends through the center of the ellipse to the other side as shown in figure 62-5), (4) click OK in the *Ellipse Protractor Window* and a 45° line in perspective will be drawn on the original ellipse. Creation of these lines is possible using other drawing programs, but the process is not as quickly or easily accomplished, and the results are certainly not as accurate.

It is easy to see that CAD provides an increasingly powerful means to render technical specifications in new and more efficient ways. Some of these ways include the ability to

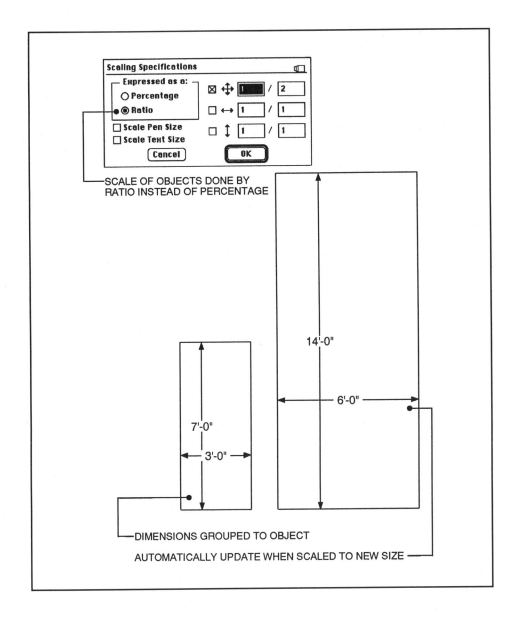

Fig. 63. Object-oriented image-scaling dialog box

automatically change dimensions of previously drawn objects when altered from one size to another. Figure 63 shows how the size and dimensions of a flat change using a Scale dialog box.

Although drafting procedures vary among scenographers, there is a general agreement as to how the above information should be drawn. Manual drafters attempt to show differing kinds of information by relative weights and thickness of drawn lines. At best, this skill is imprecise. Since most drafting is done in pencil, manual drawings invariably contain widely differing line weights and thicknesses. A distinct advantage of computer-generated working drawings is that individual objects can automatically be created in precisely drawn sizes with precisely sized line weights. An even greater advantage to computer drafting is that changes to these drawings are quickly accomplished with no residual traces of the old drawing remaining visible; this is seldom the case with manually drawn graphics.

A primary skill required in manual drafting is the ability to draw consistently lines that have different thickness. These differing thicknesses are called *line weights*. The manual draftsman need only master a few: object lines, dimension lines, hidden lines, and interrupted lines are the basic ones used in most architectural or mechanical drawing. All computer CAD and object-oriented applications employ lines that are generated from preprogrammed mathematical instructions. These result in object-oriented (vector) graphics, used to differentiate this kind of drawing from bit-mapped graphics, which are only collections of individual square units called *pixels*, a computer term that derives from two words, *picture element*, and is used as the basic unit of measurement for bit-mapped graphics and computer screen displays. Object-oriented graphics give the drawer an ability to specify precisely a wide variety of line weights that do not vary until the line weight is purposely changed. For this reason, lines can be used as deliberate elements in graphic communication. Purposely varying the line thicknesses of drawn objects makes it easier to comprehend relationships between objects. This is especially true for objects contained in complex assemblies.

Specifying line weights varies from program to program. Figure 64 shows the common line weights available in Canvas 3.5. Line thicknesses are always specified in terms of numerical *points* or decimal fractions of a single point. A point, as noted earlier, is the word inherited from printing terminology to denote both letters and lines in increments of 1/72″ in width and height. This measurement, coincidentally, corresponds to the width and height measurement of the pixel. Figure 64 also shows the mechanism for changing weights in Canvas 3.5. Note that the right hand of the dialog box (shown at the top of figure 64) applies primarily to object-oriented lines, whereas the left side of the dialog box shows the effect of effect of bit-mapped lines. Also note that both bit-mapped and object-oriented lines not shown in the main dialog box can be specified using the *Custom* option at the bottom of the line. When this option is selected another dialog box opens— the *Custom Pen Manager*. Using this option, numerically specified line thicknesses can be entered. In figure 64 an 8-point line is shown at the left of the *Custom Pen Manager* box.

Line thicknesses are changed in two basic ways: (1) by using dialog boxes, such as those shown in figure 64, or (2) by using pressure-sensitive styli with graphics tablets (see figure 10). Using a Wacom's SP-210 stylus (as shown in figure 11), it is possible to draw lines that vary in thickness as the line is being created, something that is not possible when drawing lines with a program's standard tools. Although the ability to create pressure-sensitive lines exists for almost all paint programs, this option is only available to a limited number of object-oriented programs. As object-oriented programs continue to be upgraded, one should expect to see the number grow. It is unlikely, however, that dedicated CAD programs will include pressure-sensitive drawing capabilities. Three-dimensional programs, on the other hand, are more apt to add these options to future releases. FreeHand 4.0 is a good example of an illustration object-oriented graphic program

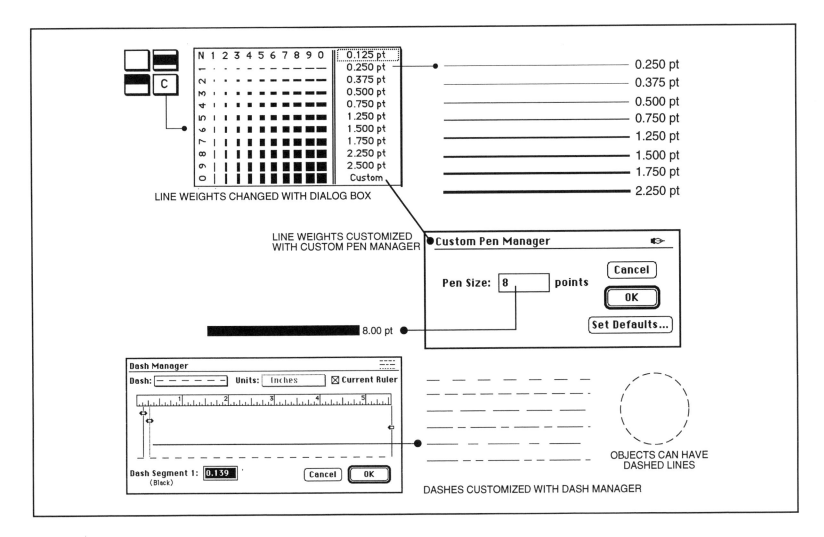

Fig. 64. Line possibilities in Canvas 3.5

that supports pressure-sensitive styli. To draw a free-form stroke in Freehand, however, parameters of a stroke width must be set to obtain precise beginning and ending points; the means to accomplish this is shown in figure 12A. By setting the stroke from a small number of pixels to a larger number, the basic size and shape of the lines are controlled. Although there is a strategy built into the basic program that allows free-formed strokes to be created without drawing tablets or pressure-sensitive styli, the technique used is, at best, a clumsy one; there is really no substitute for a graphics tablet and a pressure-sensitive stylus. For computer drawing that approaches the freedom of hand-drawn images, the graphics tablet is a wise investment.

Lines in both bit-mapped programs and object-oriented programs can be changed to the installed bit-map patterns such as those shown in figure 28. These patterned lines should not be confused, however, with PostScript pattern lines that are only possible in programs such as FreeHand and Illustrator.

One cannot read the above lines without thinking, *How in the world does anyone ever master drawing when so many things must be kept in mind as the drawing is made?*

The answer is that very little of what we have just been discussing ever presents itself directly to the computer drawer. Most of a computer's capabilities are—to use computer terminology—"working in the background." The choice most drawers make are simple ones that differ little from those made when drawing images by hand. Despite the initially daunting aspects of procedures, computer graphics are becoming increasingly more understandable to those trained with traditional tools and materials. Be certain, however, that in the future computer graphics will become more and more necessary to a scenographer's work procedures.

At this juncture, an obvious but nonetheless important point needs to be made: different CAD and drawing programs implement differently the possibilities listed above. As noted in *Interface: The Door to Computer Worlds,* the willingness of most companies to use the Macintosh interface in familiar ways ensures for the most part that the user of one drawing program can use the skills learned there in other programs. Yet this has been true only up to a point. Now, however, there is a growing trend for developers of one commercial drawing program to incorporate successful features of rival applications into their own upgrades and new versions. Competition for a customer's favor, therefore, causes a leapfrog mentality to persist in the development of drawing software. Over time, the features of one developer's programs tend to merge with those of other companies. We might reasonably expect that in the not-too-distant future there will be a master program available that accommodates every imaginable drawing need. There are good reasons, however, why this will not or should not happen, the main one being that not all drawing is of the same kind or geared to the same purpose; that is, a program that gives painterlike effects necessary for a scenographic illustration is useless for technical specification drawings. There will always be a need for specialized programs for specialized needs. Although an all-inclusive program is possible—and a few companies seem bent on achieving one—such a program could only be attained at the high cost of disk space, of sophisticated computers to run it, and, not least, of a user's ability to learn its complexities.

Let us now turn our attention to some of the positive developments that competition in the drawing application field has produced so far. Chief among these is the subject we examine next.

Automatic Alignment Features for CAD Programs

One of the most important developments in CAD technology since 1980 is a feature shared by a growing number of dedicated drafting applications that uses a form of artificial intelligence during the construction and alignment of objects as they are being drawn on the computer screen. Programs having this feature provides drawers with continual information during the drawing progress. Different companies give unique names for this feature even though they all provide the same kinds of information to the drawer and perform essentially the same kinds of actions: for MiniCad+ 5.0, these actions are labeled *SmartCursor*, Claris Cad 2.0 has adopted the designation *Guideliner*; Ashlar Vellum's feature is aptly called *Design Assistant*; and although not a dedicated drafting program, Canvas 3.5 also supports automatic drawing alignment with its *smart mouse* option. The results of these various approaches are almost identical.

The basic attribute of all these procedures is that as the drawer creates any form of object—line, rectangle, oval, arc, circle, Bézier curve, or polygon—information automatically appears near the objects affected showing possible relationships or connection options between them. This information is displayed both as key words near the objects and as guidelines (horizontal, vertical, or angular) that also show visual alignment coordinates resulting from the drawer's actions. The artificial intelligence element of these actions lies in the assumption that as the drawing is constructed, the actions of the drawer are anticipated. While this may or may not be a good example of artificial intelligence theory at work, it does significantly aid in making more accurate drawings faster than they could be done were this feature not present. For instance, if a rectangle has been created and the line tool is afterward selected, the moving cursor will, as it approaches within a few pixels of a vertex point, present the drawer with messages to indicate that that particular vertex is within snapping distance (another useful feature of object-oriented drawing programs for some time). Further, if the mouse is released while the message is still visible, the line's starting point will attach exactly to the vertex point. If, on the other hand, the line is taken to the interior of the rectangle, another message appears telling that the exact center of the rectangle is within snapping distance. If the line is released during this message, then the line's end point will automatically attach itself to the center. Figure 65 is an illustration of what the drawer would see in any of the programs using this form of guidance. One of the best features of the MiniCad+ 5.0 application is that this form of help operates in the three-dimensional phase of the program as well as in the two-dimensional phase.

It is reasonably certain that all drawing programs written in the future will incorporate the options just discussed. Aldus IntelliDraw is one of the earliest of the general drawing programs to have sophisticated artificial intelligence-like elements that heretofore were only part of high-end CAD applications. It takes little imagination to see that this form of aid not only hastens any drawing process but also makes the resulting drawings significantly more accurately constructed.

Many drawing programs provide rulers above the top and at the left side of the main window. Programs that have rulers usually allow the default scale (usually $1''=1''$) to be set to other scales. All CAD programs have rulers that can be customized, since working drawings are made in various scales. The scale of rulers must be set in dialog boxes; the mechanisms for doing this varies from program to program. Figure 66 shows the way Canvas 3.5 implements ruler-scale change. After the scale is reset, the onscreen rulers reflect the new scale. Some programs, particularly illustration programs such as FreeHand 4.0 and Canvas 3.5, permit drawers to extract from these rulers magnetic nonprinting guidelines that provide vertical or horizontal lines to which objects adhere when brought within proximity to the line. These proximities are set as default features; three to five pixels are a standard many programs providing magnetic guidelines follow. These guidelines are especially useful when creating accurately measured polygon objects like that shown in figure 66. In this illustration we see a polygon object being constructed using horizontal and vertical magnetic guidelines that extend to the rulers; this allows for precise calculation of an object with irregular elements in its makeup. The example in figure 66 was drawn in Canvas 3.5; for higher-end CAD programs, such as PowerDraw 5.0 and MiniCad+ 5.0, more options for accurate drawing are available.

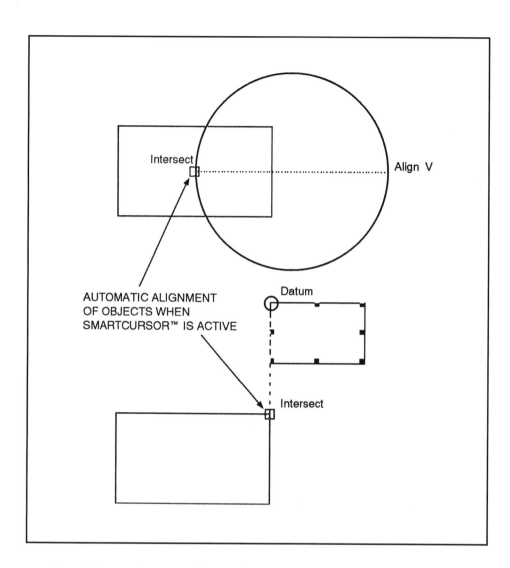

Fig. 65. Automatic alignment in CAD programs

Computer Scenographic Drawings: Size and Accuracy

One of the most important changes the computer makes in scenographic work lies in its ability to create highly accurate drawing in scales smaller than those normally used in manually made drawings. Although most scenographers will continue to use familiar scales such as 1/2″ and 1/4″ = 1′, it is very possible to make those drawings, usually done in 1/2″ scale in 1/4″ scale, without a loss of accuracy. Since few scenographers can afford the cost of a good plotter, output options become limited to printers that use considerably smaller paper sizes. Printing drawings on these smaller-size machines also means that manually made drawings which often contained many details on a single page will have to be subdivided into a greater number of smaller sheets. Large drawings can, of course, be made on the computer but can only be printed out as separate portions of the larger drawing. This option—called *Tiling*—means that any large drawing must be pasted together after printing to re-create the drawing that existed on the computer screen. This restriction applies to drawing sizes such as U.S. letter-size pages (8 1/2″ by 11″)

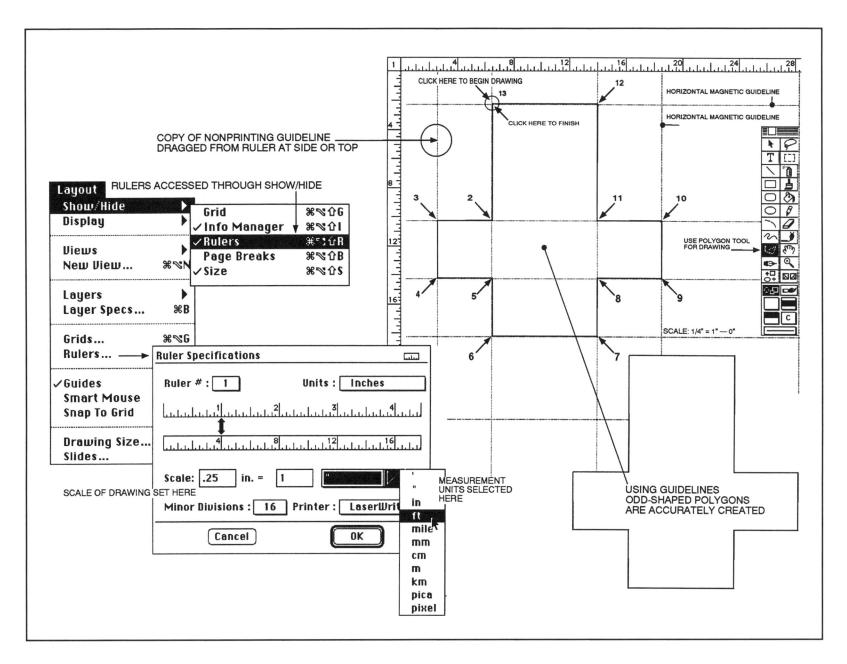

and U.S. legal-size pages (8 1/2″ by 14″), which will be the most common-size pages scenographers use. Plotter drawings have few restrictions as to size but plotters are extremely slow in printing and very expensive to maintain.

The Macintosh interface is to date the most effortless interface to read and use. Introduction of the menu system revolutionized how computer graphics are perceived on monitor screens. Still, for scenographers to design at optimum efficiency, methods of

Fig. 66. Drawing objects with guidelines in Canvas 3.5

Power Users

work must be learned that go beyond menu use. For maximum effectiveness, scenographers need to become *power users*. What are power users? the Microsoft Press *Computer Dictionary*—a book recommended for all computer users—defines the term this way: *power user: A person adept with computers, particularly on an applications-oriented level rather than on a programming level. A power user is someone who knows a considerable amount about computers and is comfortable enough with applications to be able to work with their most sophisticated features. Often power users are especially familiar with a specific type of application, such as spreadsheets or word processors, and can push these production to the limits of their capabilities.*

Power users in computer graphics are those who have taken the time to learn the quickest, most effective ways to create computer graphics. These users have found not only the means to tap the computer's hidden capabilities but also the ways to use specific applications efficiently. To voice a desire, however, is not equivalent to achieving it. In order to attain the high level of productivity suggested here one must consciously consider *all* the ways particular work methods are structured for each application used. The following recommendations are made to scenographers who desire to become power users:

1. Thoroughly learn the keystroke equivalents of all menu options that have them.

2. For those menu options frequently employed that have no default keyboard alternatives, program them with a reliable macro-making application. QuicKeys 3 is the program recommended; no macro-making application matches it. With QuicKeys 3 it is possible not only to create keystrokes that substitute for menu actions but to program the function keys—that row of keys at the top of the extended keyboard—for single-key commands.

3. Take full advantage of an application's programmable macro capabilities—such as those found in Canvas 3.5—and library options. While many graphics programs come with ready-made objects installed in libraries, all allow new objects and symbols to be created and stored.

4. Many graphics programs have *tear-off menus*. This beneficial feature allows frequently used menus—such as alignment options, line sizes, fill patterns, magnification views—to be *torn off* the original menu and placed on the drawing space in full view. When a selected line size needs to be changed, the alteration is made in the now-visible appropriate menu by a single click of the cursor.

Perhaps the most distinguishing feature that power users share is the day-to-day concern they show for both the computer and the materials created on it and for the habits they form that keep their operation at peak performance. Some of the strategies power users employ are simple common sense; others require sustained investigation of new opportunities that make the use of the computer operating at maximum efficiency. For anyone who wishes to become a power user these simple steps should be rigorously observed:

1. *Save work often.* Use the Command-S until it becomes second nature.

2. *Keep two (at least) floppy disk backup files for all work.* Update these files at the end of every session. This is the only way to ensure that work is secure.

3. *Frequently examine the state of fragmentation of the hard disk.* When necessary, defragment the disk. This operation takes time. Optimization of hard disks are possible

with several software programs. The two recommended here are Disk Express II, by Alsoft, and Speed Disk, part of the Norton Utilities package.

Calculation on the Computer

Numerical calculation is a normal part of all theatrical design and technical production processes; working drawings that detail objects and materials for scenographic designs must be carefully drawn in specific scales that accurately reflect their full-scale measurements. For this reason there are many times during the design of a production that the scenographer needs a calculator near to hand. Although small-desk or hand-held calculators are increasingly accessible, powerful, and inexpensive, computer users should take advantage of those desk-accessory applications that provide computer calculation. A program called Calculator is a standard application shipped as part of basic computer operating systems (fig. 67, top). Installed, this program resides under the Apple menu and is available to users in any program at any time. It is possible, however, to obtain other more sophisticated and powerful computer calculators that provide advanced functions. One such program—Calculator+—is available through many shareware networks. The best commercial application named Calc+ is available from Abbott Systems (fig. 67, bottom). This calculator includes more options than either the basic Calculator or the shareware Calculator+. Calc+ features larger resizable displays and—a valuable option— the ability to print out hard copies of calculations. In addition to usual numeric values, Calc+ has the ability to convert various kinds of measurements from one to the other, that is, from inches to centimeters, from inches to pica points, or ciceros. Information can be entered in all calculators from the numeric keypad on the computer calculator or from the regular keyboard keypad. Calc+—unlike the other two calculators—can not only be dragged to any size but also has a minimize button that allows it to be collapsed into a small icon that sits on the desktop.

While few scenographers are totally responsible for keeping exact records of a production's costs, some do need database capabilities. For these scenographers, or for the technical staffs that have the responsibility of building the scenographer's designs, one program—MiniCad+ 5.0 has database and spreadsheet functions integrated into its basic program. The distinct advantage of using this program is that drawings can be linked to the spreadsheet functions of the program; this means that changes made to the graphic portions of the designs will be automatically upgraded to match the new shapes or number of the drawn objects. This highly sophisticated program feature is unique to CAD applications at this level of cost. In order to take advantage of such advanced features, both the scenographer and the technical staff who rely on such information must use MiniCad+ 5.0.

Building Shapes and Forms on the Computer Drawing Board

All technical scenographic drawings created in computer graphic programs are constructed using specific kinds of tools. While implementation of these tools may vary from program to program, all have a basic set: line, rectangle, oval, arc, and rounded rectangle are basic to computer drawing. In order to obtain horizontal and vertical lines (and known angle lines such as 30°, 45°, and 60°), squares, circles, rounded squares, and circular arcs, constraining keys—most usually the Shift key—are used in conjunction with the basic tool set. Tools that provide more specialized shapes, such as polygons and free-

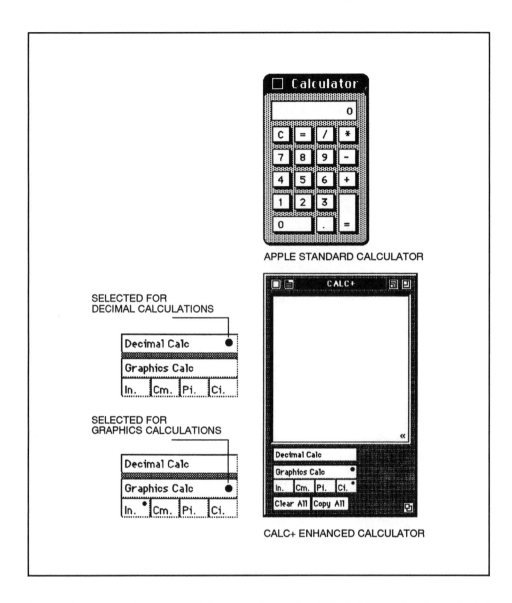

APPLE STANDARD CALCULATOR

SELECTED FOR
DECIMAL CALCULATIONS

CALC+ ENHANCED CALCULATOR

SELECTED FOR
GRAPHICS CALCULATIONS

Fig. 67. Computer calculators

form spline curves (known as Bézier curves) are also included in most object-oriented programs. It is possible with this set of basic tools plus a rudimentary knowledge of geometry to create any shape imaginable. Most object-oriented programs, however, provide menus that allow the user to specifically create multisided shapes. Objects that have equal sides—such as regular triangles, and octagons—or that have equally spaced points—such as stars—must resort to these specific menu options. Figure 68A shows the specific option in Canvas 3.5—named the *Multigon Manager*—that creates regular-sided figures. The number of sides the object will have is set in the number dialog window at the right side of the box. When a number of sides are set, the appropriate figure is highlighted to the left of the box and remains until the dialog box is reset to a different number. NOTE: Dialog boxes of this kind can often be accessed directly from the main Toolbox Menu

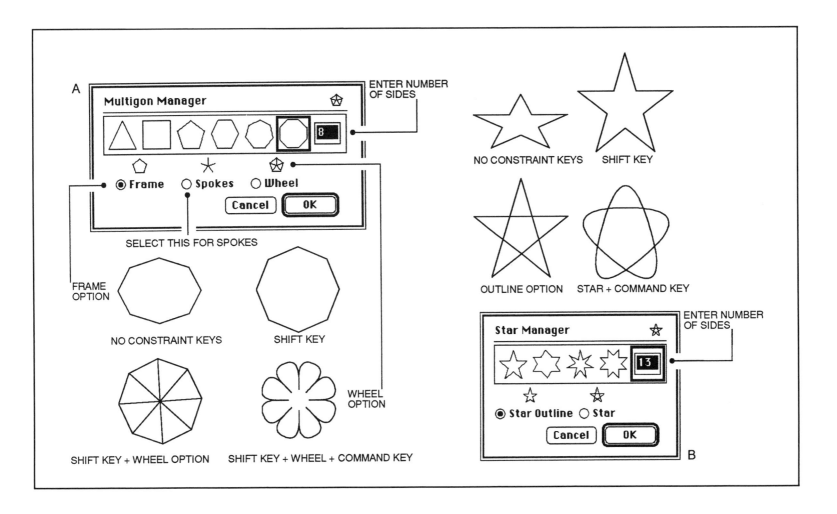

A

Multigon Manager

ENTER NUMBER OF SIDES

`8`

○ **Frame** ○ Spokes ○ Wheel

Cancel   OK

SELECT THIS FOR SPOKES

FRAME OPTION

NO CONSTRAINT KEYS

SHIFT KEY

SHIFT KEY + WHEEL OPTION

SHIFT KEY + WHEEL + COMMAND KEY

WHEEL OPTION

NO CONSTRAINT KEYS   SHIFT KEY

OUTLINE OPTION   STAR + COMMAND KEY

Star Manager

ENTER NUMBER OF SIDES

`13`

● **Star Outline** ○ Star

Cancel   OK

B

Fig. 68. Drawing complex object-oriented images

by double-clicking on the icon. Most object-oriented application programmers leave clues in the icon box itself: that is, if a small dark triangle is contained within the boundary of the icon, it can be assumed that an accessible menu will appear when the appropriate double-clicking option is invoked. These dialog boxes frequently include other options. In the examples shown below in figure 68*A*, the octagon is shown in four configurations: drawn without using a constraining key, drawn using a restraining Shift key, drawn with the Wheel option selected, and drawn using a restraining Shift key plus Command key with the Wheel option selected. Figure 68*B* shows another dialog box in Canvas 3.5: the *Star Manager*. This option operates in ways similar to that of the *Multigon Manager*. Figure 69 demonstrates two ways an octagon (*A*) with spokes can be transformed into other shapes. In figure 69*B*, double-clicking on the octagon will allow the drawer to pull out separate shapes from the main body of the object. In figure 69*C*, a circle can be used to slice the main figure into separate objects that can then be filled, in this case with a hatch pattern.

Canvas 3.5—along with MiniCad+ 5.0 and PowerDraw 5.0—provides options to

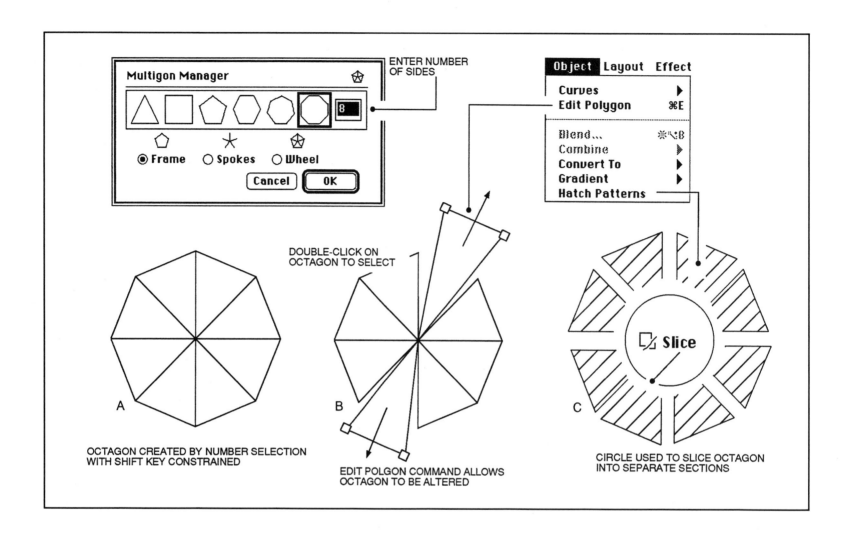

Fig. 69. Drawing and altering complex
object-oriented images

create complex single shapes from simple elements such as ovals, circles, rectangles, squares, triangles, and trapezoids. In Canvas 3.5, object combinations and transformations are made using the *Combine* option under the *Object Menu*. Figure 70 shows this menu along with the ways the various options contained operate. Figure 71 shows the difference between the way a detail is drawn using manual tools and the way the same object is drawn using computer options. Figure 72 demonstrates the steps needed to create the complex shape shown in figure 71 from basic components: the rectangle, oval, polygon, and rounded-rectangle tools. Figure 73 shows how a complex shape once created is modified by stretching (fig. 73A) the selected object. (NOTE: Objects can also be collapsed by dragging. While holding down the Shift key produces a proportionally resized object, it is advisable to use the Scale dialog box to ensure that objects are rescaled to known percentages.) Figure 73C shows how a complex form is modified through editing. In Canvas 3.5, the shortcut for placing an object in an editable mode is reached by double-clicking on the object; this reveals the controlling points that govern the outline's vertices

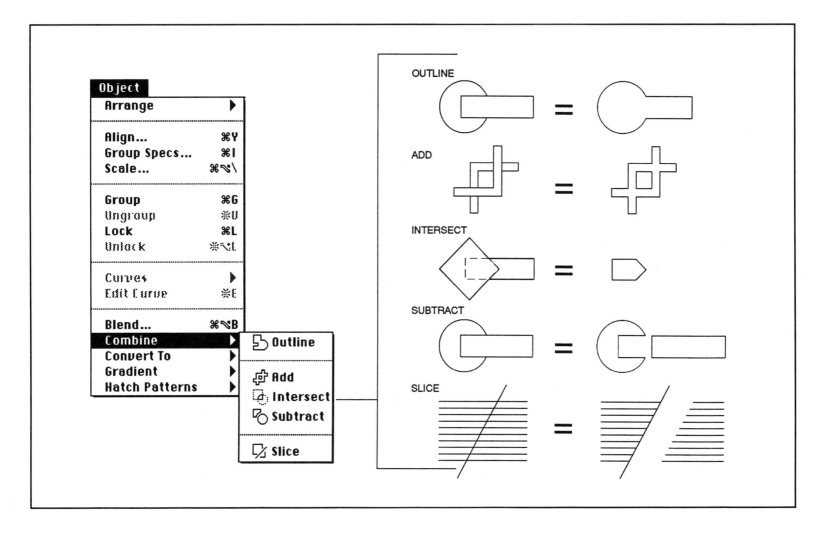

Fig. 70. Manipulating object-oriented images in Canvas 3.5

and control Bézier control points. As in other object-oriented programs these object points are of three basic kinds: corner points (junctions of two straight lines), connector points (junctions of a straight line and a curved line), and Bézier points (junctions controlled by handles that extend from the central point).

One of Canvas 3.5's shortcomings is its inability to combine shapes that have common boundaries (see "IMPORTANT NOTE" in figure 72). Two boxes, for instance, if strictly aligned by bottoms or sides could not be combined, cut, added, intersected, or sliced. Aldus IntelliDraw, a program noted in *Computer Graphics Programs,* places no such restrictions; aligned objects can be reshaped using the same options to those in Canvas 3.5. Unlike object-tool use in Canvas 3.5, Aldus IntelliDraw provides access to these options in floating palettes (fig. 74A). Once two or more objects are selected—as shown in figure 74C—it is a simple matter to click on one of the icons (in this instance the *Add* option) displayed in the palette (fig. 74B). When this is done, objects— regardless of their alignment—are changed into the new configuration (fig. 74D). PowerDraw 5.0 also

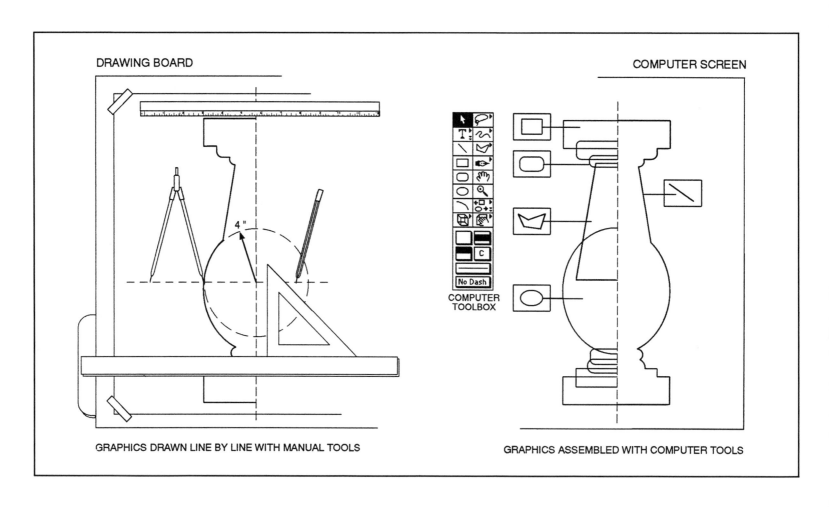

DRAWING BOARD

COMPUTER SCREEN

4 "

COMPUTER
TOOLBOX

GRAPHICS DRAWN LINE BY LINE WITH MANUAL TOOLS

GRAPHICS ASSEMBLED WITH COMPUTER TOOLS

Fig. 71. Diagram showing graphic image construction differences

puts its basic modification tools—combine, cut, intersect, and slice—into the Toolbox palette; Canvas 3.5 requires the use of a pull-down menu. Since these functions are basic to construction of complex objects, they can be made into QuicKeys commands; the better strategy, however, is to assign them to function keys.

IntelliDraw also provides object-creation features not found—or, at least, not as easily utilized—in any of the other programs recommended in this book. The most important of those features is a tool called *symmetrigon* (fig. 75A). Using this tool, complex objects like those shown in figures 75C and 75D are relatively easily drawn. To accomplish the same work even in a high-end CAD program involves more work. Setting the parameters of the object drawn is obtained by double-clicking on the *symmetrigon* icon; this brings into view the dialog box shown in figure 75B. When this dialog box appears, a choice is given to the drawer for the kind of object needed to be made: radial or mirror. When one type has been selected, the drawer returns to the main drawing screen to create the object. Figure 75C shows how a *mirrored* object looks when completed; figure 75D shows how a *radial* object looks when completed. The complexity of both objects is governed by the number of points entered into the window at the top right of

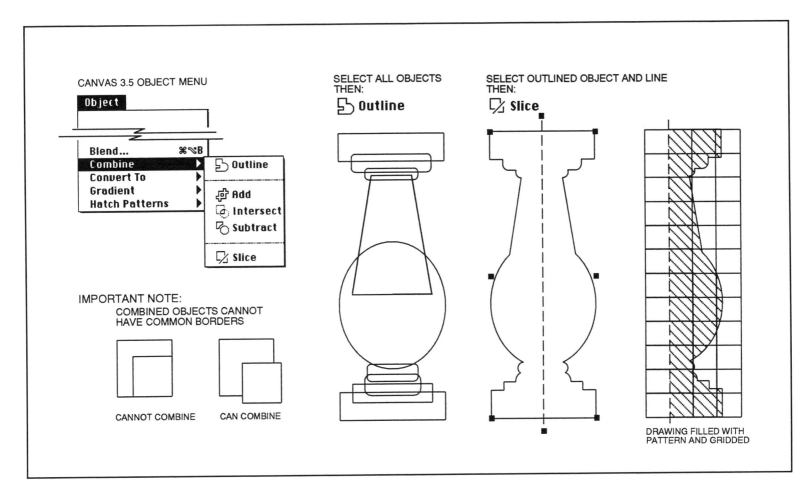

SELECT ALL OBJECTS
THEN:

⤷ **Outline**

SELECT OUTLINED OBJECT AND LINE
THEN:

✄ **Slice**

Object

Blend...   ⌘⌥B
Combine   ▶   ⤷ Outline
Convert To   ▶
Gradient   ▶   🔲 Add
Hatch Patterns   ▶   ⬚ Intersect
                         ◌ Subtract

                         ✄ Slice

IMPORTANT NOTE:
COMBINED OBJECTS CANNOT
HAVE COMMON BORDERS

CANNOT COMBINE   CAN COMBINE

DRAWING FILLED WITH
PATTERN AND GRIDDED

dialog box shown in figure 75*B*. Both *mirror* and *radial* objects are editable at any time after initial creation; that is, vertex points or control points can be added to, or deleted from, these objects at any time to create new profile outlines.

While IntelliDraw has many tools and options, it is most useful as a specialized program where specialized objects—like the images shown in figure 75*C* and 75*D*—are first fashioned and then exported to other programs. Neither Canvas 3.5 or IntelliDraw, however, supply all the features found in true CAD applications; both programs function best as experimental environments or—in the case of IntelliDraw—as "custom-made parts shops" where pieces are fashioned for use in a CAD-program drawing.

NOTE: It is not possible to include here all the instructions needed to make use of the charts, grids, and templates discussed in the ensuing sections. A familiarity with computers as well as a general knowledge of computer graphics programs is assumed for full comprehension of what follows. The grids, charts, and templates shown were constructed to be used as repeatable files. Those shown must be constructed by the individual

Fig. 72. Constructing complex objects from basic forms in Canvas 3.5

Templates

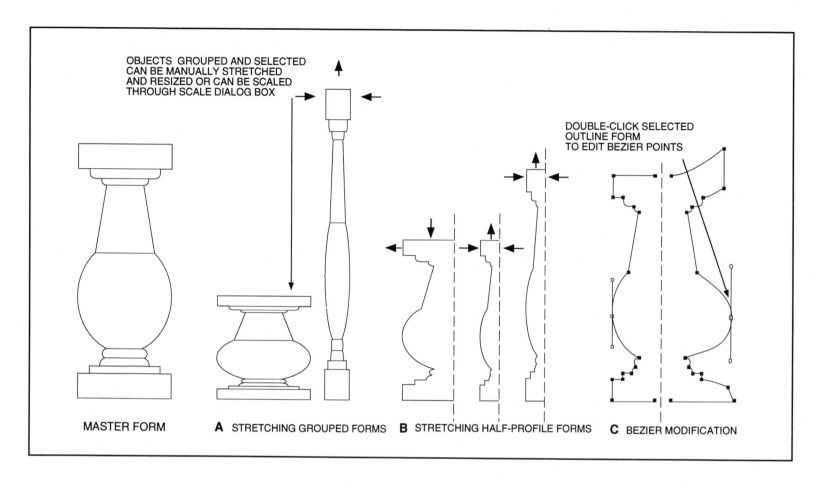

Fig. 73. Altering complex objects in Canvas 3.5

user in the program recommended; they do not come as part of any commercial program and are not to any great extent usable from program to program. The instructions included, although precise for the resident program of the template, should be considered as only approximate guides for creating grids, templates, and working tools in general.

All computer programs open new files with abilities to perform certain tasks. These basic assignments—called defaults in most applications— represent some of the options the program possesses. Most of these defaults can be changed by the user. For instance, all objects drawn in a new Canvas 3.5 unaltered file will be in a 1″ = 1″ scale; printed, these objects will measure exactly what is indicated by the program. It is possible, however, to permanently change this default scale to another one so that any object drawn thereafter exists in terms of the new scale. For instance, when a square 1″ box drawn in full scale (1″ = 1″) has the scale changed in the dialog box that affects measurement (the *Rulers* option) to a scale of 1/4″ = 1′ the box will now be a 4′ box. The default, in other words, has been changed to reflect the user's desire to draw all objects in this file in the 1/4″ = 1′ scale. Architects and other graphic designers, such as scenographers must draft objects in scale simply because one cannot draw big structures and objects at full scale. One of the basic principles of drafting is *the larger the detail, the smaller the scale.* All

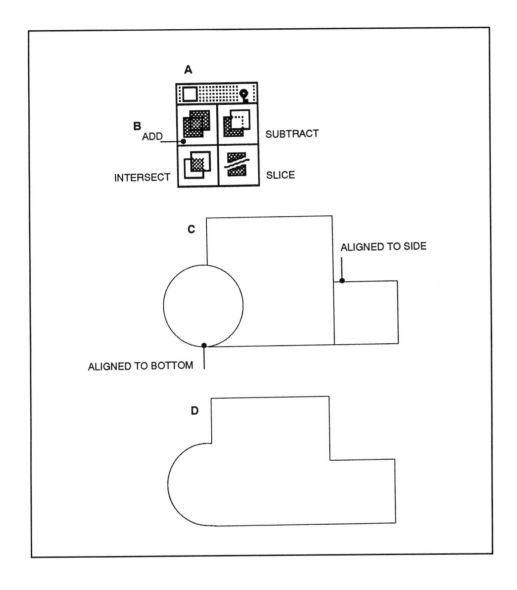

A

B ADD

SUBTRACT

INTERSECT

SLICE

C

ALIGNED TO SIDE

ALIGNED TO BOTTOM

D

Fig. 74. Aldus IntelliDraw 2.0 combine option

defaults in a computer program, in fact, can be changed to alternative options. The ability to make these changes is the basis for *templates*.

In computer graphics, *template* takes its meaning from a definition employed by other crafts. The words *pattern, guide, locating device*—all common terms in various mechanical trades—point the way we use it in computer work. The exact meaning of the term in computer language is this: *A saved document stored in the permanent memory of either a hard disk or a soft disk capable of being returned to repeatedly.* For our purposes, a template is just a number of preferences saved as a starting point for the making of drawings that have common formats and similar characteristics: scale, line size, fill pattern, kind and size of a font. Just as scenographers often reuse visual ideas from earlier productions, drawings from these often have usable parts. It is possible,

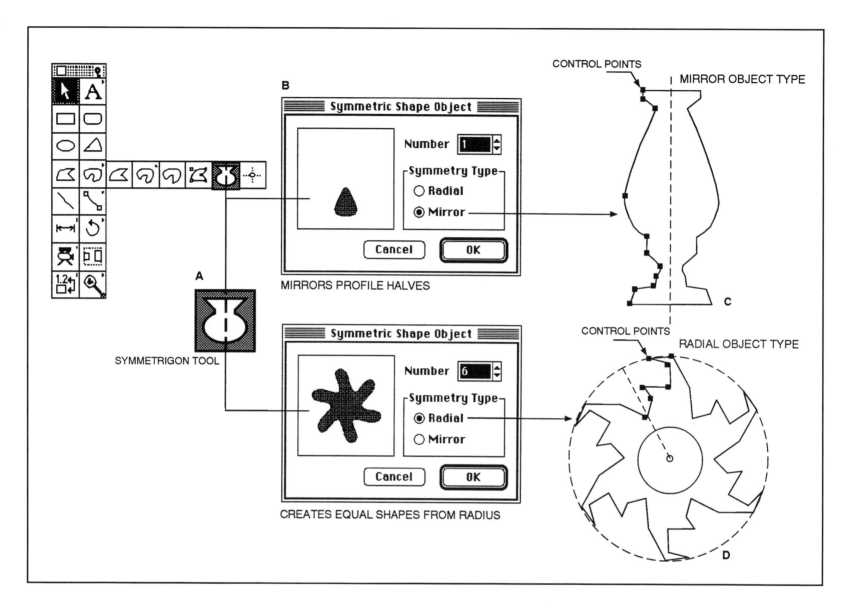

Fig. 75. Aldus IntelliDraw 2.0 symmetrigon objects

therefore, to think of templates as a form of recycling in that they permit us to use parts of previously created work for new projects, a practice not possible with physical drawings.

There are two major ways to use computer templates. These are:

1. Electronic manipulation on screen. (More detailed explanation of these procedures will be given below in the section "Scenic Change on Floor Plans".)

2. Manual manipulation using real-world tools and materials with printed computer-generated templates. Copies of an unused grid can be printed in any number desired as work sheets. Templates such as floor plans, perspective charts, elevation views can also be printed in any number needed. Using tools such as scissors or X-acto knife with No. 11 blade, items from different templates—floor plan, furniture, or scenic units for

instance—can be cut manually. Individual items can then be affixed with rubber cement, wax, or transparent tape. These can be used in this state or, if a more permanent record is desired, copied on an office copier. Manual cutting and pasting is an option with all templates; in many instances making printouts of on-screen templates allow scenographers to give directors an opportunity to participate more actively in the construction of floor plans, the drawing that must be agreed upon before any other work can proceed. Most scenographers welcome the considered opinions of directors who are willing to actively participate in the construction of an appropriate stage space. Directors who are specific in their thinking about space are often the most reasonable. For directors who plead they know little of the graphic processes scenographers use, having the director present while working on the computer floor plan saves time. It is very difficult for directors not to respond to such questions as: *"do you want this chair here. . . . or here,"* or *"is the door best placed in this position or . . . over on the opposite side,"* when the choices are quickly accomplished as they watch. There is also the added incentive to the director to actively participate in the process, since it is possible to provide almost immediately a hard copy of what is being discussed.

Of the many technical drawings scenographers make, the floor plan is of prime importance because it is the first technical drawing made by a scenographer. All other drawings depend on the information included in it. In manual drawing this set plan is invariably preceded by numerous small crudely drawn unscaled drawings; often directors of a production or with the technical director or members of the technical staff participate in their construction. Usually these preliminary drawings undergo extensive changes before an official floor plan is accepted. The process of making floor plans is similar to that of playwriting itself, of which the famous stage director George Abbot said, "Plays are not written—they are *rewritten*." It is just as true to say that a production's floor plan is not drawn, it is redrawn; in most productions many times. Even after an agreed-upon plan is made, duplicated, and distributed among those who need its information—the director, the technical director, lighting designer, and properties and special effects personnel—changes are necessary. Although these become less frequent—that is, if preliminary planning was thorough—hard copies of the plan must frequently be added to or altered. Before computer graphics, these changes had to be made by hand; at times the entire plan was redrawn. With the computer, directors can have, almost instantaneously, hard copies of floor plans that show precise positions of furniture, set properties, and where necessary effects are placed. If these prove unsatisfactory, changes to the computer plan are made, and an entirely new corrected copy of the plan is printed. If the computer performed no other function than to make floor plans, most scenographers would consider the option valuable. Multiscene productions present special problems for traditional drawers; making separate drawings for each scene or change requires time and repetition of labor.

Over the years scenographers have worked out various schemes to minimize the labor required to modify drawings. In television production, for instance, acetate drawings of frequently used settings in series productions are kept on file; these are taped to printed basic floor plans of specific studios that house the production. If a certain week's shooting

Interactive Computer Graphics Floor Plans

schedule calls for a stock setting, acetate copies of the setting are taken from the file, placed onto the master floor plan, and copied. The computer makes these procedures even more effective and timesaving. Scenographers working for the stage would do well to emulate these practices.

The Multilayered Floor Plan

The early stages of production planning is always an experimental time. During this period, the floor plan is the primary focus for both the scenographer and the director. It is critical to the progress of this planning period that scenographers and directors be able to move, add, change, or discard furniture and set properties on the plan as needs change or concepts alter. Scenic structures of the setting—walls, windows, doors, platforms— must also be capable of change; as the production's concept evolves these structures are added, shifted, or removed from the floor plan to reflect changes of thought. How best, then, do we make this process more efficient in terms of time and more effective in terms of operation? Since it is time-consuming to create from scratch the basic floor plan area of the theater space, or to draw individually the items listed above, having already installed on the computer previously drawn templates containing essential features of the stage is a wise method to conserve time both at the beginning of a project and during its development.

Floor plan templates can be made in many programs: PowerDraw 5.0, MiniCad+ 5.0, and ClarisCad 2.0 are three. Although these programs are well suited for making highly structured working drawings, I prefer to make experimental floor plans in a program that is not a true CAD application: Canvas 3.5. This program has distinct advantages for making exploratory floor plans. These advantages give (1) an "offstage" area—commonly known as the *pasteboard area* in page-layout programs—where furniture and stage units can be temporarily parked or used as permanent storage areas for scenic units such as predrawn platforms, turntables, (2) an ability to create separate layers (or "floors") that can be—as with the pasteboard area—used to store the different layers of the theater structure (stage house grid, turntable, line sets), and (3), an effective means to move items from one layer to another, in effect, an "elevator" that goes to all floors. Although furniture, platforms, and other scenic units can reside on the same layer as the floor plan, it is a better plan to have the basic floor plan dedicated to one layer and other theater functions relegated to separate layers. A distinct advantage of layers is that every setting of a production can have its own layer. This allows a series of different settings to share a common floor plan. With the basic floor plan on the bottom layer, each different setting can be "turned on," that is, made visible as required, and "turned off" when not being viewed.

Since computer-drawn floor plans provide traditionally trained scenographers with complex capabilities not possible with manually drawn floor plans, it is necessary to provide them with understandable reference points—a "metaphorical shell," as it were— so that they do not lose their prior graphic understandings. It is not necessary, however, to go too far afield to find a workable metaphor; the physical theater building itself— with its multiple floors, overhead grids, offstage areas—provides the prime image for our computer-generated floor plan.

The layers of the drawings can be considered floors of a building; our libraries—

saved scaled images of furniture and other features of the real-life stage such as platforms, steps, or scenic units like maskings and battens—can be placed in separate "storerooms" from which we take what we need; the layer managers in all three major programs have options that function as "elevators" by which any object of any size, shape, or complexity can be transported from one floor to another. A computer floor plan, in short, has all the capabilities of the most advanced theater plant.

The ability for scenographers to construct computer drawings, such as the interactive "theater building" template just described, demonstrates just how flexible and useful computer graphics have become. Earlier, in figure 47A, we saw how an interactive floor plan appears in our computer theater; B, C, and D in figure 47 also show how the layers of the file mirror floors in an actual theater building.

Most scenographers fall into one of two categories; free-lance designers working for many organizations and staff designers working primarily for one. Free-lance scenographers especially need a floor plan template easily adapted to the requirements of different theater plants. Even staff scenographers frequently have more than one theater to design for. Thus two such basic kinds of floor plan templates are discussed below: generic floor plan templates and theater-specific floor plan templates.

Generic Floor Plan Templates

The first step for most free-lance scenographers is to obtain copies of the basic stage plan and elevation from the resident house managements; these serve as guides for drawings of a commissioned production. It is not necessary, however, for the scenographer to begin the computer floor plan only after these hard-copy plans are received. Since many theaters have common features, it is possible to get a head start on the proposed production if an untitled generalized floor plan template already exists in the scenographer's resident computer.

An *untitled file template* simply means that every time it is opened, a new file is begun. All the drawing programs recommended in this book allow for the making of untitled templates. (Previous to System 7, templates were made by choosing specific file formats; in Canvas 3.5 this format carried the name *Canvas Prefs*.) Once a drawing is saved as an untitled template file, it becomes a sort of pad of forms from which new sheets are taken each time a new floor plan is begun; the pad of forms itself never changes.

System 7 also has another option to save any document as a repeatable template. The mechanism used is to change a document—such as a basic floor plan—into a format called *Stationary Pad*. This must be done *after* the basic file is closed. To effect the change, one selects the file, opens the Get Information Window, and selects the box at the lower-right corner named *Stationary Pad*. The file is converted into the new format. When a new copy of the generic floor plan template is opened, it can be modified to reflect the features of the theater that hosts the current production. This is a much more timesaving procedure than constructing a computer "theater building" from the beginning. Figure 76 shows a generic computer floor plan template based on a theater plan like that shown in figure 47. Although all the elements of the floor plan seem to be on a single layer, they are, in actuality, on separate layers, each of which can be worked on, displayed, printed, or hidden as necessary. The "warehouse" of scenic units shown to the right of the main stage area can be stored on the nonprinting area on the same level as the stage

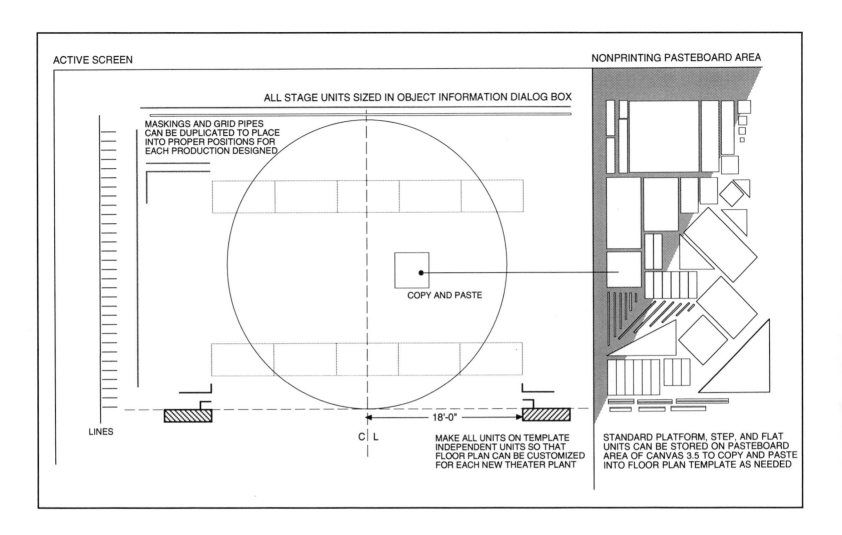

ACTIVE SCREEN

NONPRINTING PASTEBOARD AREA

ALL STAGE UNITS SIZED IN OBJECT INFORMATION DIALOG BOX

MASKINGS AND GRID PIPES
CAN BE DUPLICATED TO PLACE
INTO PROPER POSITIONS FOR
EACH PRODUCTION DESIGNED

COPY AND PASTE

LINES

18'-0"

C L

MAKE ALL UNITS ON TEMPLATE
INDEPENDENT UNITS SO THAT
FLOOR PLAN CAN BE CUSTOMIZED
FOR EACH NEW THEATER PLANT

STANDARD PLATFORM, STEP, AND FLAT
UNITS CAN BE STORED ON PASTEBOARD
AREA OF CANVAS 3.5 TO COPY AND PASTE
INTO FLOOR PLAN TEMPLATE AS NEEDED

Fig. 76. Generic floor plan template

or, alternatively, can be stored on a discreet layer below the stage. It is also possible to store objects as macros (Canvas 3.5's version of a library) or as independent files. The saving of an untitled template should be done early after it is opened with the name of the project being designed. In effect, the template loses its general quality as it becomes a specific drawing.

Theater-Specific Floor Plan Templates

For scenographers working primarily in one theater plant, a template should be made of the theater's basic plan. As with the generic floor plan, it is recommended that permanent features of the plant be placed on specific layers that match the theater's physical layout: grid on the top-most layer, stage floor on the layer below, turntable on the layer below that, and so on. Maskings should be left on the stage-floor level but traps should be placed on the lowest level, and only those in use for a particular design sent up to the stage level as needed. Furniture and stage scenic units can be stored on a separate layer, on the nonprinting pasteboard to the side of the main drawing area, or—an option I

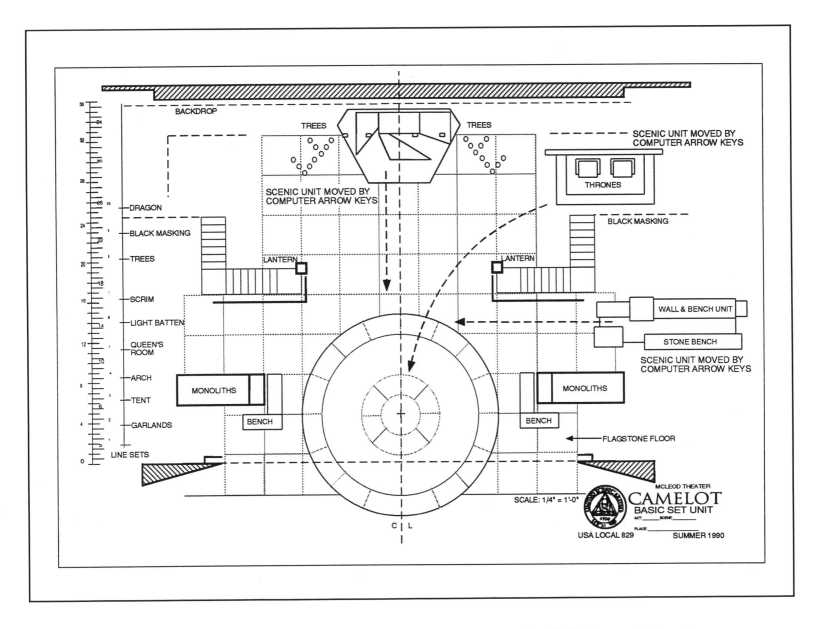

Fig. 77. Theater-specific floor plan

prefer—stored as a macro file that can be loaded as needed. It is also possible to create a separate furniture template like the one shown in figure 78. A good practice is, when a floor plan is finished, to jettison all layers and stored objects contained in the basic template not used. For instance, if the production does not need traps or the turntable, these items can be deleted. The smaller the file size, the easier it is to manipulate on screen what is drawn into it. Smaller file sizes also take up less space on backup disks.

An important part of most floor plans is the placement of furniture and set properties. It is very difficult, however, to keep available in one's head the relative sizes of sofas,

Furniture Libraries and Templates

chairs, tables, and beds. One of the most important manual tools the scenographer uses, therefore, is the scaled furniture template. These helpful tools allow scenographers to quickly draw accurately scaled shapes and sizes of objects that frequently appear on floor plan drawings. Furniture templates shorten the time to make these drawings. They also provide more accurate renderings of the objects they represent than those constructed from memory; objects drawn without furniture templates frequently do not match the floor plan scale.

The most common scale of commercially made furniture templates is $1/4'' = 1'$; most include not only basic furniture outlines but kitchen and bathroom object outlines as well. Templates for specialized spaces—offices, bathrooms, kitchens—are also available.

Computer floor plans also require furniture templates. These are available to the scenographer through two main channels: commercial files and individually made files. Commercial furniture files are not recommended here; in the first place, they are almost always expensive, and, in the second, they do not adequately meet the needs of scenographic design. What is recommended is the construction of computer furniture files by the individual scenographer.

The primary ways computer furniture templates are created and stored in computer drawing programs are:

1. *As independent files*. These files must be constructed by the individual designer in the same object-oriented program that the floor plan uses. Furniture templates like that shown in figure 78 allow the scenographer to add, modify, or delete objects as needed. Additionally, when the furniture template file is opened, only those items required for the floor plan being constructed need be copied and pasted into the drawing. The original furniture template can then be closed until needed again. Although scenographers use a scale of $1/4'' = 1'$ for floor plans, at times it is necessary to use other scales, $1/2'' = 1'$, for instance. All programs suggested in this book have scaling options so that objects pasted into a floor plan drawing can quickly be changed to match a floor plan's current scale.

2. *As libraries or macro sets*. Programs such as Canvas 3.5, PowerDraw 5.0, and MiniCad+ 5.0 allow designers to create libraries of repeatedly used objects, such as those above, and to store them as an integral part of the application's normal operation. Some applications call these integrated files *libraries*, while other applications use the term *macros*. Regardless of what they are called, the options are similar. While some programs have no limit to the number of objects that can be stored, other programs place a limit on the number of objects in one library. Canvas 3.5, for instance, places a limit of thirty-two objects per macro set. (Sets are loaded into a drawing via the Library Menu.) This number is adequate for practically all floor plans. In more specialized drawings, however, other objects, such as platforms, turntables, steps, can be stored as independent macro sets. Although in Canvas 3.5 only one macro set is available at a time, it is easy to load and clear sets as needed. Other programs allow independent libraries to be available continuously.

3. *As integral parts of a basic floor plan template*. It is possible—although not recommended—to store furniture templates on a separate layer of floor plan templates. These templates mirror their real-life counterparts in that the various layers represent

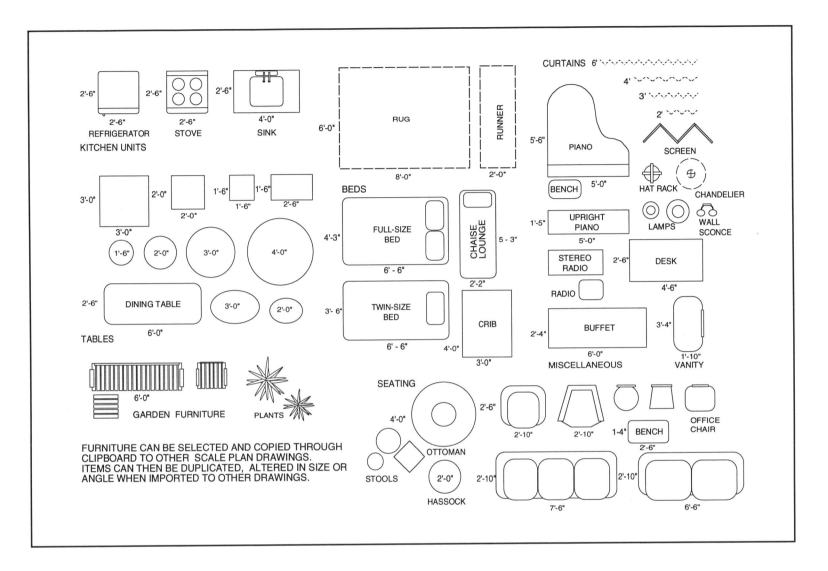

Fig. 78. Computer furniture template

floors of an actual theater building: the top layer contains grid lines and battens, the layer immediately below contains the turntable, the layer below that the stage floor, with sublevels for storage of furniture and platforms. In Canvas 3.5 there is even a convenient "elevator" to move objects from level to level. While floor plan templates allow the scenographer to operate in an understandably familiar context, the number of the objects stored in the basic template take more memory than do those drawings where objects are brought in only as needed.

Unlike objects on paper drawings, computer-drawn items of furniture have properties identical to their physical counterparts. That is, scenographers and directors can add, take away, or move furniture or scenic objects about the screen floor plan as they would in a real space. To accomplish the same effect on paper drawings involves a great deal of messy erasing and redrawing.

Most scenographers welcome the considered opinions of the director and find that those who are specific in their thinking are often in the long run the easiest to work with and the most reasonable when points of contention occur. The mutability of the computer drawing is most helpful when the director is not sure where something should go or wishes to experiment with alternative placements. For those directors who plead that they know little of the graphic processes a scenographer uses—and more often than not one must read *know little* for *not really interested to learn*—having them present while placing objects on the template floor plan saves time and frustration for both. It is difficult, in fact, for directors not to respond to direct questions such as, *Do you want this chair here . . . or here?* or *Is the door best placed in this position or . . . over here?* Decisions directors make can immediately be printed out allowing alternative possibilities to be taken away for further study. On paper drawings, changes are only made by time-consuming effort. On the computer screen, adding, deleting ,and moving objects about the floor plan stage is considerably easier and ultimately more productive for both scenographer and director.

Scenic Change on Floor Plans

One of the greatest advantages of computer floor plans is that scenic units can be moved on the computer screen drawing in similar ways as in real-world theaters. Sliding units, turntables, small revolves, jackknife stages, can all be made to move precise distances or to conform to identical patterns of movement as scene-shifting devices found on the physical stage. Moreover, by the use of levels, entire settings can be brought from storage layers to the main stage to test for effectiveness during the run of a performance. These capabilities give rise to a term that describes possibilities not possible with manual graphics: *interactive drawing*.

Interactive floor plan templates constructed in Canvas 3.5 make scenic units movable in several ways: by rotation of single or grouped objects, by arrow keys that move selected objects horizontally across, up, or down a stage floor, by keystroke options, or simply by selecting the object and moving it manually with the mouse. Physical conflicts between moving scenic units or sightline problems resulting from the movement of scenery can be tested while the floor plan is being drawn. Although it is possible to do all the above on the manually drawn floor plan, it is not nearly as quick, certainly not as easy. Let us examine more closely how scenic change is effected on the interactive floor plan.

Scenic Unit Rotation on Interactive Floor Plans

In the physical theater, it is often necessary to move scenic units as audiences watch. This movement is accomplished in four basic ways:

1. By placing scenic units on *revolving stages,* which are large mechanized disks built into the stage floor as permanent features of a particular theater plant.

2. By placing scenic units on *turntables,* which are disks similar to revolving stages but only constructed for specific productions. These units sit on the stage floor, not built into it as is the case with revolving stages. At times the area immediately surrounding these disks is built up to give the effect of a flat floor; in effect, the advantages of permanent revolving stages are gained in temporary structures.

3. By placing scenic units on casters that rotate freely. This allows the unit to be either moved onto or around the stage manually or to be rotated manually.

4. By placing scenic units on fixed casters—which restrict movement of the wheels

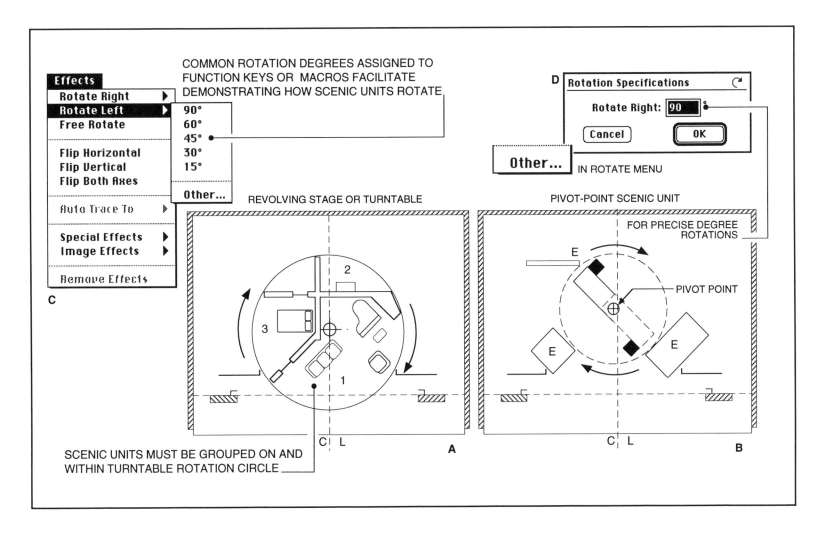

Effects

Rotate Right ▶
Rotate Left ▶
Free Rotate

Flip Horizontal
Flip Vertical
Flip Both Axes

Auto Trace To ▶

Special Effects ▶
Image Effects ▶

Remove Effects

C

90°
60°
45°
30°
15°

Other...

COMMON ROTATION DEGREES ASSIGNED TO
FUNCTION KEYS OR MACROS FACILITATE
DEMONSTRATING HOW SCENIC UNITS ROTATE

D **Rotation Specifications**

Rotate Right: 90

Cancel   OK

Other... IN ROTATE MENU

REVOLVING STAGE OR TURNTABLE

PIVOT-POINT SCENIC UNIT

FOR PRECISE DEGREE
ROTATIONS

PIVOT POINT

SCENIC UNITS MUST BE GROUPED ON AND
WITHIN TURNTABLE ROTATION CIRCLE

C L   A

C L   B

Fig. 79. Rotating scenic units in Canvas 3.5

to forward or reverse motion—or on pivot-point units temporarily fixed to the stage floor.

Mimicking their real-world counterparts, grouped scenic units can be rotated on interactive floor plans. Careful construction and placing of the units on these drawings, however, is very important. Great care must be used in making these drawings; unless precise procedures are followed, interactive floor plans that have either rotating stages or pivot-point scenery rapidly become unsynchronized, no longer reflecting real-world actions.

Two methods of accomplishing rotating scenery are discussed below (fig. 79). The first shows how revolving stages are used in theaters having permanently installed revolving stages (similar to the generic floor plan shown in figure 76). For turntables installed for specific productions, the procedures are identical since floor plan drawings do not distinguish between units built into the stage floor or turntables sitting on stage level. The second demonstration (fig. 79B) shows how pivot-point scenic units are constructed and used.

Revolving Stages and Computer Turntables

Revolving stages are relatively easy to create and use on interactive floor plans; care must be taken that they are positioned properly. In both the generic floor plan template (fig. 76), and in the theater-specific floor plan (fig. 77), revolving stages are included. What is not evident in a casual examination of these drawings is that in both instances the revolving stage is stored on the level *below the stage floor layer*; in other words, on the "floor" immediately beneath the main stage. In both templates, it is possible to render the layer holding the revolving stage invisible. If required for particular productions, the revolving state unit can be brought to the stage level via the Send to Layer option using, in effect, the "elevator" shown in figure 48 to bring them up to the active floor plan level. When the revolving unit has been placed on the active stage floor level, it is then possible to begin placing platforms, furniture, and other scenic units—walls, set properties, and the like—on the turntable disk. After all desired items are placed, the turntable and all on are grouped (by Shift-Selection) into one unit that has a bounding box, as shown in figure 79A. (NOTE: *It is important that no item on the turntable disk be outside the circle's perimeter*. If any item lies outside the perimeter, when the whole is grouped, a new bounding box is created with a new center point not necessarily that of the original revolving stage. When rotated, the new center point causes *the whole disk to move its position relative to the stage floor*. It is imperative, therefore, that the bounding box of the turntable be restricted to the diameter of the turntable's disk; otherwise the turntable will continue to become out of synchronization with the rest of the stage unit.)

Rotation of the turntable is controlled by:

a. Direction. The default setting of the rotation direction is clockwise. To rotate the turntable counterclockwise, the dialog box *Rotation Manager* (fig. 79D) is used. The Rotation Manager makes it possible to rotate objects to any degree (from 1° to 360°), either clockwise or counterclockwise.

b. Degree. Rotating by degree can be done in four ways:

1. *By using keystroke Command-R*. This option rotates the selected unit clockwise 90 percent.

2. *By using the Rotate° command from the Effects Menu* (fig. 79C): This option reveals a hierarchical menu that allows the rotation of any object or group of objects in predefined increments. Selecting this option produces another dialog box (see figure 79D above).

3. *By using the Free Rotate command from the Effects Menu*. Since all objects are grouped within the diameter of the turntable disk, the Free Rotate command allows manual rotation of the disk either clockwise or counterclockwise to any degree desired. Rotation degree can be monitored by watching the information bar at the bottom of the screen. (NOTE: Turntables in an actual theater plant are best controlled with regular degree settings. It is advisable, therefore, to use regular degree increments on computer floor plans as well. It is then possible for the scenographer to give precisely the degree settings necessary for the design when realized on the stage.)

4. *By using QuicKeys function keys for preset degree settings*. Since QuicKeys allows each program to have its own set of function keys settings, it is possible to set keys to selected settings—45°, 60°, and so on. Along with the Command-R setting, it is possible to have the necessary rotations available with a minimum effort. This can be

helpful when showing others—such as the director or the technical director—how the floor plan will appear at any given moment. Even two settings, 45° and 90°, give a number of position shifts (fig. 79-1,-2,-3) while only using one QuicKeys configuration.

Unlike revolving stages or turntables, specifically placed pivot points are used to rotate individual scenic units. Although these units do not often have circular bases, a circular path is created as the unit revolves around its fixed point. The diameter of the path is determined by two factors: the pivot point and the scenic unit's most distant point from the pivot point (shown as a dashed line in figure 79*B*). This imaginary circle is called the *master circle,* since it assumes control over the virtual space within its circumference. When drawing a floor plan that contains pivoted scenic units, it is necessary both to draw the master circle and to group it with the scenic unit that, in effect, brought it into being. The basic measurement that gives the circle's diameter is the precise distance between the pivot point, which (like the revolving stage or turntable) is grouped with all elements within its boundaries. A number of pivoted scenic units can be present on the stage at one time. The only rule that governs the size or shape of these units is that *master circles cannot overlap*. Since master circles contain all elements of the units being rotated, conflicts that result from overlapping boundaries can easily be resolved on the ground plan during the design stages of drawing.

The steps in creating pivoted scenic units are as follows:

1. Draw scenic unit or draw composite elements of scenic unit and group into single object.

2. Create pivot point by drawing a short single line, duplicating it, rotating it 90°, grouping the two lines, and placing it at a point on the scenic unit about which it will revolve. This point may have to be moved several times to get the exact effect desired. The process is one of trial and error: repeated grouping and ungrouping of a scenic unit, its pivot point and its master circle, and testing each result afterward are the only ways to arrive at a satisfactory result.

3. Measure from pivot point to point farthest from pivot point. This can be done by selecting the circle tool, placing the cursor precisely on the pivot point, and drawing a circle *while holding down the Shift and Option keys*. After the outer line of the circle has passed over all points but one, the mouse button can be released, and the master circle will be in place.

4. Master circles for pivot-point units differ from those in typical turntable units in that they must be changed to invisible lines before the scenic unit it serves is attached to it. The circle must also have no FILL. This is an easy task, since that only involves going to the Pen Pattern dialog box and selecting NONE. The line is still there, and the circle still operates as a circle, but it cannot be seen on the screen, nor will it print on the hard copies of the floor plan.

5. In order to make the unit work as a pivot-point object the circle and the objects contained within its circumference must be grouped into a single unit. Use the arrow cursor to drag a selection box around circle and scenic unit to select all bounding boxes (this can also be accomplished by Shift-clicking both). Since the line of the circle is invisible, and since the circle has no fill, it is difficult to select it so that it can be linked with the scenic unit it is to pivot. In Canvas 3.5 a handy feature makes this task much

Computer Pivoting Scenic Units

easier. A keystroke built into the program allows all objects to be viewed as wire frames. This includes invisible objects as well. This view can be accessed by using Command-1. The screen immediately changes to show all objects as very thin lines, including the invisible ones such as the circle. This allows the designer to select it as well as the other necessary objects. After this is done, use the keystroke Command-G to group all selected objects into a single unit.

6.   The unit is now ready to be rotated or moved to a new location. Rotation of unit is accomplished by means discussed above.

7.   If other pivoted scenic units are to be used, steps 1–5 are repeated. All units are then tested for master circle conflicts and adjusted until conflicts are resolved.

8.   An alternative to using an invisible line for the circumference of the circle is to use a dashed line. This is helpful to show the path the unit makes as it moves. If more than one pivoting unit is employed, or if there are fixed scenic units in proximity to the pivoting unit, conflicts in rotation can be ascertained and resolved.

9.   If pivoted scenic units are set or removed during the course of a production— or if scenic units are placed on other movable platforms—units for any one scene can, as with individual settings in a multiscene production, be given a specially named separate layer that can be turned on or off (made visible or invisible) using the Layer Manager option. All three applications mentioned above have layer capability and can be used as storage areas when rotating units are not needed. Canvas 3.5's ability to move units from layer to layer easily makes it especially attractive as an interactive floor plan option.

Moving Scenic Units by Arrow Keys

Figure 80 shows how scenic units, such as sliding stages, are moved using the arrow keys of a drawing program. When scenic units are selected (fig. 80*A*, *B*, or *C*), their movement—either horizontally or vertically—is controlled by these keys. A good reason to use Canvas 3.5 for making interactive floor plans is that this program has arrow-key options not found in other programs; some drawing programs do not support movement of selected objects at all. In Canvas 3.5, however, a selected unit is moved one pixel point in a desired direction by clicking on the arrow key that indicates the direction (see bottom right of figure 80). If, on the other hand, the selected arrow key is used in conjunction with the Command key or with the Option key, the selected unit moves either ten pixel points (arrow key + Command key) or fifty pixel points (arrow key + Option key). This allows the scenographer to show a director both where a scenic unit "lives" offstage and its position when in use. In figure 77—a floor plan for a production of *Camelot*—the wall and bench unit seen offstage left and the large scenic unit seen at the rear of the playing area were moved using the left-facing arrow key and the down-facing arrow key, respectively. If no intervening moves are made after a unit is shifted, the unit can be restored to its starting position with a single Undo (or Command-Z) command.

The directions for all the moves listed above sound complicated in print. They become quickly understandable, however, when working with actual programs. Although it takes some time to set up options to work in the manner described, it is work that does not have to be repeated. Template stages do, in fact, save scenographers a great deal of time and labor. More important yet, the ability to show directors or technical staffs during the planning stages of a production exactly how scenic changes operate prevents misunderstandings later on.

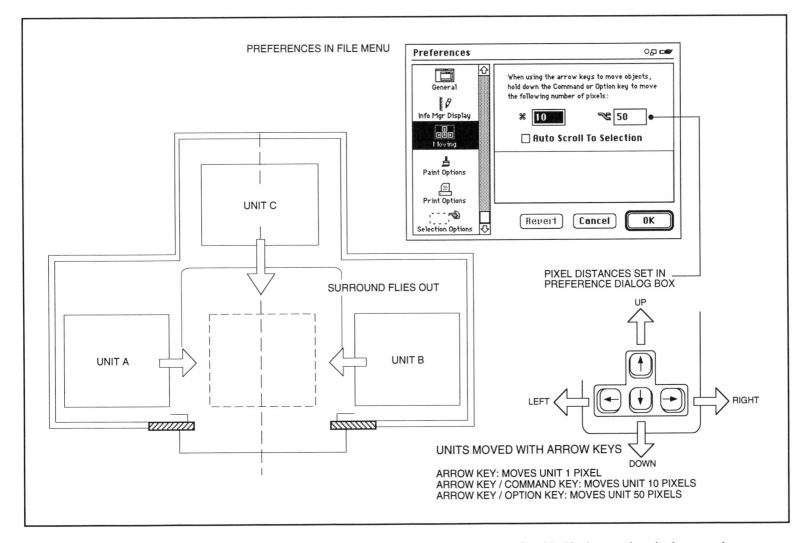

PREFERENCES IN FILE MENU

Preferences

General

Info Mgr Display

Moving

Paint Options

Print Options

Selection Options

When using the arrow keys to move objects, hold down the Command or Option key to move the following number of pixels:

⌘ 10   ⌥ 50

☐ Auto Scroll To Selection

Revert   Cancel   OK

UNIT C

SURROUND FLIES OUT

UNIT A

UNIT B

PIXEL DISTANCES SET IN
PREFERENCE DIALOG BOX

UP

LEFT   RIGHT

DOWN

UNITS MOVED WITH ARROW KEYS

ARROW KEY: MOVES UNIT 1 PIXEL
ARROW KEY / COMMAND KEY: MOVES UNIT 10 PIXELS
ARROW KEY / OPTION KEY: MOVES UNIT 50 PIXELS

Fig. 80. Moving scenic units by arrow keys

General Working Drawings and Specifications

Most scenographic projects are broken into phases—(1) conceptual work: quick sketches, diagrams, analyses of various sorts, oral and written communication; (2) illustrative work: finished perspectives, scenographic renderings, collages of colors and textures; (3) technical specification work: plans, elevations, projections of various kinds, lists of materials, schematics showing operation of parts or interaction of units, time schedules; and (4) supervisory work: monitoring the progress of shops, locating specialized objects and materials, supervising working of settings on the stage. These separate phases are accomplished with programs best suited to the work at hand; few scenographic projects can be completed within the confines of a single program.

Traditionally phases of a project do not overlap; for instance, modelmaking is usually done near the end of the design process. With computers, however, accurate three-dimensional electronic models are available for viewing or modification over the entire

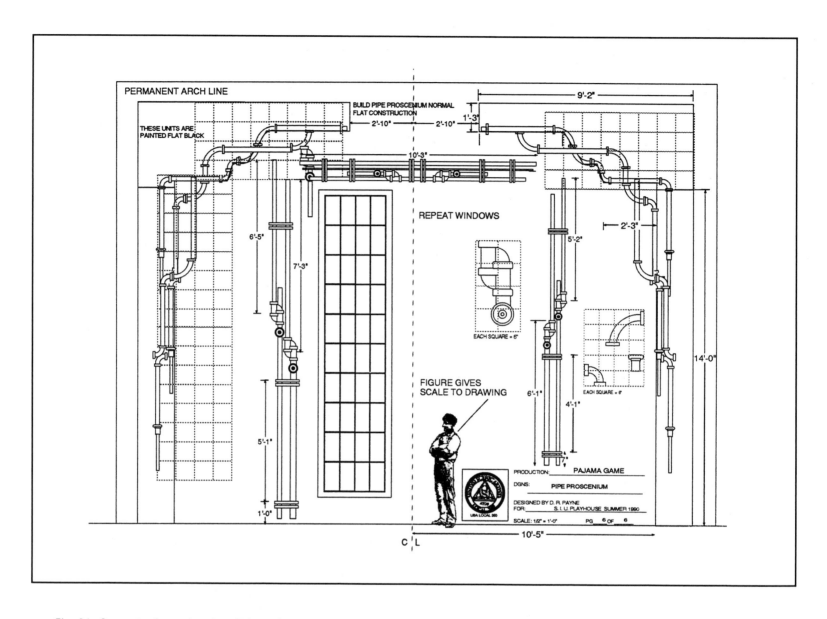

PERMANENT ARCH LINE

BUILD PIPE PROSCENIUM NORMAL
FLAT CONSTRUCTION

THESE UNITS ARE
PAINTED FLAT BLACK

REPEAT WINDOWS

EACH SQUARE = 6"

EACH SQUARE = 6"

FIGURE GIVES
SCALE TO DRAWING

PRODUCTION: PAJAMA GAME

DGNS: PIPE PROSCENIUM

DESIGNED BY D. R. PAYNE
FOR: S. I. U. PLAYHOUSE SUMMER 1990

SCALE: 1/2" = 1'-0"   PG 6 OF 6

C L

Fig. 81. Computer front elevation: Pajama Game

design process (see "Interactive Computer Modelmaking" in chapter 4 for discussion of this subject). Computer drawing has radically changed many old work routines. Let us now examine some of the ways that technical specification drawing has changed since the introduction of computers into the scenographer's studio.

Figure 81 shows a typical front elevation drawing made for scenic shop instruction. This kind of drawing can be done on real-world drawing boards as well as on the computer screen. Figure 82 also shows a typical elevation detail for a production flown unit that could also be done manually. This drawing, however, benefits from the capabilities of the computer; not only is the scenographer saved the time of drawing the highly detailed image (it was taken from a scanned library previously recorded), printouts of the image

LINE 15   LINE 15

6'-9"

9'-8"

USA LOCAL 829

THE BEAUX STRATEGEM   ELEVATION: 1ST ARCH   DESIGNED BY D. R. PAYNE
SCALE: 1/2" = 1'-0"   PG __6__ OF __12__

can be used for scenographic model parts and for a painter's elevation. Figure 83 shows another detail drawing for a scenic unit. Included with the elevation, however, is an imported view copied from a Virtus WalkThrough model PICT image. This image—although originally created for other purposes—costs the scenographer little extra time and effort to include it into the technical drawing. The advantage gained from this extra step is that the builders gain a better idea as to how the unit will be employed in the production. Although this information is not absolutely necessary to the construction process, it makes the unit's purpose a little bit clearer. Any visual information scenographers provide to shop workers during the construction ensures better results on stage.

Another advantage computers give to scenographers is the ability to create accurate drawings of irregular profile outlines. Figure 84 shows the steps necessary to turn an image into an outline form using the tracing possibilities of an application dedicated to

Fig. 82. Elevation detail: The Beaux Stratagem

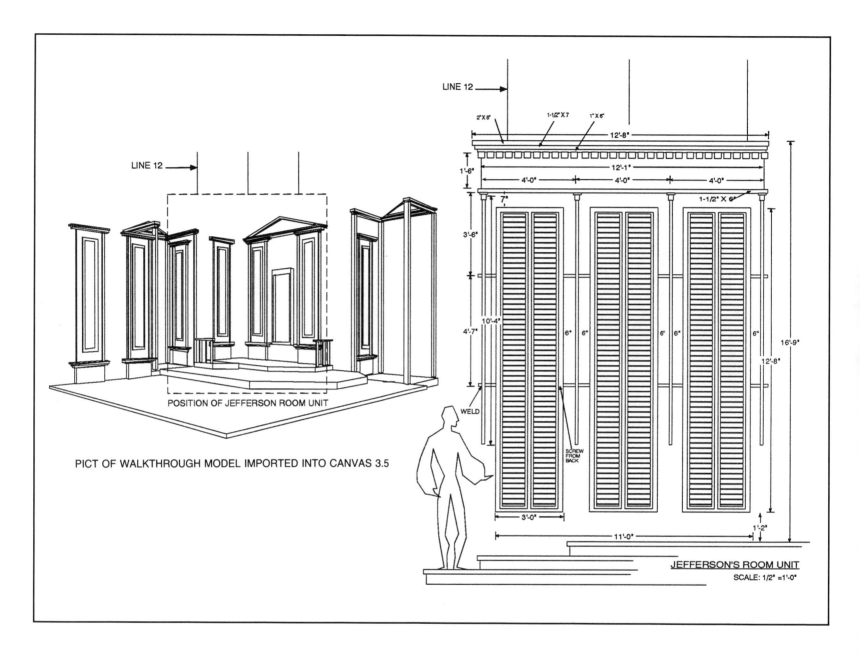

LINE 12

POSITION OF JEFFERSON ROOM UNIT

PICT OF WALKTHROUGH MODEL IMPORTED INTO CANVAS 3.5

JEFFERSON'S ROOM UNIT
SCALE: 1/2" =1'-0"

Fig. 83. Working drawing detail with model view: 1776

the conversion of bit-mapped images into high-resolution objects: Adobe Streamline 3.0. Saved as an Illustrator 1.1 File (a file format that can be read by many object-oriented programs), the image can then be exported to more sophisticated CAD programs such as MiniCad+ 5.0 or PowerDraw 5.0. These outlines can then be saved, dimensioned, and given to a scenic shop for full-scale execution. Here the drawing has been placed behind a grid to make the full-scale construction of the scenic unit more manageable. The actual drawing of the outlines in full scale in the scenic shop can be done in three ways: (1) by manually drawing grids over the computer printout, (2) by printing off the file directly

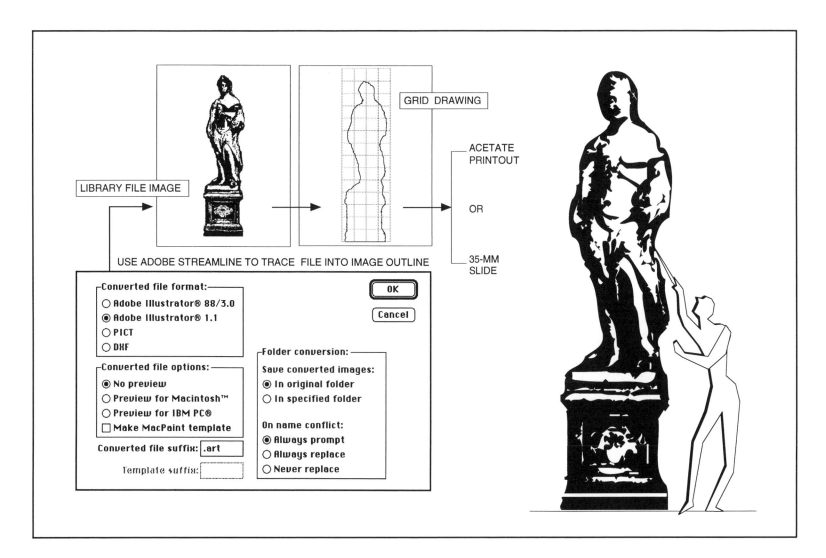

GRID DRAWING

ACETATE PRINTOUT

OR

35-MM SLIDE

LIBRARY FILE IMAGE

USE ADOBE STREAMLINE TO TRACE FILE INTO IMAGE OUTLINE

┌Converted file format:─┐
○ Adobe Illustrator® 88/3.0
● Adobe Illustrator® 1.1
○ PICT
○ DXF

[OK]

[Cancel]

┌Converted file options:─┐
● No preview
○ Preview for Macintosh™
○ Preview for IBM PC®
☐ Make MacPaint template

Converted file suffix: .art

Template suffix:

┌Folder conversion:─┐
Save converted images:
● In original folder
○ In specified folder

On name conflict:
● Always prompt
○ Always replace
○ Never replace

from the computer on acetate on a PostScript printer to be used with an overhead or opaque projector as shown in figure 128, or, (3) to have a 35-mm slide printed directly from the computer on a slide-making printer.

Individual working-drawing details—such as that shown in figure 84—are also valuable as computer library files; at a later time these details are usable for other projects. It is extremely important to keep 3.5 disk backups of previous work, since computer drawings over time accumulate into hundreds and hundreds of hours of work. These backup disks become a way to share work with other scenographers or designers.

The lighting plot for a production consists of two main parts: (*a*) a list that gives types of instruments needed and numbers of each along with information concerning medium colors—if any—and (*b*) a plan view of instruments used showing electrical connections and focus angles. In some instances, this view includes the scenographer's

Fig. 84. Converting bit-mapped image to object-oriented graphic

Computer Lighting Plots

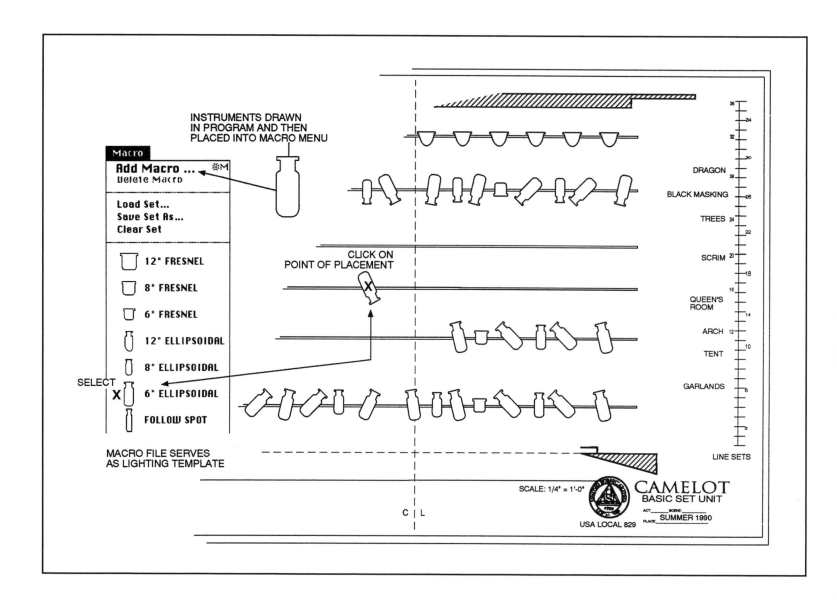

Fig. 85. Computer light plot diagram

floor plan; in others, only the lighting instrument distribution is shown. Figure 85 shows a typical plan view for a lighting plot.

The first part uses spreadsheet forms of listing giving the type of instruments needed and the number of each, the second part—the plan view—was, until the past three decades, considered an extension of the scenographer's work. Increasingly scenography and lighting have been separated into distinct professions although many scenographers still consider the lighting of a production as an integral part of the total design. Past scenographers like Robert Edmond Jones and Jo Mielziner were convinced that scenographic design and lighting design were inseparable parts of a single vision; modern-day pressures in the theater—not least of which is the expanding complexity of lighting technology—have given rise to new standards of production that recognize lighting designers as full-fledged artistic contributers.

Regardless of the philosophy adopted, whoever is responsible for the lighting for a production knows that the work needed to make light plots is extensive and complicated. Creating light plots have in many ways been facilitated by the introduction of the computer. For instance, the lighting designer can take full advantage of the scenographer's work; using the floor plans of a production—and these always precede those of the lighting designer—the time saved in making new plan drawings is reduced significantly. If the lighting designer shares the scenographer's computer file of the production, the master light plot can occupy a unique layer—most usually the top—of the drawing in the same manner that the scenographer assigns different scenes. Just as the scenographer is able to show separately each setting in relationship to the basic stage layout (and to print out those views as unique hard-copy drawings), the lighting designer can use the same strategy to create individual light plots for each scene showing as little or as much of the scenographer's drawing as is deemed necessary. If lighting designers share the same basic CAD software—and those working in a permanent theater organization quite probably do—they are able to introduce into the scenographer's drawing their own libraries of specialized instruments and symbols. The computer makes interaction between scenography and lighting attainable in ways not possible with regular real-world drafting practice.

Although the scenographer's floor plan may have dozens of objects drawn on it, the plan view of the lighting plot frequently requires hundreds of lighting instrument symbols. The repetitive job of hand-drawing the numerous instruments on manually drawn plots is alleviated by using commercially made templates. Even with these, the task is time-consuming and tedious. To move instruments once drawn or to change type of instrument or angle of focus adds considerably to the chore. On the computer lighting-plot construction is considerably more manageable. Here are some advantages of computer-generated lighting plots:

1. For the listing part of the plot, computer spreadsheet programs permit designers to create instrument lists that can be automatically sorted into appropriate configurations. When lighting designs are changed—as inevitably they must be—new arrangements are automatically updated. Spreadsheet applications also give an added advantage of accounting: instruments can be totaled as aggregates or as separate groups; again, when changes are made, updating of the list is automatically entered. Cue sheets for running a production also benefit from spreadsheet technology; being able to add cues, to delete cues, or to rearrange their order is facilitated if stored on computer files. If the scenographer and the lighting designer use programs such as MiniCad+ 5.0 or PowerDraw 5.0, the listing part of the light plot can be accomplished without leaving the CAD part of the program, since this application has database/spreadsheet options built in.

2. The graphic plan view part of lighting-plot construction also benefits when rendered on the computer. By using clones of instruments duplicated from lighting instruments on master lighting templates (that is, library or macro files)—the electronic equivalents of physical lighting instrument templates—lighting designers significantly cut the physical work in making lighting plan views. The left side of figure 85 shows the way clones of instruments are obtained from Canvas 3.5's macro library. Although we tend

to think of libraries as collections of small objects such as furniture, or lighting instruments, It is possible to have entire plan views of the stage showing lighting battens complete with circuit boxes and other permanent features of a theater, such as floor pockets stored as a single library object. Having such an independent layer stored as a library object in a lighting designer's personal files alleviates the necessity for scenographers to dedicate a distinct layer on their own basic floor plan templates. This practice allows lighting designers to take the scenographer's floor plan file and to customize it according to their own ways of working using as much or as little of that plan as needed. Some lighting designers only show the layout of the lighting equipment used, leaving out the scenographer's scenic units; other designers include the scenographer's complete floor plan as part of the lighting plan view.

When the scenographer serves as the lighting designer of a production, undoubtedly the same program that created the floor plan will be used for the lighting plot. When the lighting designer is a separate designer, however, the same computer program may not be used. Different CAD and other drawing programs do, however, "speak" to one another, that is, make it possible to transfer information from one program to another or from one computer to another. It is perfectly possible for the lighting designer using MiniCad+ 5.0 to take a floor plan created in ClarisCad 2.0 and convert it to a MiniCad+ 5.0 document. It is becoming increasingly possible to exchange information from one type of computer to another, although in most cases this can only be done by using special applications that create interface links. This is especially true for PowerDraw 5.0, which requires that a separately purchased translator program be used to effect transfers of one file format to another.

3.   Almost all present-day lighting boards use computer technology to store and run cues electronically, although interfacing between studio computers and these lighting boards is rarely possible. In the future such interaction is only a matter of time. In the meantime, however, even at this level of integration, the computer CAD programs greatly enhance construction of lighting plots.

The Computer **4** Scenographic Model

It is interesting to speculate what Gordon Craig or Adolphe Appia would have made of the computer. That they valued the aesthetics of drawing is evident in every design they made; both took delight in applying atmospheric effects to their sketches. But atmospheric effects were not the sole concern for either artist; both experimented extensively with three-dimensional form, both were intrigued with the use of space in the theater. Craig in particular devoted considerable time to scenographic models. The care he took to keep photographic records of his experiments clearly demonstrates that his interest in the world of form ranged beyond nebulous two-dimensional image making. Appia's prime concern lay more with the effects light and shadow produced in time on three-dimensional form. His drawings clearly demonstrate the ways he thought the scenography of the future should be approached. There is ample reason to believe that both visionaries would have sought the opportunity to explore on the computer screen those evocative theatrical structures they imagined on paper and built on model stages. Still, innovative and far-seeing as both were, they were artists tied to their own time; their visions understandably could not include the possibilities we readily accept today. They worked—like most designers of the past—within the assumptions they inherited: that scenographic designs and scenic sketches were synonymous terms; that static drawings provided true illustrations of what scenographers intended on the stage and as such were the best means for communicating their intentions to other minds.

Two fundamental problems exist with these assumptions: (1) two-dimensional drawings cannot adequately reveal a scenographic design's three-dimensional nature; and (2) almost always the prime viewing point of a scenic sketch is placed at the exact center of the theater's auditorium—a view that provides little indication how designs appear from other vantage points.

Just what, then, *can* a scenographic sketch show? Is it really worth the effort to make such limited drawings at all? For no matter how sophisticated a sketch's rendering, no matter how much it is a work of art in itself, these drawings provide little workable information to other production workers. Directors, for instance, cannot adequately determine space available for movement; scenic shops cannot determine size or shape of forms; scenic painters cannot discriminate painted detail from three-dimensional construction; costume and lighting designers—whose work should be closely integrated with that of the scenographer's—are not able to discern separate colors from complex tonalities embedded in a painted sketch's atmospheric effects.

For all these reasons, two-dimensional scenographic sketches have been supplanted by three-dimensional scenographic models. A main reason for this change is that fewer and fewer productions are produced on the proscenium arch stages that dominated the theater from the middle of the seventeenth century until the middle of the twentieth. During the past fifty years, moreover, both theater structures and the stages within them have altered radically. It makes little sense, scenographers working in other forms reason, to create static pictures of settings from one position only when the design is to be viewed from numerous vantage points. Will scenographic sketches entirely disappear? Probably not. But what has changed since the time of Gordon Craig and Adolphe Appia is not only that newer technologies have found their way into our present-day theaters, but that the computer has significantly altered the scenographer's perceptions of what sketches and models are and how they relate to scenographic processes.

It should not be assumed, however, that illusory drawing has lost all value for the scenographer. Learning the principles and mastering the techniques of perspective drawing is still a subject every student of scenography should study and master. The advent of the computer, however, has for many scenographers changed the way of making perspective drawings; in some ways the computer has extended the old methods into new opportunities to communicate the thoughts of the scenographer. Best of all, the drudgery of creating accurate perspective views of a setting has in large part been assumed by the internal workings of computer software.

Despite the growing use of computer graphics in scenographic work, as late as 1990 less than 20 percent of professional designers in the United States and Canada used computers as a regular part of their practice. Fewer still are using the computer as a modeling environment. By the year 2000, if present trends hold, it is probable that most scenographic designers—as well as other theater artists—will employ integrated two- and three-dimensional programs to create, experiment with, and store most of their work in computer graphics form.

In this section we will explore some of the ways three-dimensional computer modeling is accomplished. We must also examine what role two-dimensional drawing plays in the development of computer three-dimensional models, since their construction is directly related to specific information concerning the size, shapes, and positions of objects that compose them. This information is frequently set down in CAD programs that do not have three-dimensional capabilities. That is, a floor plan of a model is created after which it is exported into a three-dimensional program so that it can be realized as a three-dimensional model. A notable exception to this procedure is a CAD application that contains both two- and three-dimensional possibilities: MiniCad+ 5.0. This program is one of the two recommended as a drafting program (the other program being PowerDraw 5.0). MiniCad+ 5.0 is the only relatively inexpensive program that also produces other

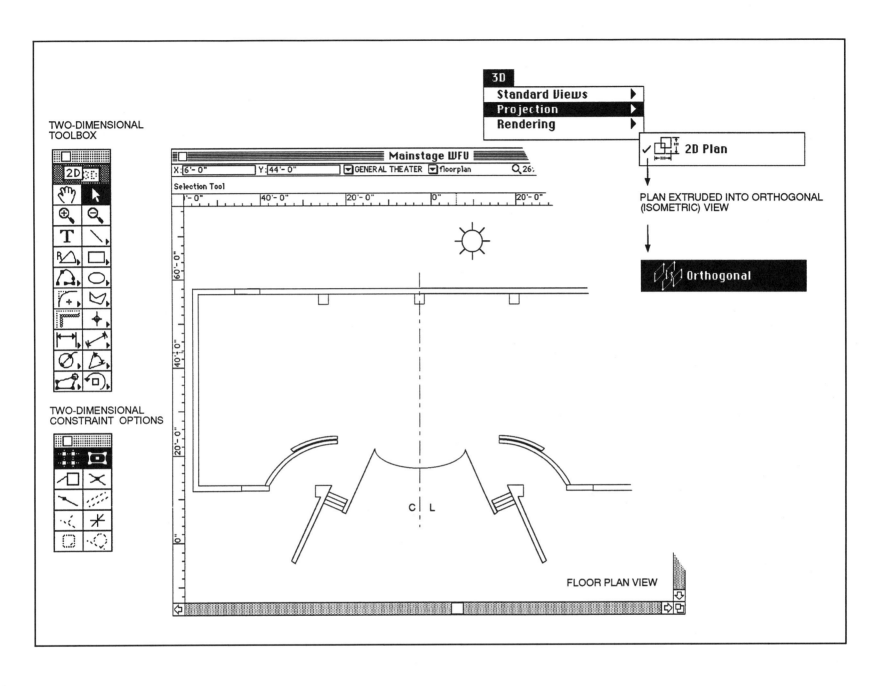

forms of working drawings necessary for scenographic design such as orthographic projections (isometrics, cabinet oblique, and cavalier oblique projections). Figure 86 shows the two-dimensional screen for MiniCad+ 5.0. Note that the Toolbox at the left of the screen uses the familiar icons for creating graphic objects. It is while in this mode that the drawer creates plans and elevations. In figure 87, however, the mode of drawing has changed; using the conversion features of MiniCad+ 5.0, the plan has been changed to

Fig. 86. MiniCad+ 5.0 two-dimensional screen diagram

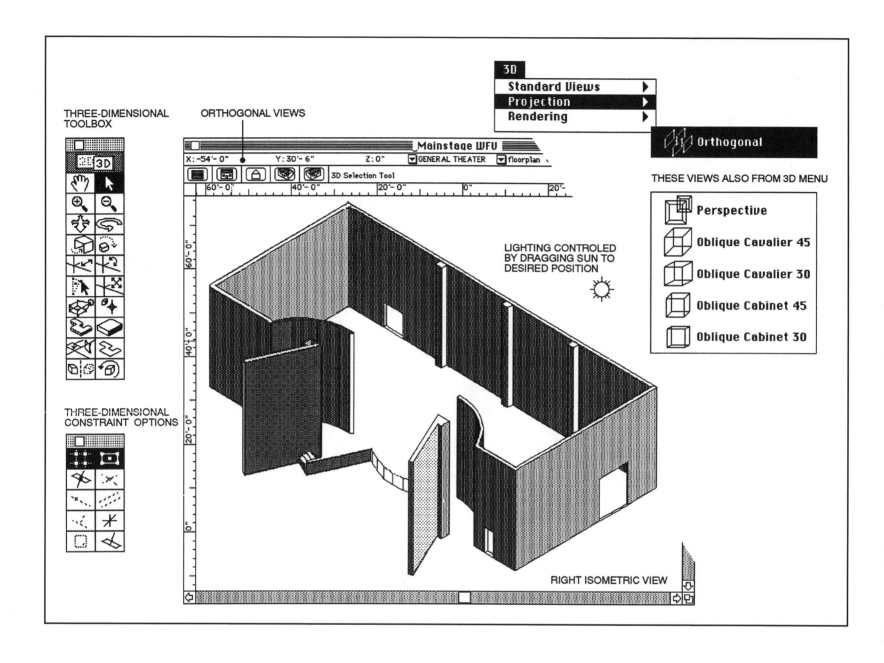

Fig. 87. MiniCad+ 5.0 three-dimensional screen diagram

a three-dimensional environment. It is also possible to change the view shown to others indicated in the pull-out menu shown at the right side of figure 87.

And yet, all programs such as MiniCad+ 5.0 are primarily used *after* concepts of a design are established or aesthetic parameters set. What is missing from almost all computer programs is the ability *to experiment with scenographic ideas in three-dimensional form.* Even the most dedicated three-dimensional programs—such as Swivel 3-D Professional, Infini-D, or StrataVision 3D to name but three in a rapidly growing field—

are not conducive to the early phases of design conceptualization. What programs would be, then, most advantageous to scenographers during the experimental stages of a production's design? This phase of the design process, more than demonstrating the ways computers aid in presenting technical specification of decisions made, is the focus of the following section.

Computer Three-Dimensional Graphics

Just as there are two kinds of graphic images possible with computers—bit-mapped images and object-oriented images—there are also two basic kinds of three-dimensional programs: those that create images that give the appearance of three-dimensionality and those that create objects on the computer screen with all the characteristics—height, width, and depth—of true three-dimensional objects found in the real world.

Of course, three-dimensional forms on computer screens are flat; they are not actually three-dimensional in the way we think of objects in our so-called real world. Still, just how much difference is there between what we see in our day-to-day experience and what is viewed on the computer screen? One of the first important thinkers to question this difference is Ivan E. Sutherland, an early investigator of the computer's ability to create electronic three-dimensional spaces using digital equipment. In a paper written in 1968 detailing his experimental work with virtual reality head displays, he says this:

> The fundamental idea behind the three-dimensional display is to present the user with a perspective image which changes as he moves. *The retinal image of the real object which we see is, after all, two-dimensional. Thus if we can place suitable two-dimensional images on the observer's retinas, we can create the illusion that he is seeing a three-dimensional object.* Although stereo presentation is important to the three-dimensional illusion, it is less important than the change that takes place in the image when the observer moves his head. (Italics mine.)

Sutherland was speaking then about virtual reality possibilities using helmets that fitted over the head into which two small television cameras were set. Hardware-based systems—those that require equipment—were the only forms of virtual reality possible at the time. We now have, however, software-based virtual reality programs that make it possible to turn our computers screens into the equivalent of physical spaces that operate on the two-dimensional surface with all the capabilities of movement that exist in the real world of everyday experience.

What makes all kinds of imagery possible is the computer's ability to describe shapes and forms using digital information and mathematical computation. Three-dimensional programs, however, require a much more sophisticated program language to create computer three-dimensional objects. Let us take a closer look at some of the basic assumptions that both real-world three-dimensional drawing and computer three-dimensional drawing share.

Since the third dimension is impossible to attain on two-dimensional surfaces, drawing systems have been devised to trick the eye of viewers into seeing objects drawn on flat surfaces as three-dimensional forms. For any system of perspective to be successful, it must provide logically coherent visual links to real-world three-dimensional visual experiences. All perspective systems—both real-world systems and computer—are based on rules and principles geared to make the flat image representation of a three-dimensional object visually coherent. Two of the three basic terms used to describe the positions of forms in three-dimensional space were first used by the seventeenth-century philosopher and scientist René Descartes. These are X (the symbol traditionally used to designate width or horizontal orientation of a plane) and Y (the symbol traditionally used to designate the height or vertical orientation of an plane); Z (the symbol derived from *zenith* is traditionally used to designate the depth or distance of a plane) has been added to this description so that any three-dimensional object can be accurately located or described in a known volume of space. Without an understanding as to how these terms apply to a three-dimensional volume, it is not possible to understand how the illusion of three-dimensional form is created on two-dimensional surfaces. These terms, however, change their designations according to the viewpoint from which observations are made.

Confusion arises when perspective drawers—such as painters and architects—use these same designations for computer three-dimensional graphics. Those trained in manually drawn perspective systems frequently do not take into account that while X retains its meaning, Y and Z change designations.

The reason for this confusion is that the coordinate system for computer three-dimensional worlds is a mathematically based system that—unlike the way art and architecture schools teach perspective—uses a plan or top view of an object as its primary observation viewpoint rather than the frontal-view system (also called a *real-world* coordinate system) employed for manually drawn perspectives. Real-world coordinate systems are customarily encountered by painters and architects and graphic artists before the math-based system used for computer three-dimensional programs.

The difference between the two systems is not all that difficult to comprehend: in the real-world coordinate system, the viewer's eye sees *directly ahead* as if looking at a transparent plane—known as the picture plane in art school language—that is vertical to the earth's surface (fig. 88A). The Z coordinate (traditionally depth in the real-world coordinate system), therefore, directly faces the viewer, who is always assumed to be in an upright position 90° to the horizontal plane of the earth. Mathematically based, or computer, coordinates, on the other hand, place the viewer's eye directly *down and over* a plane horizontal to the earth's surface (fig. 88B). In computer perspectives (and in the programs studied in this book), the Z coordinate (height in the math-based system) places the viewer's eye directly over the horizontal plane of the earth. This difference in primary viewing point constitutes the main difference between the systems; in both systems the X coordinate (width) retains its basic relationship to the other two.

Figure 89 is a diagrammatic view showing the various views all computer three-dimensional programs have; the specific program illustrated is Virtus WalkThrough 1.1.3. Direct access to these views can be obtained by using the keyboard commands (shown at the upper-left corner of figure 89). One of the most important advantages of using computers for creating three-dimensional perspective views is that all that has been discussed above is automatically calculated by the computer programs we choose.

Now let us proceed to the main subject of this section of the book: computer scenographic models.

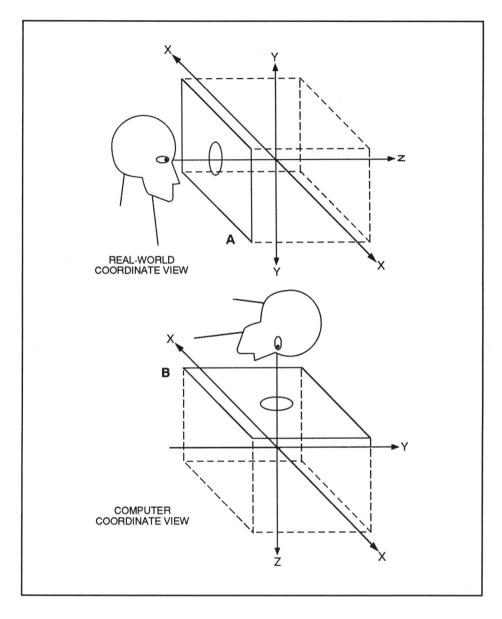

REAL-WORLD
COORDINATE VIEW

COMPUTER
COORDINATE VIEW

Fig. 88. Diagram of three-dimensional coordinates

Computer Scenographic Models

Prior to the availability of computers with powerful graphic capabilities, scenographic design was manually generated. Modelmaking was—and to a large extent still is—accomplished with materials and techniques little changed during the past six hundred years. During that past, modelmaking almost always proceeded only after floor plans were fixed. Scenographers who now employ computers in their work process have seen those basic options extended in ways that would not have been envisioned even ten years ago. In this section we will examine a few basic ways in which modelmaking has changed during this brief period and suggest how that the craft might change during the next decade.

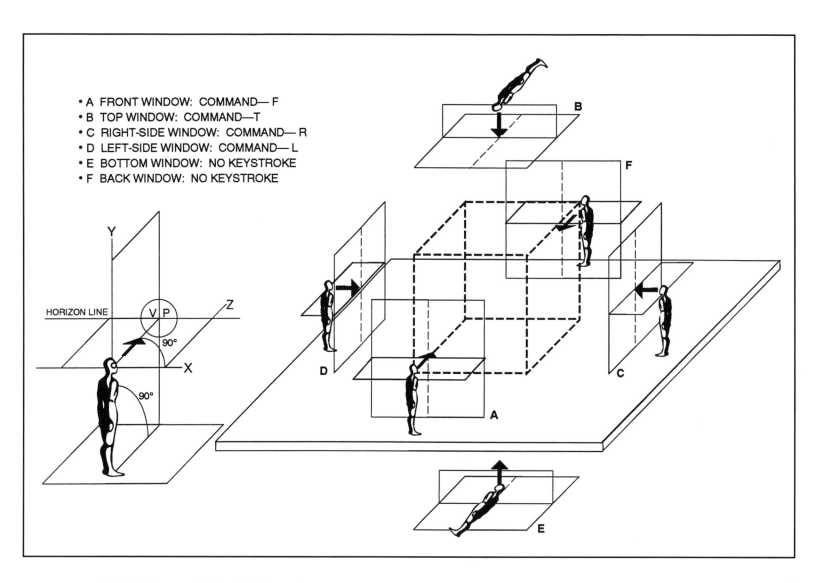

Fig. 89. Diagram of Virtus WalkThrough basic windows

Modelmaking has been part of scenographic practice for at least six centuries. The term *model* has been used from the Middle Ages on to denote those kinds of plans that are made in miniature to be realized at a later time in a larger scale. A scale model more specifically relates those plans drawn in a known set of measurements to actual three-dimensional structures that are constructed in either larger—and sometimes smaller—dimensions. Another use of the word *model*, however, links conceptual planning—such as the structure of a written work or the description of physical laws or the behavior of objects or events—to possible or probable outcomes. These are generally referred to as *mathematical models*. Unlike physical scale models—primarily intended to show size and visual relationships—mathematical models allow one to accurately predict complicated mathematical estimations such as the orbit of planets, the flow of rivers, or the reaction of one chemical element to another. Artists, for the most part, only have to contend with the first of these kinds of models: physical scale models. With the advent of computer graphics and computer modeling, one is forced into contact with aspects of modelmaking that depend entirely on abstract computation and calculation. Fortunately for most of us trained as visual artists used to working with our eyes and our hands, the complex mathematical systems necessary for computer modelmaking are incorporated into the invisible structure of specific applications by complex codes created by programmers. If one had to learn *how* a computer graphics program works in order to use it, few artists could avail themselves of the numerous advantages embedded in even the simplest of computer applications.

In this book we examine two kinds of three-dimensional programs: (1) those that create drawings using predrawn perspective grids—an extension of manual graphics technique—and (2) those that generate three-dimensional drawings on the screen by specifically formatted programming code.

The first kind of perspective drawing mirrors principles and techniques employed in traditional perspective drawing, the kind of drawing learned in art school perspective classes and demonstrated in chapter 3. These grids are mechanically constructed by the scenographer using a standard computer drawing program like Canvas 3.5.

Programs especially designed to automatically create three-dimensional objects, on the other hand, do not require of users a familiarity with, or comprehension of, perspective rules and principles. The only requirement of these programs is a specific knowledge as to how the program works along with an ability to provide precise information essential to the running of the application. Although these programs are our main concern in this section—since they allow scenographers to automatically construct correctly displayed three-dimensional objects on the computer screen—we should not completely abandon the computer perspective grid system described in the previous section. Even in the computer environment, templates made by traditional methods retain a value for many scenographic design projects.

The concept of interactive scenography—as a way for artists to conduct a dialog with different parts of the individual mind and also as a means to interact with the minds of others—is an important newer way of working that the computer has engendered. In this book, therefore, the term *interactive* is used in two ways: first, the interaction of the computer and the artist, and, second, the interaction of artist to artist, with the computer used as both the interpreter of individual ideas and the reflector of differing points of view. One of the best uses of the computer lies in its ability to arbitrate decisions between outlooks by providing quick alternative views of elements in question. Therefore, if we dismiss at the beginning the autocratic dictates of either the director or the scenographer, the sharing of visual ideas can be accomplished on several levels:

Interactive Computer Modelmaking

1. Through verbal communication alone; talking out a production in terms of the authors instructions—both explicit and implicit—and technological requirements
2. Through the use of metaphorical analogy; seeking imagery through poetic visions
3. Through rudimentary diagrams and shared visual or physical artifacts

4. Through study and manipulation of prepared models or model parts
5. Through use of interactive images and interactive computer-generated three-dimensional models

In all cases above, the need to share information and concepts produces specific kinds of results. But it is only with the last category listed—when the computer enters into the discussion process—that interaction produces immediate tangible results, that is, changes to projects or printed materials for participants to use for future study.

Although all designers know that any artistic process needs periods of unstructured gestation, there comes a point when the various strands of a project must be given form and direction. It is at this point the computer proves to be most helpful. While all designers have individual work procedures, the closer to project completion the more likely these procedures are to become similar.

For most scenographic projects, designers assemble a body of information prior to beginning a scenographic model: scaled plans and elevations along with unscaled visualizations of form and detail. This preliminary work is usually done using two-dimensional drawing techniques on two-dimensional materials. Scaled models are not, strictly speaking, absolute necessities for scenographic design. During the past fifty years, however, with the awareness that scale models serve such an important function in the creative process of a production's design, using models has become an invaluable way to explore problems not possible to solve with flat drawings alone. Scenographers have also discovered that the very act of modelmaking *without* prior concepts or detailed plans often proves advantageous to those who evolve ideas in ways more directly attuned to the most basic theatrical elements: time, space, and movement. Direct modeling has fostered a new paradigm for both scenographers and directors who view scenographic design as an interactive creative process. As a result of the shift in emphasis from two-dimensional form to three-dimensional experimentation, the concept of *interactive exploration* developed, and the term *interactive model* has become current in scenographic practice. But just what is an interactive model?

Interactive models are not so much things as they are processes made visible. This holds true for both physical models made with actual materials and the kinds of models explored in this book; however, both have fundamental purposes. Horace Freeland Judson, in *The Search for Solutions*, gives a good explanation of just what those purposes are:

A model is a rehearsal for reality, a way of making a trial that minimizes the penalties for error. Playing with a model, a child can practice being in the world. Building a model, a scientist can reduce an object, a system, or a theory to a manageable form. . . . modeling, however serious, enshrines an element of play. Watching a child, one turns that observation the other way around: for the child, absorbed in play, modeling has an essential aspect of seriousness—it's a way of grasping the ways things are. For the scientist or engineer, conversely, the seriousness of modeling retains something of the youthful delight. Scientists are incessantly saying to each other "let's play around with that"—and modeling is the quintessential way of playing with the way things might work and might be. . . . Curiously, model-building can also be a way to create a theory. . . . *The performance of objects. The behavior of elaborate systems. A kind of theory-making. Modeling performs at these three levels.* (Italics mine.) (Horace Freeland Judson, *The Search For Solutions* [Baltimore, MD: Johns Hopkins University Press, 1987])

When one first approaches the computer as a tool for modelmaking, there are a number concepts to master as well as a number of obstacles to overcome. Some of these involve matters just discussed; the individual nature of the designer to a large extent decides what the mix between preplanned and interactive modelmaking will be. A more troublesome aspect of computer modelmaking lies in the unavoidable fact that new techniques as well as new concepts of work must thoroughly be learned if one is to access the possibilities offered by the computer. This situation is not helped by the realization that one can never learn a program entirely but only that part the developers have thus far assembled; that every application is a work in progress, the end of which is not easily predicted. This brings us to a concept that is basic to computer modelmaking: additive and subtractive modeling.

Regardless of the techniques, materials, or technology used, the scenographer's task in most instances requires that these basic jobs be accomplished:

1. The construction of technical drawings (elevations, axonometric views, detail specifications, etc.)
2. The construction of perspective views either with manual graphics or in a three-dimensional program suitable for architectural views
3. The construction of scaled models

Before the advent of computer graphics modelmaking, scenographic models could be roughly broken into three distinctive categories: experimental models, working models, and exhibition models.

1. *Experimental models.* The experimental model is not so much a type of model as it is an activity. Often the scenographer will begin to search for a design concept with three-dimensional forms and materials directly on a scaled model stage. He does not, when working in this manner, first draw out a predetermined design and then build a scale replica of it. Rather, experimental models are assembled with found materials and objects, with little regard as to measurement or scale. The object of this activity is, as its name implies, to determine scenographic concepts in an experimental way without using prior sketches or preconceived concepts. In this book we are assuming that the primary creative search for solutions begins on the computer. It is well to keep in mind that scenographers may in some projects work in one way and in others use an entirely different approach. The path is determined by a number of factors: time available for a project, complexity of a project, and, not least, the visual-spatial imagination of others with whom the scenographer works. While most directors only see (or want to see) more completed projects, some directors take an active part in the design process during the earliest possible stages. When three-dimensional models are constructed on the computer, interaction of others becomes a much more feasible possibility than when the scenographer

works with actual real-world materials. It is reasonable to say that computer-generated models—unlike their physical counterparts—never lose their status as experimental models; that is, that as long as the file in which they reside remains unlocked, changes can be made. This gives the computer model a distinct time advantage over more finished models that usually are altered only with considerable difficulty.

2. *Working models.* The physically constructed working model's primary function is to show how a scenographic design appears onstage. Working models evolve from a limited selection of experimental model possibilities. Unlike experimental models, however, working models must have a known scale and need to be presented in a fixed context: on a correspondingly scaled stage structure that allows the design to be tested for its appropriateness or feasibility in a specific space. Working models are constructed from a wide range of materials (paper, plastics, balsa, illustration board, wire, modeling paste, etc.). It is customary to finish all units of the working model with a uniform covering of gesso—a white coating that gives a unified color and surface to the model— being the most common material used. Working models often are done in units that correspond to ways they are built in the scenic shop; this practice allows technical directors or stage managers to analyze any necessary movement of the units on the actual theater stage floor.

3. *Exhibition models.* The exhibition model is the type of presentation one most often sees displayed for public view: its basic purpose is to show how the setting will actually appear on the stage. For this reason it is painted in the same colors as will be the eventual set onstage. It is also used by many scenographers to "sell" a design; the highly detailed exhibition model frequently has a fascination for viewers that overrides its value as an appropriate solution to a production's real needs. This model often includes scaled representations of furniture and set properties, and it is common also to include representations of performers in order for the observer to see the relationship of the setting's size to the human being. It is possible—as stated above—to make many of the elements of the exhibition model on the computer. Since the line-drawing detail capabilities of the computer are superior to manually drawn graphics, exhibition models that have intricate flat graphic elements—highly detailed panels, image backgrounds, intricate floor patterns, elaborate grillwork designs, or curtains—incorporated into the design are the models best suited to utilize computer-generated images.

And now to these traditional categories has been added a fourth: *computer scenographic models.*

Constructing Computer Scenographic Models

For many scenographers—like myself—the next step after agreement on floor plans is to construct detailed accurately scaled models. After the model (or models) is completed, a period of time usually exists to discuss with the director and others concerned how original concepts and sketches work when experienced as three-dimensional structures. Only after this period, and necessary modifications are made to the model, are technical drawings made. Integrating computer technologies into my working plan has caused fundamental changes to long-established work habits and procedures. I now find that it is possible to accomplish on the flat screen many tasks that could only have been done by physical model experimentation; for example, checking sightlines of a setting, viewing a setting from various heights or angles, changing shapes and placement of setting forms.

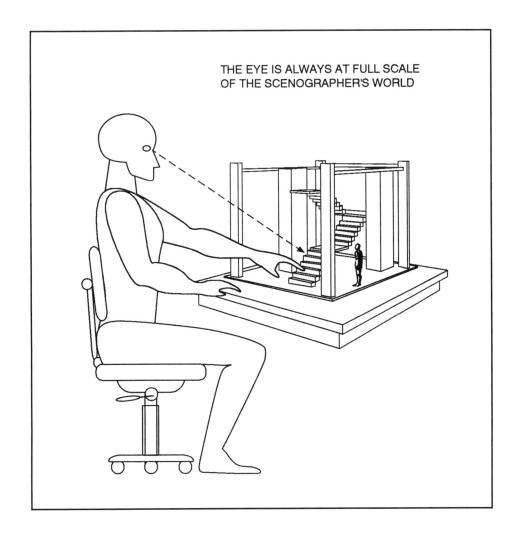

THE EYE IS ALWAYS AT FULL SCALE
OF THE SCENOGRAPHER'S WORLD

Fig. 90. Real-life scenographic model view

For evocation of a production's mood, few computer programs today can match the atmospheric qualities of a trained scenographer's manually painted sketch. But this part of the scenographer's job is at best tangential to the main tasks required; renderings of settings are limited in the information they give. Scale scenographic models, on the other hand, show intended spatial relationships in ways unmatched by drawings (fig. 90); even the most sophisticated three-dimensional computer graphics program will not change this situation. What constructive role, then, does the computer play in the planning and execution of a design? I see its use as an interactive testing device for three-dimensional views. In the future of scenography this function is apt to prove the computer's most important contribution. After all, computers possess the ability to *see* in the same manner as the single lens camera and the camera lens sees in identical way to the human eye. The computer screen is, in fact, little different from the flat surface of a photograph; perspective principles operate on the computer in exactly the same way they do in photography, including the ability to set a computer view to exactly match lens measure-

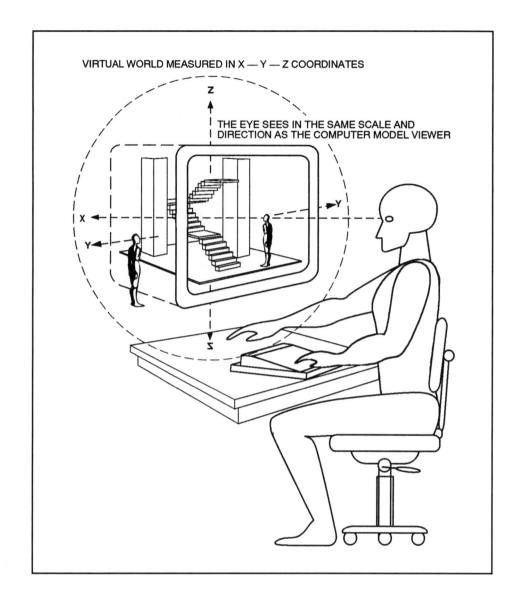

VIRTUAL WORLD MEASURED IN X — Y — Z COORDINATES

THE EYE SEES IN THE SAME SCALE AND
DIRECTION AS THE COMPUTER MODEL VIEWER

Fig. 91. Virtual reality model view

ments. The computer can, using the proper program, become an extension of the human eye (fig. 91).

It should also be noted that while all computer three-dimensional graphics share certain basic similarities, the underlying technologies of individual programs give differing results. Virtus WalkThrough 1.1.3 and MiniCad+ 5.0—two of the important programs mentioned in this book—have distinctive ways of accomplishing similar objectives. Since it is not possible to demonstrate fully all the programs recommended, only a few possibilities taken from one program—Virtus WalkThrough 1.1.3—will be discussed and demonstrated. MiniCad+ 5.0 is a powerful three-dimensional program that gives possibilities not found in Virtus WalkThrough 1.1.3 and is one of the best of the architectural drawing programs that allows scenographers to translate a highly accurate drafting environment immediately into either orthogonal or perspective three-dimensional views. Virtus WalkThrough 1.1.3, on the other hand, is not a CAD program and has as its prime goal the modeling and viewing of forms in space, and that is more to our present purpose.

All scenographic concepts must be converted into drawings that allow a scenic-building shop to realize in full-scale structures the visions of the scenographer. The more elaborate the vision, the more detailed these drawings must be; accurate measurements and precise details of assembly must be specified if the image on the stage is to correspond to the image drawn on paper. What precedes the making of detailed plans, however, is almost always a long period of unstructured visual experimentation. Exact measurement of objects or calculation of spatial arrangement is not or should not be the focus during this exploratory phase; *not* thinking too precisely is more to the purpose of scenographer and director. It is during this phase, then, that modelmaking plays its most important role and has its greatest impact on what is eventually codified in technical drawings.

The making of a scale model—either manually or on the computer—requires two major decisions: (1) the scale to be used, and (2) the kind of model to be constructed. Although it can be assumed that when one reaches the model stage of a project all decisions have been made, and little remains but to actually construct the model completed in the imagination; such is rarely the case. Most scenographers find that it is much easier in the scenographer's studio, rather than in the shop or the theater building, to move a scale model piece to a new position on the model stage floor or cut a new window in a model's wall.

It should be pointed out that modelmaking in the future will most likely proceed along two paths: (1) making models using real-world materials and (2) making models that exist only in the memory of the computer. It is probable, however, that scenographers will find that a composite of these two approaches is necessary. Before proceeding to the later option, let us first examine some of the ways that computers aid in the making of physical models:

1. Floor plan printouts used as scenographic model bases
2. Shop elevation printouts used as scenographic model walls
3. Shop elevation printouts used as color elevations (with computer-generated grids superimposed over these drawings)
4. Acetate printouts used as transparent drops, windows with subdivisions, and so on

The materials that computers are capable of handling are, of course, substantially different from those normally used for modelmaking; computer-generated models are by necessity paper models. An advantage of computer-drawn graphics, however, is the computer's ability to draw with great accuracy; even a $1/4'' = 1'$ model is significantly more accurate than hand-drawn ones. Using this smaller scale, it is possible to print, as a contiguous form, an entire box setting on a legal-size page; using larger scales—such as $1/2'' = 1'$—requires the model to be printed in sections with manual assembly of the sections. If the scenographer has access to a plotter, the task of assembling the computer model is simplified; figure 92 shows a flat elevation printed on a plotter. (Note that tabs have been added at the bottom of the section to facilitate attachment of the model wall to the floor plan base.) Using plotters permits printing out larger sections of a drawing—such as the wall shown—at standard working-drawing sheet sizes, something not possible using most laser printers that require drawings to be printed in sections that are assembled afterward with tapes or paper cements. It is possible, however, to obtain laser writers and ink-jet printers that print drawing sheets up to 22″ in length. These machines almost always cost more than standard printers.

Using heavier stocks for printouts makes more substantial paper models. Since laser printers differ in ability to process paper stock weights, it is necessary to determine precisely the stock that individual printers process. An important advantage computer printouts give paper models is that architectural detail included is more accurate. Although paper models are generally white, tinted papers that match the basic tonality of the design can also be used. And, of course, these printouts can be hand-rendered to approximate more accurately a scenographer's intentions. In the future, color printing will be more affordable to individual users; "painted" printouts, showing not only color but also textures and shadings, will also become available to those scenographers unable to afford them at the present time. Printing computer images onto acetate stocks allows designers to show the effects of different color tonalities using the same image.

Figure 93 shows a scenographic image derived from a computer three-dimensional model; figure 94 is a model of the same design constructed with real materials and finished as an exhibition model. Both works are based on identical floor plan measurements. It takes little reflection to see that as similar as they are in two-dimensional form, they have visual differences. Although possible to make computer simulations that rival the photographic realism of the model seen in figure 94, the procedures require a significantly greater investment in time, skill, equipment, and software than is intended in this book. We should keep in mind that the main purpose here is to suggest to scenographers ways to enhance communication during the conceptual stages of a production, not ways to create images that rival those of other technologies. What is apparent even at this level of attainment demonstrated in figure 93—an image created as a WalkThrough 1.1.3 model and rendered in Adobe PhotoShop 2.5—is that the world of two-dimensional drawing and the world of three-dimensional modeling are beginning to overlap in ways not possible previous to the advent of the computer.

The viewpoint of scenographic sketches almost always shows how settings appear from the center-most seat of the auditorium. Traditionally, scenographers during the seventeenth, eighteenth, and nineteenth centuries used this viewpoint—known as "the king's seat"—to establish their primary vanishing point focus. Perspective sketches for open stage, arena, or black-box stages do not, however, have so clearly defined a focus; in these theaters no one seat corresponds to "the king's seat" of the proscenium arch theater. For this reason, models are more often used for designs in these theaters than are perspective sketches. Virtus WalkThrough 1.1.3 provides these views in a fraction of the time it takes to draw them using traditional techniques. Figure 95 shows a perspective drawing of an arena setting with three alternative viewpoints.

Planning sessions between scenographers and coworkers—such as directors—are

Fig. 92. Printout of computer paper model parts

Fig. 93. *Virtual reality model image:*
Incident at Vichy

typically accompanied by on-the-spot quick sketches that attempt to show three-dimensional structures on two-dimensional materials; from the inception of scenery until now, this practice has little changed. But even when made by skilled artists, these drawings give no more than rough approximations of what eventually appears onstage. Although scaled models progressively modified and refined usually follow these initial planning conferences (and accurate scale models have all but replaced flat renderings as final scenographic indications), modelmaking at these first sessions is—if attempted at all—necessarily limited to playing with blocks or unscaled paperfolding. Even when detailed models are later made, they present other problems, the main one being that all scenographic models are done in scales significantly different from those in which designers and directors live. Jean Cocteau obliquely warns of this danger when he notes, "*To*

Fig. 94. Scenographic model: Incident at Vichy

reproduce a model too precisely on the stage is one of the greatest faults in theatrical craftsmanship." What he means is that when one goes from one scale to another perceptions radically change. His advice is sound: very few people—scenographers and directors included—give enough attention to what these differences are. Fewer still can visualize the effect of a model rendered in full scale. Scenographers with years of experience are frequently surprised as they see their models take form in the scenic shop; sometimes they are surprised again when a design reaches the stage. Even with the most accurately rendered scale models, our judgment—like Gulliver's viewing Lilliputians—is as grossly distorted as scales are different.

What scenographers need during design conferences are these:

1.   A means to demonstrate quickly and accurately the graphic intent of the scenographer as well as ways to modify these drawings in any manner when requested by others concerned.

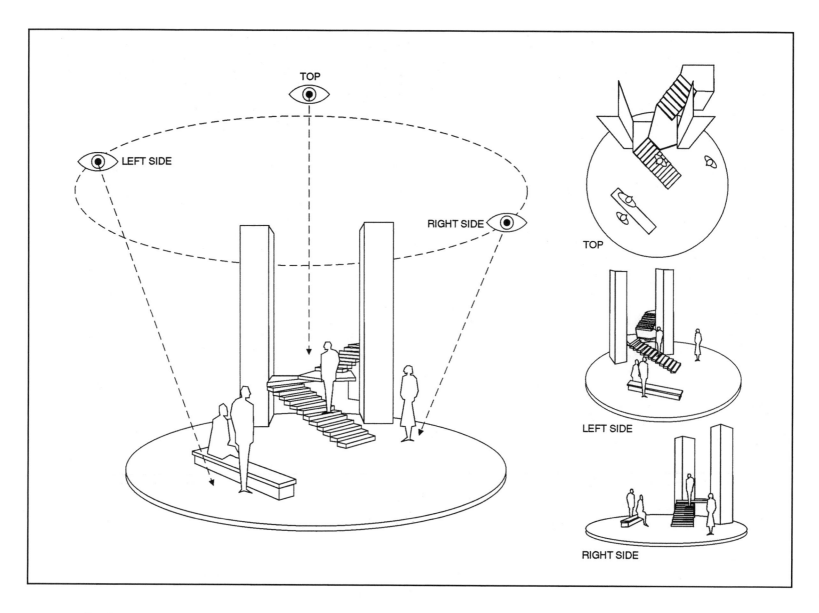

Fig. 95. Virtual reality arena theater views

2.   A method to show scenographic concepts from any viewpoint in true perspective; that is, to view quick sketches in three-dimensional form at real-life scale. Using Virtus WalkThrough 1.1.3, these views are easily obtained. Figures 96 and 97, for instance, show alternatives to flat drawings of floor plans and front elevations. The bird's-eye view (fig. 96) is especially useful to those working in nontraditional stage environments— arena theaters (fig. 95), for instance—or in cinema or television studios (fig. 98). Showing a setting from a single central fixed point of view, as most scenic sketches do, makes little sense for those designing film or television studio settings. Bird's-eye views can, in fact, provide several kinds of information at the same time: (1) they can be read as correctly dimensioned floor plans; (2) they can be turned in any direction so that a shooting

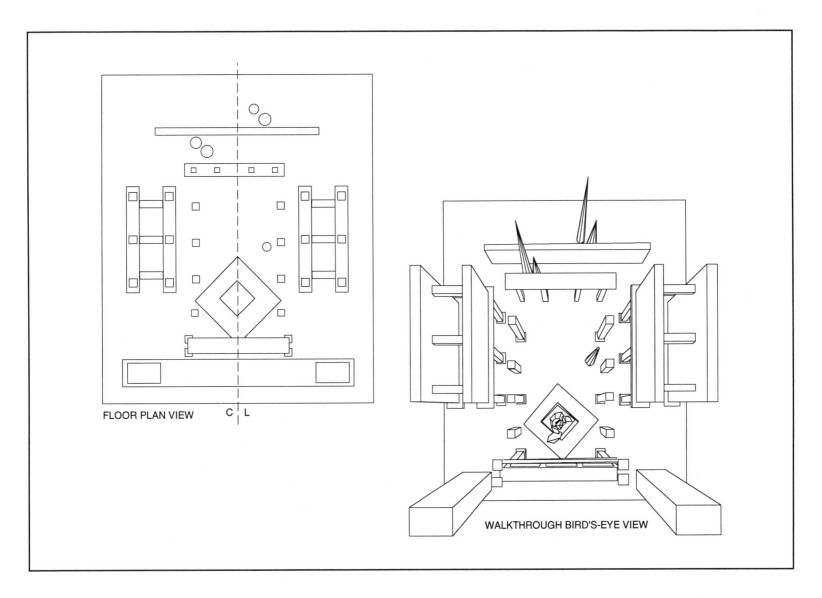

FLOOR PLAN VIEW   C L

WALKTHROUGH BIRD'S-EYE VIEW

angle is approximated; (3) they can provide other workers—properties or special effects personnel, for instance—with a means to determine what the designer wants on the set. Several major cinema studios have begun using computer-generated virtual reality programs as substitutes for traditional storyboard planning.

What is proposed here is nothing less than a radically new approach to scenographic design; a method of work wherein the act of graphic sketching and the purpose of modelmaking are combined into a single interactive procedure; a process that allows the eye of the scenographer and others to *enter into a what is essentially a scenographic drawing, and while there to explore both the visual and the spatial possibilities of a scenic environment and to make changes to that environment as concepts alter or technical needs vary.*

Fig. 96. Virtus WalkThrough top views

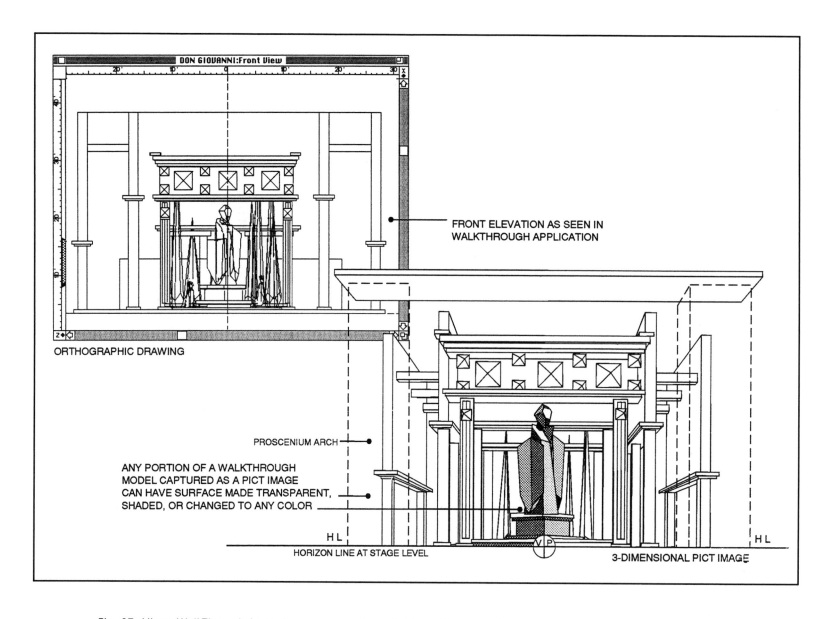

DON GIOVANNI:Front View

FRONT ELEVATION AS SEEN IN
WALKTHROUGH APPLICATION

ORTHOGRAPHIC DRAWING

PROSCENIUM ARCH

ANY PORTION OF A WALKTHROUGH
MODEL CAPTURED AS A PICT IMAGE
CAN HAVE SURFACE MADE TRANSPARENT,
SHADED, OR CHANGED TO ANY COLOR

H L

HORIZON LINE AT STAGE LEVEL

3-DIMENSIONAL PICT IMAGE

H L

Fig. 97. Virtus WalkThrough front views

Improbable as this proposal seems, for approximately three decades computers have had the capability to accomplish the processes listed above. Until recently, however, the cost of the necessary hardware was exorbitantly high—from $50,000 to more than $500,000—and the required software unavailable to all but a few researchers working in small development centers. Now a reasonably priced program exists that allows scenographers, directors, and technicians to create quickly and to explore immediately any view of a computer-drawn three-dimensional environment. The technology that makes it possible to combine graphic sketching and computer modelmaking into a seamless process is a rapidly developing field of computer science called *virtual reality*. While a relatively large number of computer programs allow designers to construct accurate representations

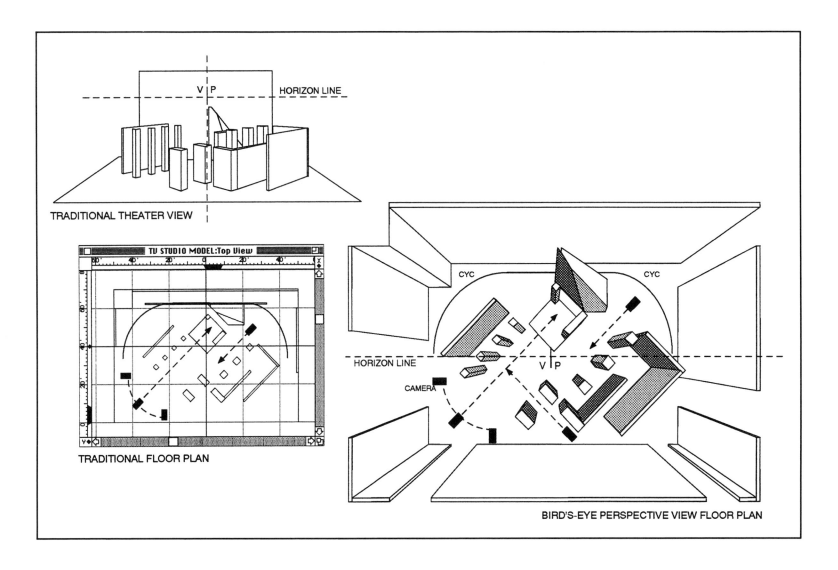

TRADITIONAL THEATER VIEW

TRADITIONAL FLOOR PLAN

BIRD'S-EYE PERSPECTIVE VIEW FLOOR PLAN

of three-dimensional forms, only virtual reality permits the drawer to view *and* to interact with the environment the drawn objects inhabit.

The organization that makes this long-desired goal possible is a small computer company called Virtus Corporation. Situated in Cary, North Carolina, this group is located about as far from Silicon Valley—the heretofore accepted center of computer technological innovation—as one can get. Virtus, one of a fast-growing number of small companies outside the California matrix, resides in that fertile area of R & D named the Research Triangle Park, the rough boundary of which is determined by three small cities in North Carolina: Chapel Hill, Raleigh, and Durham. (Chapel Hill is the home of the University of North Carolina, which supports one of this country's most advanced centers for virtual reality technology. Although UNC's approach to virtual reality is based on expensive hardware, Virtus's program is software-based.)

Fig. 98. Virtus WalkThrough bird's-eye perspective view

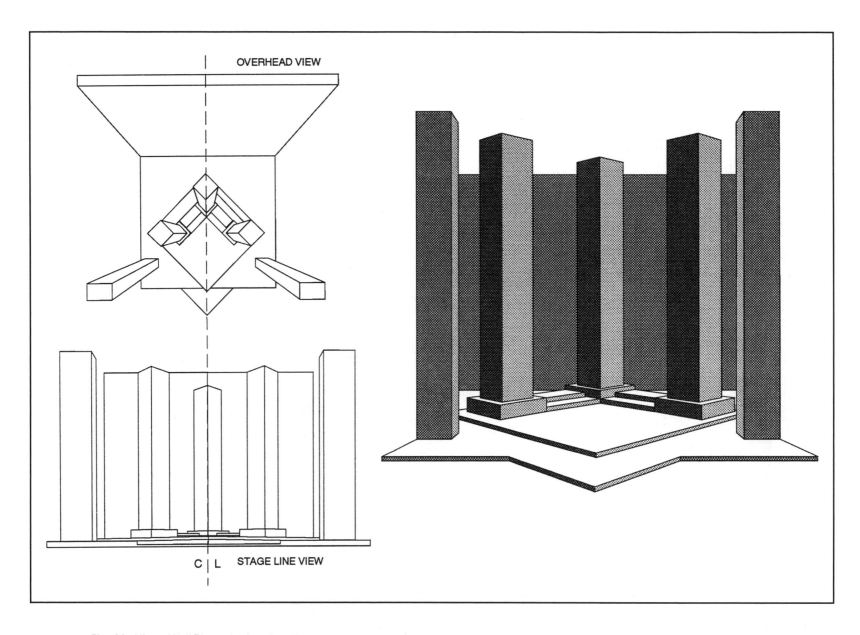

OVERHEAD VIEW

C | L   STAGE LINE VIEW

Fig. 99. Virtus WalkThrough virtual reality model

Virtus WalkThrough 1.1.3 allows designers to interact directly with representations of three-dimensional objects in the same manner as they would in the real world in real time. By guiding the program's observer—the cursor of the input device used—designers can take the eye to any conceivable vantage point; viewpoints are virtually unlimited. Almost instantaneously the designer can obtain an accurate perspective rendering of a setting from any point of view. For instance, changing the viewpoint from the center of the auditorium (fig. 99, right), to an overhead view showing the floor plan in perspective (fig. 99, top left), to a floor-line view (fig. 99, bottom left) is accomplished in the time it takes to move the cursor. It is even possible to look onto the stage from the wings as

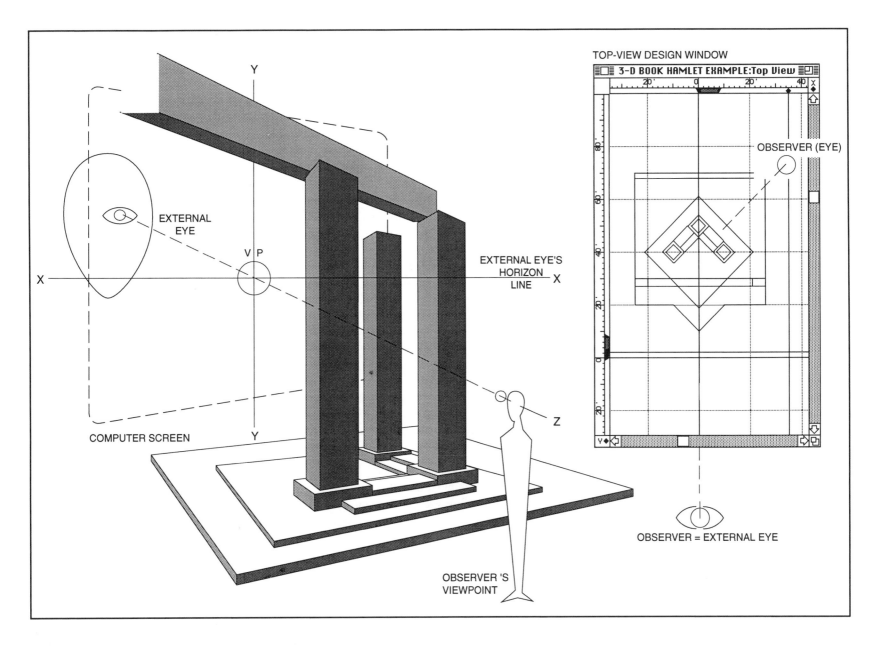

Fig. 100. Virtus WalkThrough model offstage view

shown in figure 100. A useful option of this program is the ability to temporarily render portions of the model transparent—such as the stage-right side of the proscenium arch shown in figure 101—in order to see objects hidden from view. (Figure 102 shows what one would see from the stage-right wings of the setting shown in figure 101.) This option is accomplished by selecting the proscenium side and double-clicking on the transparent icon in the *Walk View Window Toolbox*.) Most remarkable of all, what the screen shows is *identical to the view seen were the viewer standing on the actual stage*. Complete three-dimensional designs are possible in minutes and hours, not days or weeks.

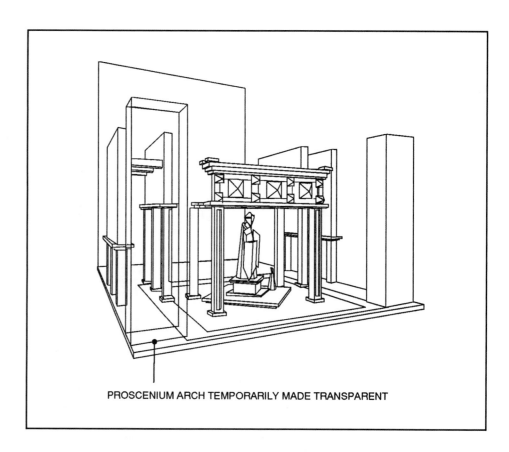

PROSCENIUM ARCH TEMPORARILY MADE TRANSPARENT

Fig. 101. Virtus WalkThrough model view

Technical problems—such as sightlines and platform-level heights—can be tested in the time it takes to move the screen's cursor to a new position. For instance, suppose a director wants to see how actors on six-foot levels appear to viewers seated in extreme left-side first-row orchestra seats. Using a virtual reality model theater like the one shown in figure 103, this view would appear as that shown in figure 103*A*. Figure 103*B*, on the other hand, shows what a viewer would see from the extreme right-side back-row balcony seat. Moreover, to the extent that the virtual reality model has been carefully crafted in the computer file, these views are directly comparable to views made in the real theater; what is seen there can accurately be determined on the computer model.

Since Virtus WalkThrough 1.1.3 computer graphics models are comparable in every way to traditionally constructed ones, real-world modelmakers can quickly test alternative forms and spatial relationships before constructing their physical counterparts.

Three-dimensional applications are notoriously confusing to many users, even to those experienced in other computer graphics applications; some few programs—*very few*—are relatively accessible. Of these Virtus WalkThrough 1.1.3 ranks high. The primary reason for Virtus WalkThrough 1.1.3's accessibility is because the program's format generally obeys a primary precept for Macintosh applications; that is that the interface of the program is easy to understand and that the methods of work it requires mirror real-world practices. For computer artists, an interface is well designed to the

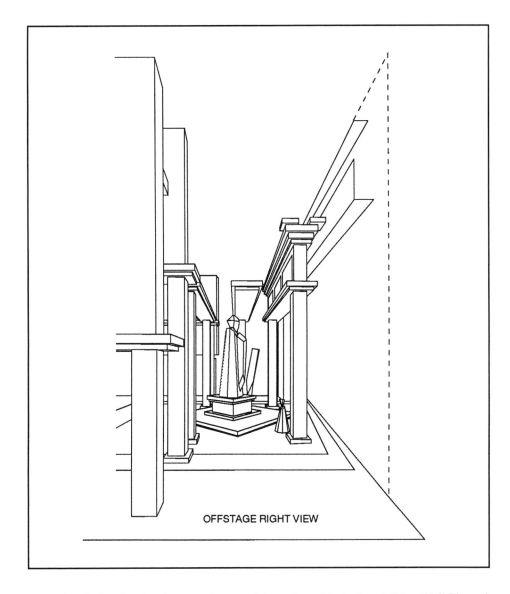

OFFSTAGE RIGHT VIEW

*Fig. 102. Virtus WalkThrough model
stage-right view*

extent it mimics the drawing practices used in real-world studios. Virtus WalkThrough 1.1.3—to use a common computer term—is *user-friendly*, its interface geared to the way many manual graphics designers think; that is, in terms of plans and elevations (front, back, side, rear). In Virtus WalkThrough 1.1.3 these views are directly accessible through the use of keyboard shortcuts (Command-T equals plan view, Command-F equals front elevation view, Command-R equals right elevation view, etc.).

Figure 104 shows Virtus WalkThrough 1.1.3's basic screens, consisting of three independent windows. These are the

1. *Toolbox*. Tools and modifiers are available for use when the *View Window* is active (seen at the left side of figure 104*A*). This Toolbox also includes a *Color Selector*, a *Layers List* that allows a drawing to be constructed in independent layers, and *Indications*

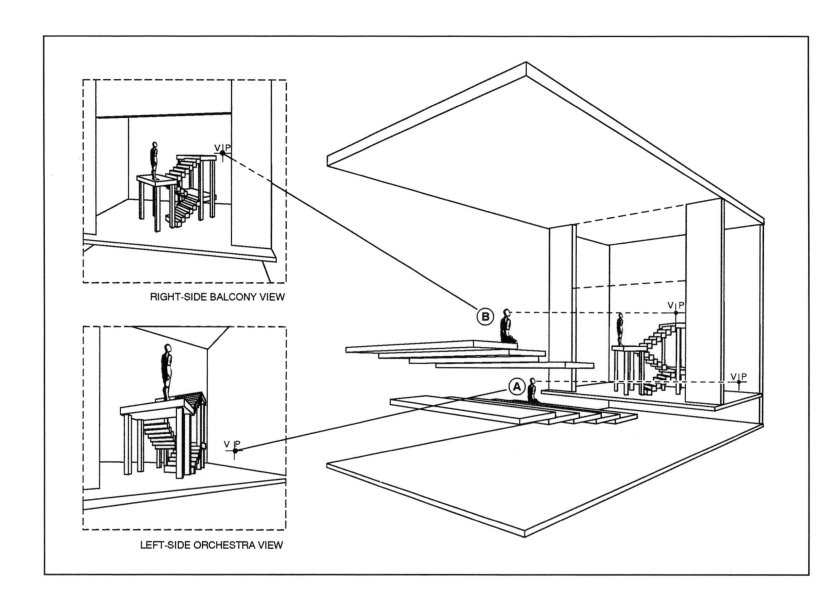

RIGHT-SIDE BALCONY VIEW

LEFT-SIDE ORCHESTRA VIEW

Fig. 103. Virtual reality model auditorium viewing positions

(a section of the Toolbox that shows the coordinate positions of the cursor or a position of an object being drawn). Although these windows present an impressive amount of data—constantly updated as a model is constructed—the user need not pay too much attention to the data displayed. At least, I do not.

2. *View window*. When this window is active (104A), objects can be drawn in six possible views (*top*, *left*, *right*, *front*, *back*, or *bottom*), all accessible by keyboard shortcuts. More than one window can be open at the same time. Since each of the views is only a keystroke away, having more than the two primary windows open only clutters up the screen.

3. *Walk View Window*. This window (104B) shows a three-dimensional rendering

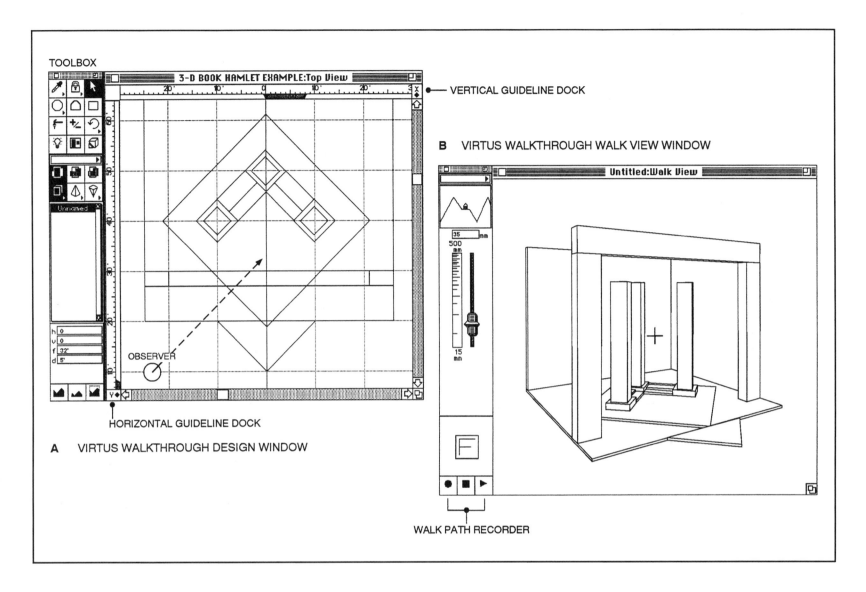

TOOLBOX

3-D BOOK HAMLET EXAMPLE:Top View

— VERTICAL GUIDELINE DOCK

B VIRTUS WALKTHROUGH WALK VIEW WINDOW

Untitled:Walk View

OBSERVER

HORIZONTAL GUIDELINE DOCK

A VIRTUS WALKTHROUGH DESIGN WINDOW

WALK PATH RECORDER

of objects as they are created. When work on any of the drawing windows is accomplished, the Walk View immediately—almost—updates the changes. When this window is selected—and only one window can be active at one time—a different palette appears on the left side of the screen. New options both for viewing and for modifying what has been constructed are available when the Walk View Window is active. The scenographer can move in and around the model with the cursor alone; no key strokes are necessary. Speed of the movement is governed by the relative position of the cursor from the center of the view, the cross in the middle of the screen that marks the vanishing point of the view. The Walk View Window also gives access to the program's animation feature called *record and playback path tools*. A recorded walk path is saved along with the file; when saved as a Voyager File (see below for fuller discussion of this option), the scenogra-

Fig. 104. Virtus WalkThrough basic screens

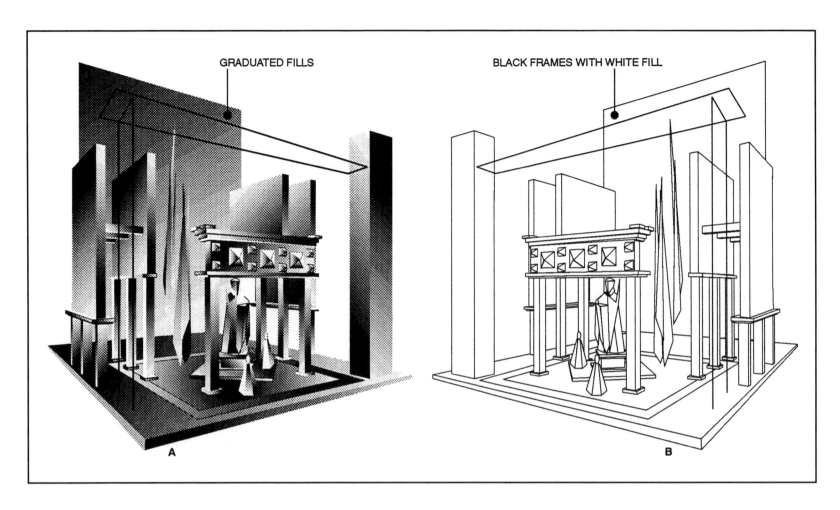

GRADUATED FILLS

BLACK FRAMES WITH WHITE FILL

A

B

Fig. 105. Virtus WalkThrough
model-rendering options

pher is able to send a model to others for viewing even if the original WalkThrough 1.1.3 program is not present.

Virtus WalkThrough 1.1.3 models are constructed as composites using primary forms known as primitives: cubes, cones, cylinders, pyramids, prisms, spheres, hemispheres. After a basic form is constructed, it can be modified in several ways: by grouping primitives into complex units, by changing the nature of the object's surface (from opaque to transparent or translucent), by placing openings of any shape and size in an object's surface so that interior spaces of the object are revealed, or by using a knife tool to slice off sections of an object to create new asymmetrical ones. Virtus includes with the basic program a number of libraries—common objects such as tables, chairs, lamps, which are nothing more than various primitives grouped into recognizable forms. In addition to these, Virtus regularly sends to registered users additional libraries of new objects. Designers can also create and save their own composite objects as library items.

Models can be viewed as monochrome-shaded images (fig. 105*A*) or as unshaded white images (fig. 105*B*). PICT images of either option are available for further manipulation in programs such as Adobe Photoshop 2.5 or Fractal Design Painter 2.0. On-the-screen models can be displayed in color. Using the unshaded mode for viewing speeds up the screen refresh; that is, when the monitor screen redraws its image after additions or changes are made to objects. In the normal mode of view—viewing the model as shaded objects—lighting of Virtus WalkThrough 1.1.3 models is possible. The two basic modes of lighting are ambient or focused. Cast shadows—such as those available in other three-dimensional programs—are not possible. Virtus will, I am certain, add extended lighting features in future releases of the program. Virtus WalkThrough 1.1.3 models can, however, be exported to other programs—such as Specular's Infini-D—to obtain cast shadows and more advanced lighting possibilities. These exportations, however, always take a great deal of time and require more effort on the part of the scenographer. The most important feature of this program is that it gives the scenographer a quick way to explore conceptual ideas. As such, it is more useful as a tool for investigation of design possibilities rather than as a means to produce photorealistic images.

Although Virtus WalkThrough 1.1.3 is not a substitution for traditional modelmaking or scenographic rendering, it is valuable at every step of the design process. Most important of all, Virtus WalkThrough 1.1.3 allows designers and directors to participate in that ideal relationship Peter Brook effectively describes in his book, *The Empty Space:* "a true theatre designer will think of his designs as being all the time in motion, in action . . . In other words, unlike the easel painter, in two dimensions, or the sculptor in three, the designer thinks in terms of the fourth dimension, the passage of time—not the stage picture, but the stage moving picture. A film editor shapes his material after the event: the stage designer is often like the editor of an Alice-Through-the-Looking-Glass film, cutting dynamic material in shapes, before this material has yet come into being. The later he makes his decisions, the better."

It is doubtful that scenographers soon will abandon traditionally made scenographic models. It is clear, however, that computers will play significant roles in modelmaking processes of the future.

In order to use any program effectively, one must have access to the full manual that accompanies the program in addition to a working knowledge of how the program works. This is only possible when the user has purchased and registered the program from either the company or a retailer of the application. (The educational price of the program—that available to both educational units or individual students—is the lowest obtainable.)

The primary emphasis in the basic manual for Virtus WalkThrough 1.1.3 is on the construction of architectural projects—individual rooms, suites, buildings—not on scenographic designs. The default extrusion, for that reason, is set to objects eight feet high, the most common height of an interior room. For scenographic work, this basic extrusion depth is not that applicable or useful as, for instance, an extrusion depth set to one foot, a thickness that is usable as a stage-floor plane. The reason for this default option is that most designers of scenic units use the stage floor as the starting point of a design. Thus the suggestions given below are intended for those who specifically use the program for scenographic purposes or related media. It is an advantage, therefore, to have a new Virtus Walkthough or Virtus Professional File open an untitled screen set to

Model-Building Principles in Virtus WalkThrough 1.1.3

preferences that more nearly approximate the needs of the scenographic designer. The ability to immediately create a base plane representing the stage floor saves several steps in the process and consequently a fair amount of time. New default settings are recommended to those using Virtus WalkThrough 1.1.3. In Virtus programs this customization is accomplished through the Preferences option in the Edit Menu. When this option is accessed, several windows become available that allow the user to reset basic preferences (including the depth of an object's opening extrusion). Figure 104 shows the first window that appears when the Preferences option is selected.

It is also possible to create files for specific theater plants that are saved as templates (that is, that have certain basic features already drawn when the template is first opened). The System 7 format allows the template to be assigned in the Get Information File; these templates are called *stationary files*. It should be remembered, however, that the amount of information included in these preset templates affects the size of the file and consequently both the speed of access to the file and any subsequent additions to the basic template. Care should be given, therefore, to making these templates, or stationary files, as elemental as possible, since every new scenic unit added to the design will alter the size of the file.

Basic Rules for Using Virtus WalkThrough 1.1.3

1. *Do not overlap objects.* (In programs such as MiniCad+ 5.0 and in other three-dimensional programs such as Infini-D, Swivel 3-D, or Swivel 3-D Professional objects can be overlapped. See Virtus's manuals for reasons why this is not possible using this program.)

2. *Nonconvex objects are not allowed.* (As with overlapping objects, such objects are possible in the programs mentioned above. The differences in the nature of the technologies involved between Virtus's virtual reality approach and these other programs are also explained in the Virtus manual.)

3. *Speed and detail are inversely proportional.* (This is true for all files regardless of the technology used to create them.)

4. *Transparent and translucent objects and surfaces drain processing power.* (The more complicated the computation the computer is required to perform, the slower the speed of working. In general, the problems that complex files engender can only be solved by faster machines, by adding more internal memory, or introduction of acceleration cards, all of which will remain expensive options for some years to come. Cost of added speed does, however, decrease year by year.)

5. *You cannot draw a line. All objects have depth.* (The effect of lines can be gained, however, by using object frame outlines as lines. This does, as noted in point 4 above, come at a cost to size of file and speed of working.)

Basic Steps for Using Virtus WalkThrough 1.1.3

Virtus WalkThrough 1.1.3's interface closely conforms to other Macintosh drawing program formats. Although commands and options unique to this program must be mastered, these are designed to correspond closely to the ways scenographers draw on traditional drawing boards. The basic steps in using Virtus WalkThrough 1.1.3 are as follows:

1. *Opening the program windows.* Double-click on the application icon. An initial screen opens showing standard Virtus information including the registrant's name and serial number. Three separate screens appear in the configuration shown in figure 104. From left to right are: *the Tools Window*, *the Design View*, and *the Walk View* (3-D

Modeling View). The *Tools Window* for creating objects is only accessible when the *Design View* is selected (see figure 104*A*). When the *Walk View Window* is selected (and all design windows are inoperative when this window is selected), a different *Tools Window* opens that allows the designer to access and set options not available in any *Design Window* (figure 104*B*). Options in this window allow viewers to set the *lens focal length tool*, thus changing the apparent closeness of the *Observer* to drawn objects. These distances are adjusted by selection of the button on the sliding bar displayed at the center of the window. The small picture at the top of the window shows the effect of the change; the small window directly below the picture gives exact readings in millimeters. The smaller the number in the box, the farther away an object appears; the greater the number, the closer an object appears. It is important when working with designs that are to be used for film media that the correct lens configuration be used. Virtus WalkThrough 1.1.3 gives the opportunity to select the proper aspect ratio. The subject of aspect ratios for film media is discussed later in "Computer Modeling for Cinema and Television."

While the observer can be selected in any design window and dragged to a new viewing position, it is only in the *Walk View* that one can freely navigate (or "walk") by depressing the mouse button in relationship to the center cross hair. Both the Shift key and the Option key modify the kinds of movements possible in the *Walk View*. To become proficient in navigation around the virtual world created by Virtus WalkThrough 1.1.3 takes some training time. Nevertheless, this program among all the three-dimensional available on the small computer is the simplest to master. It is also the best suited to showing others such as the director or the technical staff of a production what the intentions of the scenographer are. Another important feature of the *Walk View Tools Window* is the ability to record the path of a walk. This feature is accessed by selection of *record and playback path tools* at the bottom of the window in figure 104*B*. These tools allow the designer to record a specific path after which the path can be played back as an animation. The round button at the left of the window begins the recording that continues until the recording is stopped by the square button in the center of the bar. To view the recording, the triangular button at the right of the bar is clicked. The path will play in a continuous loop until the mouse button is clicked again. An advantage of this option is that at any time while viewing a recorded path, it may be stopped, modified, and immediately played again with the new changes incorporated into the previous recording. This allows scenographers to show to others a previously designed environment capable of almost instant alteration. By using this system a director not only can see a setting from various audience viewpoints but can modify the elements of the setting within a brief span of time.

2. *Accurate drawing and placing of objects.* Computer models are built in many ways similar to the design of settings using traditional methods and materials. In both processes the floor plan is usually the first drawing where exact scale is recorded. One of the handicaps of most computer three-dimensional programs, however, is that although constructing objects is not difficult, knowing exactly where they exist in the computer's world space is. The scenographer should, therefore, establish a base plane—the floor of the model's stage—before construction of objects begin. After a base is created, it is possible—as with physical models— to create and place objects (i.e., scenic units).

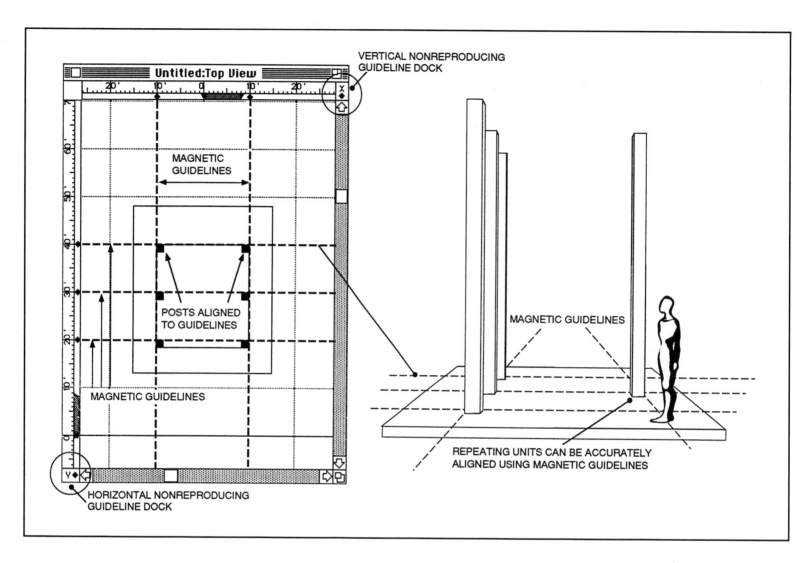

VERTICAL NONREPRODUCING
GUIDELINE DOCK

Untitled:Top View

MAGNETIC
GUIDELINES

POSTS ALIGNED
TO GUIDELINES

MAGNETIC GUIDELINES

MAGNETIC GUIDELINES

REPEATING UNITS CAN BE ACCURATELY
ALIGNED USING MAGNETIC GUIDELINES

HORIZONTAL NONREPRODUCING
GUIDELINE DOCK

Fig. 106. Virtus WalkThrough magnetic guidelines diagram

Objects can visually be tracked in the *Walk View Window* as they are drawn in a *Design View Window*. Objects being drawn also show their positions in the side and top rules. This allows one to start at a known position and to size an object visually. In all *Design Views,* nonreproducing magnetic guidelines are available. Using these guidelines facilitates accurate placement of objects under construction. *Guidelines* are accessed from two places called *docks* in all *Design Windows* (see figure 104A). *Docks* have the letter *X, Y,* or *Z* at its center depending on which *Design Window* is active. By clicking on the *dock* with the mouse and holding down the mouse key, guidelines are drawn into the window view; they can also be moved to new positions in the same way as an object. *Guidelines* are not objects; if left in the file they do not print. Setting (or changing) the color of the guidelines is done in the *Editor* dialog under the *Preferences* option. The left side of figure 106 shows how guidelines are set up in the *Design Window* to facilitate drawing an aligned row of pillars. The right side of figure 106 shows the effect as seen in the *Walk View Window*.

Objects drawn in Virtus WalkThrough 1.1.3 appear to be solid things and similar to objects in other three-dimensional programs. Appearances, however, cannot always be trusted. Surfaces of Virtus WalkThrough 1.1.3 objects are, in reality, calculations that describe mathematical objects in terms of points in space. The surfaces of these objects, unlike those in the real world made of physical materials, are infinitely thin *representations* of planes. It is possible to think of Virtus WalkThrough 1.1.3 objects as *visible volumes of space*.

There are three ways Virtus WalkThrough 1.1.3 surfaces are altered: (1) changing of an object's color, (2) placing holes of differing shapes and sizes in a plane—such as a door or a window—so that the interior space of an object becomes visible, and (3) changing the surfaces of a form's basic nature (opaque) to translucent (an effect similar to seeing through lightly frosted glass) or to transparent (an effect similar to seeing through plain glass). These changes are made using specific tool options in the Toolbox palette displayed when the *Design* windows are active. The tool that allows holes to be put into a surface is called the *surface editor*. Placing holes in objects does no irreparable harm to the surface of any object into which they are placed; any breach of a surface can be moved later, sized differently, or removed entirely, leaving the surface as it was originally. By selecting an object and double-clicking on one of the three surface icons that control the opacity, translucency, or transparency of an object's surface, it is possible to change the basic nature of all surfaces. This is an advantage when showing parts of settings blocked by opaque foreground objects; the foreground objects become wire-framed structures revealing the objects behind. The original nature of the surfaces are restored using the same procedure. It is also possible to change surfaces of an object's individual planes. Figure 107 shows many of the features of surface manipulation just discussed.

Figure 108 shows a PICT image created for a production of *Hamlet*. The original image was derived from a virtual reality model created in Virtus WalkThrough 1.1.3 using the following procedures:

1. Go to *Front Design Window*. Set top extrusion marker on 0 and bottom marker at 6″ or 1′ below 0.

2. Go to *Top Design Window*. Using the *rectangle tool*, drag open a rectangle to desired size. (In the example shown, the size of the stage floor is 50′ wide and 50′ deep.) This stage should be so that it rests symmetrically on the 0 vertical line. This 0 line becomes the center line of the floor plan. The bottom edge of the rectangle should be placed on the horizontal 0 line. Placed on these coordinates makes it possible to return to this basic view by use of the *Center Home* command. This is most helpful when the stage has scrolled out of screen view. This command along with the *Center Observer* are quick ways of finding your bearings when working on a design. One of the common frustrations in working with almost all three-dimensional programs is the experience of being lost in the world of computer space; having a quick way to find one's way to a

Object Surfaces in Virtus WalkThrough 1.1.3

Steps in Building a Virtual Reality Stage Model

Building Stage Floors

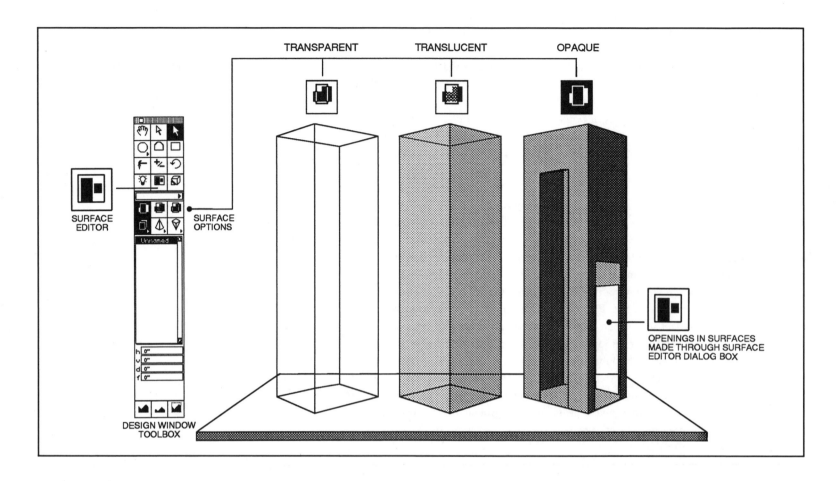

TRANSPARENT   TRANSLUCENT   OPAQUE

SURFACE
EDITOR

SURFACE
OPTIONS

OPENINGS IN SURFACES
MADE THROUGH SURFACE
EDITOR DIALOG BOX

DESIGN WINDOW
TOOLBOX

Fig. 107. Virtus WalkThrough surface options

Building Platforms on Stage Floors

starting point is a hallmark of a carefully thought-out three-dimensional application interface.

3.   Build forestage with the *N-sided tool*. Even though it is on the same level, the forestage is a separate part of the stage. This is because in WalkThough it is not presently possible to create nonconvex objects. Future versions will allow such objects to be constructed and have the ability to overlap objects into complex shapes.

Platforms, like that shown figure 108, are built using the same procedures as those to build stage floors. The steps are identical; only the extrusion markers must be reset to make sure a platform unit rests on the stage floor or—for platforms at heights above the stage floor—at the correct level height. If several platforms of the same dimensions are required, duplicates of the first can be made by selecting the platform and using the Duplicate command (Command-D is the keyboard equivalent). A WORD OF CAUTION: Large platforms on the actual stage are usually composed of smaller units; a single level may have a large number used in its construction. In Virtus models, it is better to construct the unit as a single entity rather than as a composite of those platforms needed in the real structure. On technical drawings these individual units must be indicated; it is not advisable to duplicate this practice in the modeling stage. The reason is twofold; first, it takes more

HAMLET ACT I SC. 1   DARWIN REID PAYNE 1993

time to draw and assemble the units; second, every unit made has six faces, all of which the program must calculate and keep in the file's memory. The fewer number of objects present in a model, the faster the computer can update changes to the model's views or changes.

Most real-scale scenery is constructed in discreet sections after which individual parts are assembled into composite forms. In the example shown, each pillar consists of two distinct forms: a short wide boxlike unit and a taller narrower form that sits on top.

Fig. 108. FreeHand 4.0 PICT model rendering

Constructing Scenic Units

Most building of computer models is done like buildings are in the real world: from the base up. In order for each new object to exist in its proper three-dimensional space, its base plane and top plane must be set in the *Front Design Window*. After the appropriate extrusion markers are set, the drawer returns to the *Top View Design Window* to determine its plan size. The steps used to construct the pillars shown in figure 108:

1. Go to *Front Design Window*. Set top extrusion marker on 1′ 6″ and bottom marker on 0.

2. Go to *Top Design Window*. Using the *rectangle tool*, drag a shape to make a 6′ 0″ square. This can be done visually either (1) by watching the size form as reflected in the top and side ruler bars or (2) by watching the *Dimensions Window* at the bottom, left side of the *Work Window*. As the shape is dragged, the size indications are displayed in the window's boxes. By holding down the *Shift key*, the shape is constrained to a square. These pillars can be constructed anywhere on the screen and then dragged onto the 6′ 0″ units for exact placement. If there are several scenic units the same size and shape, it is not necessary to build each individually; after one has been made, the units can be grouped and duplicated into any number desired. In the example shown, there are three identical units. After one unit is finished, grouped, and selected, the *Command-D* keystroke will produce the number needed; in this case, two duplications.

3. In the example shown, both the main platform and the pillars that set on top are at a 45° angle to the front edge of the stage. This can be accomplished by this procedure:

   a. Select an object (either single or grouped).
   b. Click onto the *rotate tool*.
   c. Hold over approximate center of object.
   d. Hold down mouse key and drag out.

It is often difficult to know precisely the angle that an object is rotated. But, as with creating precisely shaped sizes, it is possible to monitor the rotation angle in the same bottom-left Design Window. Also, holding down the *Shift key* will restrain the object's rotation to certain set angles, 45° being one of those.

Because different drawings often use basically similar objects, it makes sense to have some means for using these previously made forms in new drawings. Most object-oriented programs, therefore, give users options to save in libraries frequently used forms and images. It is customary for the makers of a program to include with its basic application ready-made library files for immediate use; these are, it should be expected, general in nature, since they are meant for a broad nonspecialized public. Most users need, however, unique kinds of images that company programmers cannot anticipate. Scenographers, for example, use many kinds of objects that even architects would not find useful. Individual libraries, therefore, must be constructed if specialized needs are to be served.

Libraries have different names in different programs; in Canvas 3.5, library files are called *macros* that are kept in *macro sets*. Macro sets become available through the *Macro Menu* in the top information bar where a *Load Set* option is visible when the menu is opened. This action takes you to an open dialog box, where various kinds of saved images

Using Libraries in Virtus WalkThrough 1.1.3

and objects are kept. It is also through the *Macro Menu* that selected items are placed into macro sets. Like objects can be placed in the same file (up to thirty-two items in Canvas 3.5) and given distinctive names such as *Furnishings, Platforms, Stairs*. When a new drawing is started, an appropriate macro file can be loaded. Although macro sets can be saved in a drawing along with other information, only one macro set at a time can be present in the *Macro Menu*. Libraries do not, unfortunately, work across applications; although it is possible to open a library, place an object from it into a drawing, copy the image (or export it in some programs), and then paste it into another compatible program. While files cannot be universally shuffled back and forth between different kinds of drawing, it is surprising just how many can be taken from one kind of program into another. Virtus WalkThrough 1.1.3 files, for instance, can be saved as PICT images and opened in Canvas 3.5 for further manipulation. Many of the images in this book were exported from application to application in order to take advantage of options not available in the native program.

WalkThrough 1.1.3 comes with a large number of library image files (and in this program are called *libraries*, not *macros*). Figure 109 shows a unit taken from a library named *Stairs* and introduced into a virtual reality model. This library assembles a number of time-consuming images ready for immediate use in a Virtus WalkThrough 1.1.3 drawing. Figure 109 also shows the steps needed to use existing libraries. These are:

1. Go to the *File Menu*. Select the *Library* option.

An open dialog box will appear showing the library files available. Double-click on the appropriate file—in this instance, *Stairs*.

2. When the *Library Window* opens, select the desired unit. (The appropriate stair will appear in the right window.)

3. Select *Copy* from the *Edit Menu* (or use the shortcut *Command-C*).

4. Return to the main *Design Window* of the drawing.

5. Select *Paste* from the *Edit Menu* (or use the shortcut *Command-V*).

6. The selected stair unit is now in the model and can be duplicated, rotated, or placed at different height levels as necessary.

Scenographers cannot totally rely on the libraries that come with a program, since they are only incidentally applicable to scenographic needs; personally constructed libraries must be made by individual scenographers. To place a new object into a library file follow these steps:

1. Draw the object using the *Design Window* views necessary. Be very accurate in the construction of individual pieces and especially careful in the grouping of pieces together.

2. After completing the object, group individual elements into a single unit if the object is composed of more than one. To place an item into the *Library*, select it and copy it to the *Clipboard*. It is through the *Clipboard* that Virtus WalkThrough 1.1.3 library items are installed or moved.)

3. Go to the *File Menu* of Virtus WalkThrough 1.1.3.

4. Select the *Library* option. When the *Library Window* appears, select an appropriate existing library or—alternately—create a new folder giving it an appropriated name: *Furniture, Platforms, Tree Forms*.

5. Paste the new library object into an existing or new library.

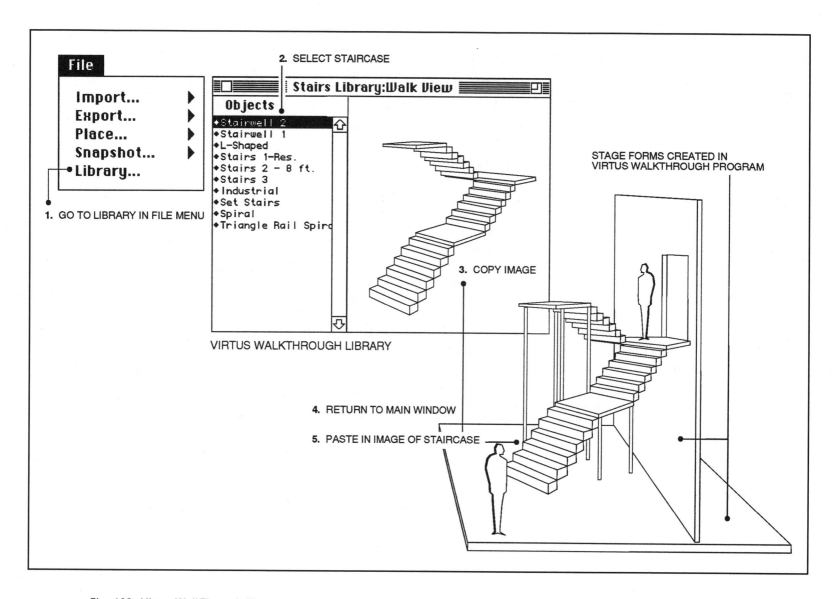

The following labels appear within the figure:

File

Import...
Export...
Place...
Snapshot...
• Library...

1. GO TO LIBRARY IN FILE MENU

2. SELECT STAIRCASE

Stairs Library:Walk View

Objects
◆Stairwell 2
◆Stairwell 1
◆L-Shaped
◆Stairs 1-Res.
◆Stairs 2 - 8 ft.
◆Stairs 3
◆Industrial
◆Set Stairs
◆Spiral
◆Triangle Rail Spiro

VIRTUS WALKTHROUGH LIBRARY

3. COPY IMAGE

STAGE FORMS CREATED IN
VIRTUS WALKTHROUGH PROGRAM

4. RETURN TO MAIN WINDOW

5. PASTE IN IMAGE OF STAIRCASE

Fig. 109. Virtus WalkThrough library screen

The library image always comes into the drawing at the height of the presently set vertical extrusion. The image—which is almost always a grouped compound one—can be pulled into place horizontally, while *Top View* or *Side Views*, or can be moved up or down in the *Front View*. The grouped image can also be rotated, slanted, or skewed. It is also possible to ungroup the compound object for its individual components or to group with other units into a new object. Figure 110 shows a step unit obtained from a Virtus WalkThrough 1.1.3 library in relationship to the two major views—*Front View* (front elevation) and *Top View* (floor plan)—used to control the placement of the stairs and to alter its shape or orientation in the model.

Building walls with thickness in Virtus WalkThrough 1.1.3 is unlike other three-dimensional programs in that basic walls of any Virtus WalkThrough 1.1.3 object are

Steps for Building Walls with Thickness

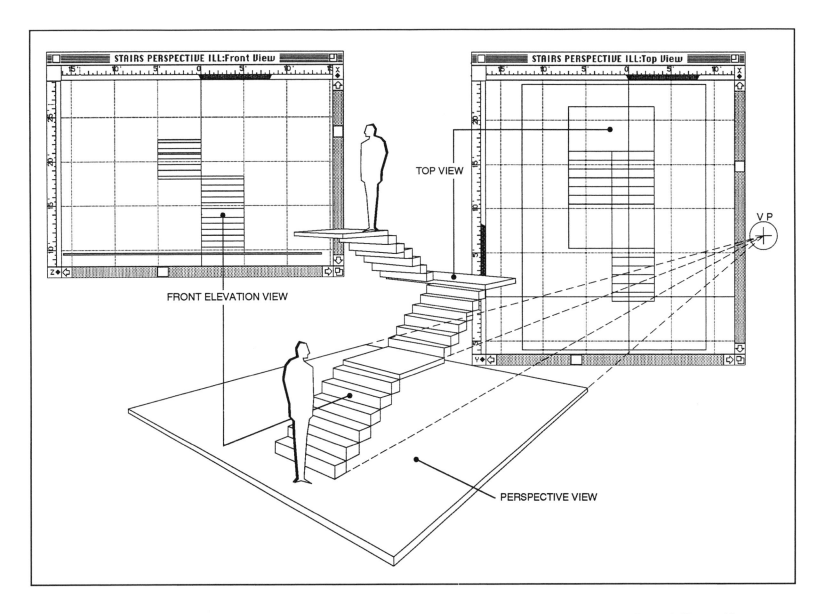

Fig. 110. Virtus WalkThrough library object

infinitely thin; they are, in fact, only mathematical descriptions of planes that define the computer's conception of space, not "walls" as we perceive them in the real world. All objects created with this program are really forms that define an amount of space whose bounding dimensions give the appearance of flat planes; they are mathematical abstractions that are represented on the computer screen as plane surfaces. Even seemingly curved objects are constructed of these flat plane surfaces that are arrayed to give an approximation of round or ovoid objects. The thickness of these plane surfaces cannot be increased. Simulated walls in models that require openings are accomplished by changing the attributes of the selected planes of the objects used. The way to create the components of these composite wall structures is not that different from creating any other group of

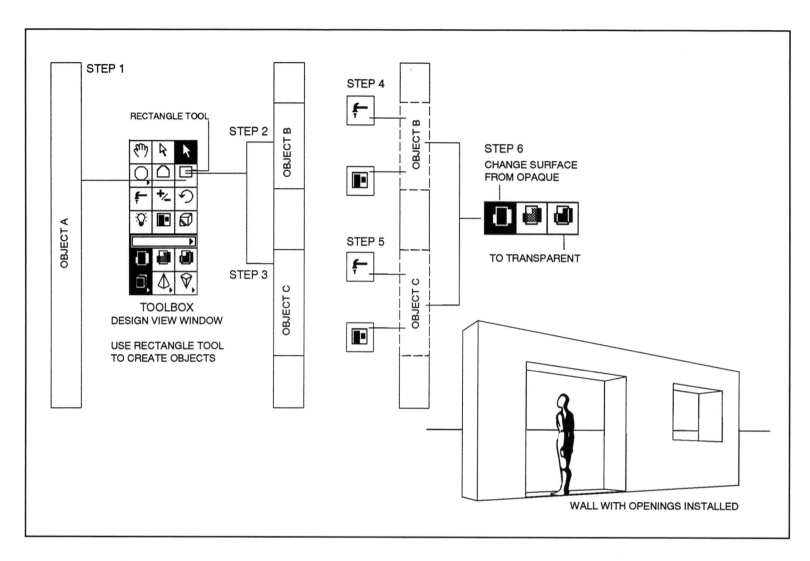

STEP 1

RECTANGLE TOOL

STEP 2

OBJECT B

STEP 3

OBJECT A

TOOLBOX
DESIGN VIEW WINDOW

USE RECTANGLE TOOL
TO CREATE OBJECTS

OBJECT C

STEP 4

OBJECT B

STEP 6
CHANGE SURFACE
FROM OPAQUE

STEP 5

OBJECT C

TO TRANSPARENT

WALL WITH OPENINGS INSTALLED

Fig. 111. Virtus WalkThrough wall thickness diagram

objects. To place openings in these walls, however, requires a particular sequence of steps. The openings in the walls so constructed are in reality smaller objects that have been placed within a larger host object. In addition, certain of the interfacing planes of these objects must be connected with the *connect surfaces tool* and then rendered transparent. The resulting walls are actually objects nested within other objects whose surfaces have been selectively modified with the *surface editor tool*. This sounds more technically complicated than it is; in actuality the creating of wall and window openings in these composite walls can be mastered in approximately twenty minutes of study. The exact technique for making walls with openings is better demonstrated, however, by graphic illustration than word description. The steps given below—and following the visual instructions shown in figure 111—should make the procedure more understandable. The techniques demonstrated in figure 111 are usable for other purposes in the making of complex Virtus WalkThrough 1.1.3 models.

Thin walls are the normal state of Virtus WalkThrough 1.1.3 objects. Walls with thickness must be created as one would with any other Virtus WalkThrough 1.1.3 structure. These are the steps necessary to create a wall with thickness:

1. Decide on the height of the wall and set the extrusion markers in the *Front Design Window* (front elevation). Go to the *Top Design Window* (plan) and with the *rectangular tool* drag open a wall object to the required size. This is designated as object A.

2. Decide on the height of window opening as well as how high from the stage-floor base the bottom of the window is to be. Now go back to the *Front Design Window* to set the extrusion markers that reflect the window's height. Go to the *Top Design Window* and draw object B as shown in figure 111, step 2. The outsides of the window should touch the insides of the wall. Making sure the *Snap to Grid* option is on is helpful when an exact interfacing of wall surfaces is necessary.

3. Decide on the height of the door open and where it is to be placed in relation to the stage floor. If the door is to be at stage floor level, set the *bottom extrusion marker* there. Now set the *top extrusion marker* at the desired door height. Perform the same steps on the door as the window. In the *WalkThrough Window* you will not at this time see the door and window within the wall unit.

In order to obtain the result shown in the perspective view of figure 111, additional steps are required. These are:

4. The window (object B) must have those plane surfaces that interface with those of the wall connected with the *connect surfaces tool*. This procedure must be performed on both sides of the window.

5. The door (object C) must in exactly the same way have the plane surfaces that interface with the wall connected with the *connect surfaces* tool. As with the window this procedure must be performed on both sides.

6. Each plane of each object interfacing with the wall must now be opened with the *surface editor tool* and changed to *transparent*. This is done by double-clicking on the *transparent* icon as shown in figure 111. The result of these operations will immediately be displayed in the *WalkThrough Window*. The bottom right of figure 111 shows a printed version of the foregoing steps.

Computer Modeling for Cinema and Television

To what extent is the education of scenographers trained for stage scenographic design usable in cinema and television? In particular, what skills and graphic practices are transferable? Most production designers for television and cinema are, in fact, trained as stage scenographers before taking employment with television stations or film companies, since many of the skills learned for stage design are directly applicable to the cinema and television. The early stages of all theatrical projects—stage, film, and television—are roughly similar. Starting with an idea or—more usually—a written text, directors, designers, and technicians attempt to define the parameters of the project in visual terms.

Fortunately for students today, computer technology and software make the process of learning many of the terms and principles of filmed media an easier task than it was even a decade ago. This section is a brief examination of some basic concepts and practices that students of scenography need to master for film media design.

In the early days of cinema production there was little difference between stage and film design. The reason for this is simple to understand: the only source of designers for the developing medium of film was the live theater. Early cinematic works betray all too clearly their stage origins. Differences between stage designs and filmed works diverged significantly, however, as cinema continued to evolve into more sophisticated forms and to explore new directions. During a relatively brief time, however, the film industry evolved principles and practices that allowed it to develop into a unique art form. Nor is the process done; the interplay of television and other technologies will continue into the foreseeable future. It is now understood, moreover, that a scenographer's work for the stage is significantly different from work done for filmed media. An excellent discussion of these differences is given in *Caligari's Cabinet and Other Grand Illusions*, by Léon Barsacq. This is a informative text that chronicles the history of design in the cinema from its inception until today. It is recommended to all students of scenography as one of the best introductions to the principles and practices of film media design. Here is a brief excerpt from the book:

> Over the last fifty years or so, the development of stage scenery has been determined by a truer understanding of stage perspective. Though still subject to all the fluctuations of literary or pictorial fashion, stage scenery has broken free from the grip of naturalism and seeks to suggest a place and an ambiance, rather than to provide the action with a precise frame. In fact, this role is the one traditionally assigned to scenery during the theater's great periods.
>
> The film set, however—originally simply canvas painted to create an illusion— has developed in the opposite direction, toward a certain form of realism, toward authenticity. This development can be explained by the existence of a film perspective very different from that of the theater. It is no longer the spectator who follows the action taking place on the stage in front of him, but the camera, which penetrates the intimate world of the characters and accents this or that facial expression, this or that aspect of an object, setting, or landscape. The film set serves as a frame not only for the movements of the actors, but also for those of the camera, which passes through doors, accompanies an actor going upstairs, takes the place of the actor by leaning over the banisters in order to show the entrance hall in a high-angle shot, and so on. (Léon Barsacq, *Caligari's Cabinet and other Grand Illusions* [New York: New York Graphic Society, 1976])

In the twenty-first century cinematic production images will no longer be recorded and stored on film but will be shot and edited on high-resolution videotape. Finished productions will be disseminated in several formats; videotape, laser disk, and compact disk will be common options, although one can expect holographic projections to be added to these in the not-too-distant future.

But just where are the cinema and television industries today; how far have the technological progresses expected in the next thirty years actually advanced?

The short answer is, the promises are far greater than the accomplishments. Still, slowly cinematic production continues to incorporate new technology into old techniques and practices. Perhaps the greatest proponent of electronic cinema production working in the last decade of the twentieth century is Francis Ford Coppola, who in 1992 released his version of *Dracula*. While it fared poorly with both critics and audiences, the film had one distinctive aspect to it that set it apart from every other major motion picture ever made: it was the first picture that employed electronically processed editing and postproduction work. That is, it was cut and sound-edited completely on videotape using computer technology developed by Coppola's own production company, American Zoetrope. Coppola, in fact, first used the term "electronic cinema" to differentiate his approach from those used today.

Computers have been used since the middle of the 1970s for creating special effects and for limited animation sequences. During the planning phases of a project, however, directors, designers, and cinematic technical personnel have continued to use practices now approaching the century mark. Inevitably, filmed projects of the future will heavily rely on computer technology during all aspects of production, not just for special effects sequences or isolated portions of a film. Production studios where live actors perform undoubtedly will continue to exist. But alongside these physical places there will also exist other kinds of studios: virtual reality studios created within the electronic world of the computer. It should also be expected that these two kinds of studios will increasingly interact, since there is essentially no impediment to the combination of filmed human beings and digitally captured or electronically created imagery. Even now it is possible to see on our relatively rudimentary computers the outlines of the new techniques that will undoubtedly become standard practice.

Although many graphics programs are usable for cinema and television design, only Virtus WalkThrough 1.1.3 gives scenographers ways of working on the computer screen that exactly match the operations of cinema and television cameras. Whereas this program's capabilities are more evident in architectural or scenographic design, they are especially applicable to cinema and television design needs.

It is possible to use the features of Virtus WalkThrough 1.1.3 in a three important ways: (1) creating storyboards during the conceptual stages of a film project, (2) finding camera positions to match planned views, and (3) plotting tracking sequences on exact floor plans. This last capability, which gives directors and technical staff an accurate opportunity to study the consequences of camera angles in terms of traffic patterns before actual equipment is placed, is one of the most important ways this program can be used.

One of the most significant areas where computers will play a major part is during the conceptual stages of a film project. It has long been standard practice to use scaled models for determining how a proposed location will appear. During the heyday of the large studios these models were painstakingly put together by resident artisans; often such models took a great deal of time to construct. These large studios have virtually disappeared and have been replaced by smaller independent groups that often are created for a single project. Production designers working for these kinds of organizations, work with stricter time lines and without the large technical staffs that were common at the major studios of sixty years ago. There has been a need—not fully realized as yet—for new methods of working that address the changing processes of film designing.

Figure 112 shows a diagrammatic view of a future cinematic studio operation. The

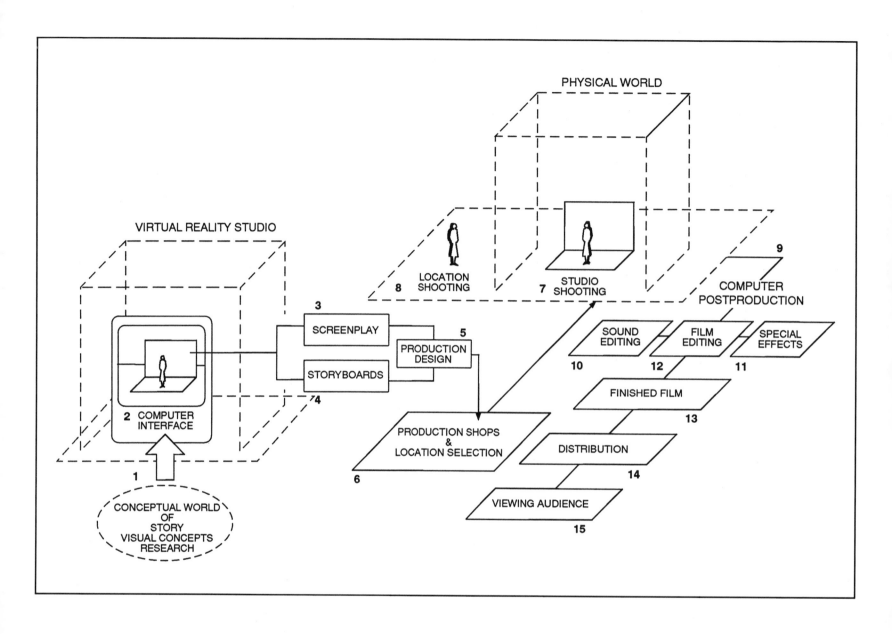

PHYSICAL WORLD

VIRTUAL REALITY STUDIO

3 SCREENPLAY

5 PRODUCTION DESIGN

STORYBOARDS

2 COMPUTER INTERFACE

4

1

CONCEPTUAL WORLD
OF
STORY
VISUAL CONCEPTS
RESEARCH

LOCATION SHOOTING **8**

STUDIO SHOOTING **7**

COMPUTER POSTPRODUCTION

9

SOUND EDITING

FILM EDITING

SPECIAL EFFECTS

10 **12** **11**

FINISHED FILM

13

PRODUCTION SHOPS
&
LOCATION SELECTION

6

DISTRIBUTION

14

VIEWING AUDIENCE

15

Fig. 112. Cinema studio functions diagram

most important feature of these studios is that—unlike the film studios of the twentieth century, which were entirely physical places—an important counterpart to the future physical studio will be an equally important virtual reality studio only accessible through the computer. And it will be in this electronic studio that much of a production will be forged: not only will screenplays be written and technical drawings made in the computer, but much of the camera positioning, tracking of shots, and selection of precise camera views will be decided in the computer's virtual studio before actual recording of the physical actors begins. Figures 113 and 114 show how computer virtual reality studios can be created that emulate their real-world counterparts.

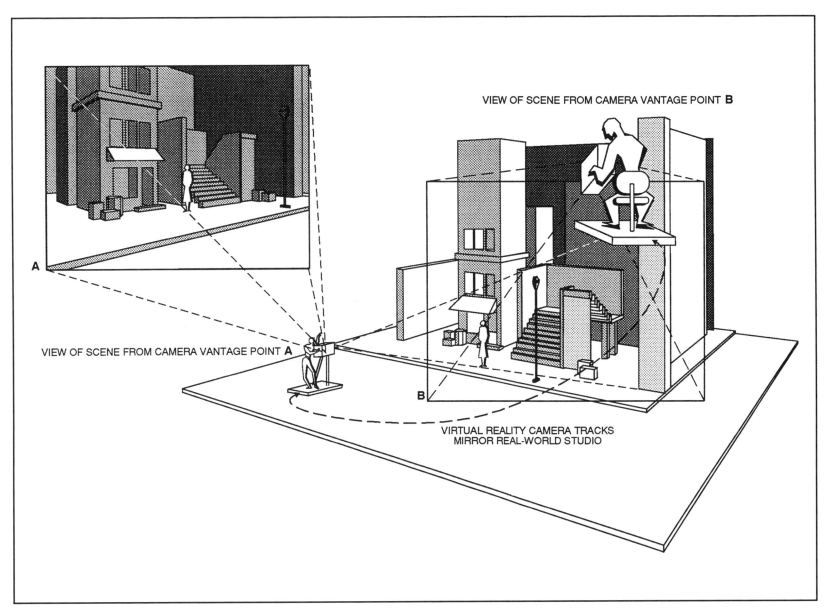

VIEW OF SCENE FROM CAMERA VANTAGE POINT **B**

VIEW OF SCENE FROM CAMERA VANTAGE POINT **A**

VIRTUAL REALITY CAMERA TRACKS
MIRROR REAL-WORLD STUDIO

Fig. 113. Diagram of virtual reality film studio

Storyboards

Since the rise of production teams in Hollywood during the 1930s almost all motion pictures since then have made it a practice to outline the continuity of the proposed film in a series of rough sketches. *Storyboards* have become an important part of filmic project planning. In *Shot by Shot*, Steven D. Katz says this:

Maurice Zuberano, one of the most respected production illustrators and art directors in the trade, has called the storyboard the "diary of the film." If so, it is a diary written about future events. What he was getting at, though, is that the

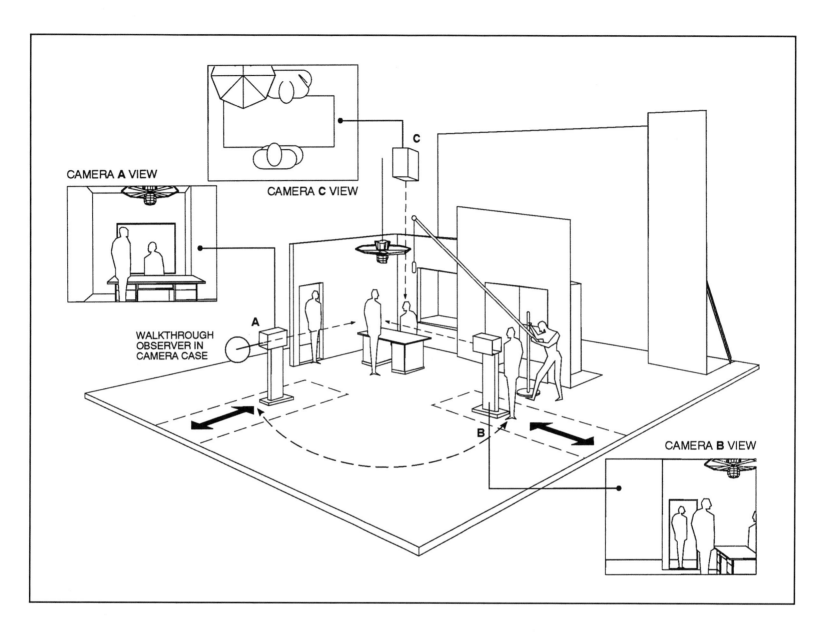

CAMERA **A** VIEW

CAMERA **C** VIEW

WALKTHROUGH
OBSERVER IN
CAMERA CASE

A

B

C

CAMERA **B** VIEW

Fig. 114. Diagram of virtual reality television studio

storyboard is the private record of the visualization process, one of the reasons so few of them survive intact. Frequently, it is the evidence that the look of a film was the work of someone other than the director. For directors without a strong visual sense the storyboard illustrator is the shot-flow designer, essential to the structuring, staging and composition of shots and sequences.

Of course, there are directors who are as visually sophisticated as any member of the production staff, and in the narrative sense, perhaps more so. Hitchcock, who is probably associated with storyboarding more than any other director, used elaborate boards to refine his vision and control the filmmaking process, ensuring that his original intention was translated to the screen. (Steven Katz, *Film Directing Cinematic Motion: A Workshop for Staging Scenes* [Studio City, CA, Wiese Productions, 1992])

By the early part of the 1990s, computer and digital technology had thoroughly and radically altered film practice at the highest levels of production. Curiously enough, however, during the earliest stages of a project's planning, artists responsible for basic visualization of the project still relied on skills and techniques perfected in the late renaissance using materials basically unchanged for hundreds of years before then. Storyboard artists, art directors, and production designers working on the largest and most sophisticated projects continued to use traditional art school procedures to record the visual thoughts that accompany these early mapping out sessions.

The reason for this lag between the high end of production and the conceptual stages of a production's planning is not difficult to find. The enabling technology that makes the effects of a *Star Wars* trilogy possible is too costly for casual use and not intuitively workable for graphic artists trained to the use of hand and eye without mechanical impedance between thought and action. While powerful results could be obtained using available computer technology, only highly trained operators—not necessarily highly trained graphic artists—could tread the way through complicated, time-consuming, often enigmatic procedures. Electronic tools were simply not available that operated with the speed and usability of the pen or pencil relying on the judgment of the trained eye.

With the advent of Virtus WalkThrough 1.1.3, creating an electronic "diary" of a production becomes a reasonable alternative to traditional methods. Using the features of this program requires several kinds of investment; some time is required to learn the program—although the program directly mirrors the way those trained in drafting work—and any workstation represents a considerable initial expense. There are a number of good reasons, however, for creative filmmakers and allied artists to use electronic programs for storyboards like that displayed in figure 115; here are a few of them:

Accuracy of proposed view. With manual drawing of each storyboard cel, the artist seeks only to give a general idea of how images fill the screen; true perspective views are not a priority and are rarely considered. Using Virtus WalkThrough 1.1.3, however, accurate perspective views of all basic forms that would be in the camera view make the process of exact visualization not only possible but unavoidable. It is possible, in fact, to determine at the conceptual stage of a project exact camera distances, tracking paths, camera angles, aspect ratios of the screen format—Television, Academy, European Wide Screen, US Wide Screen, Anamorphic—as well as focal length of lens and film-type specifications. (Although not part of the storyboard process, Virtus WalkThrough 1.1.3 includes in the same menu with the film aspect ratios still-picture ratios. These are 35-mm horizontal, 35-mm vertical, 2.25″ square, 4″ by 5″ horizontal, and 4″ by 5″ vertical.) Figure 116 shows how aspect ratios, focal length of lens, and film specification are set.

Ability to alter individual image cels. After a camera shot is introduced into a cel of an electronic storyboard, the basic view can be altered either electronically or used as a printed outline to be enhanced manually. Again, accuracy of intention is much more possible at an earlier stage of the planning process than with manual storyboard procedures.

Ability to alter storyboard arrangements. Making changes in a project during the

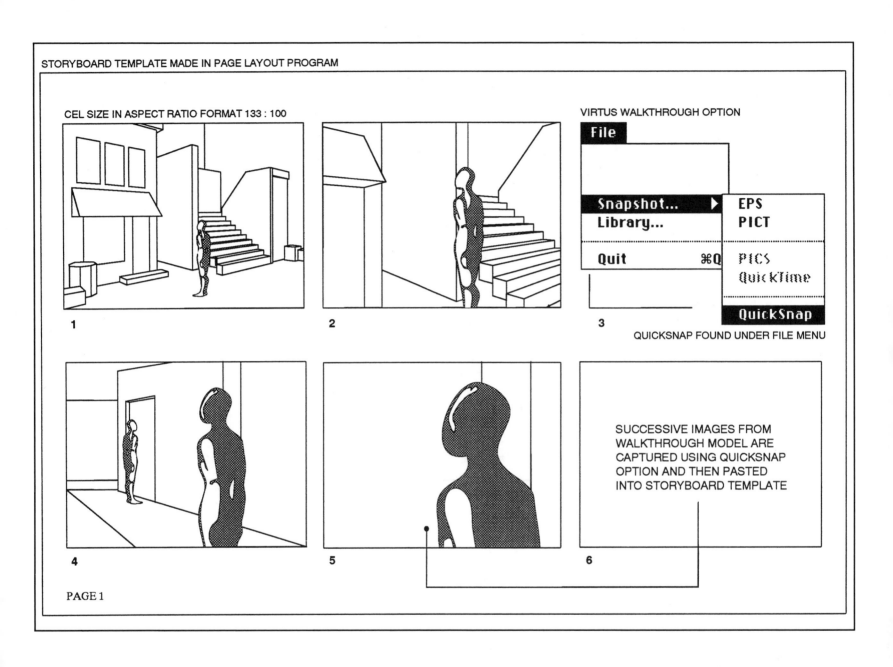

STORYBOARD TEMPLATE MADE IN PAGE LAYOUT PROGRAM

CEL SIZE IN ASPECT RATIO FORMAT 133 : 100

VIRTUS WALKTHROUGH OPTION

File

Snapshot... ▶   EPS

Library...   PICT

Quit   ⌘Q   PICS

     QuickTime

     QuickSnap

QUICKSNAP FOUND UNDER FILE MENU

1

2

3

SUCCESSIVE IMAGES FROM WALKTHROUGH MODEL ARE CAPTURED USING QUICKSNAP OPTION AND THEN PASTED INTO STORYBOARD TEMPLATE

4

5

6

PAGE 1

Fig. 115. Filmed media storyboards

storyboard phase of a project often avoids costly delays in production schedules. Arrangement of proposed camera shots is much easier to do electronically than manually changing the images on traditional storyboards. Using a computer storyboard also allows planners of a project—such as the director who may or may not have graphic skills—to rearrange individual shots without aid of a storyboard artist. The process of editing the film during the conceptual stages of a project becomes feasible for those with only minimum graphic training. The ability to freely manipulate the flow of images is an invaluable tool for

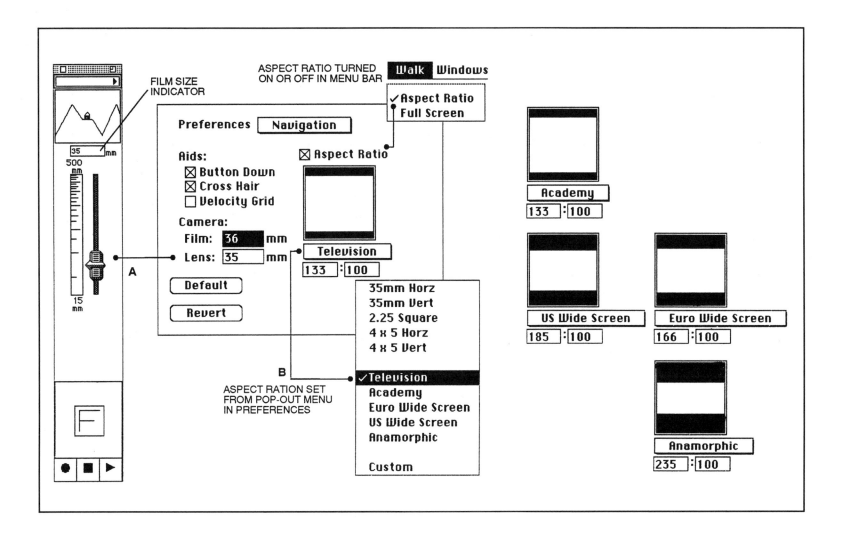

Fig. 116. Diagram of aspect ratio options for filmed media

directors and coworkers and encourages experimentation, a vital element in all creative processes. Through the use of a page layout program such as Publish It Easy 3.0 or PageMaker 5.0, master pages of storyboard cels can be created that will automatically number individual pages or renumber them as alterations are made.

Virtus WalkThrough 1.1.3 is most valuable to the scenographer when the program is used as a communication tool; that is, when all concerned with a production share ideas and concerns in the same place at the same time. There are occasions, however, when coworkers are separated in time and place. Then scenographers need methods to share images with these other workers. Ideally all those working on the project would have access to identical computer workstations with Virtus WalkThrough 1.1.3 installed; this situation rarely exists. How, then, do scenographers transmit computer models to distant viewers? A number of ways are possible. These are:

Exporting Model Views

1. As a file on the scenographer's own workstation.
2. As a floppy-disk copy viewed on another computer that has Virtus WalkThrough 1.1.3 installed.
3. As hard copies printed directly from Virtus WalkThrough 1.1.3 or as hard copies printed from PICT files created in compatible graphics programs.
4. As Walk Paths. These are short animations recorded within the model's resident Virtus WalkThrough 1.1.3 file. Recording these animations is accomplished while in the Walk View Window.
5. As animation files created in applications capable of rendering Walk Paths into animations. Some of these programs are PACO Producer, PICS, and QuickTime. While there are other animation programs that process Virtus WalkThrough 1.1.3 files—Adobe Premiere and MacroMind Director for instance—these are not as suitable to scenographic work.
6. As Virtus Voyager files. These files are created in a separate program that augments the basic capabilities of Virtus WalkThrough 1.1.3.

PICT Images from Virtus WalkThrough 1.1.3 Model Views

PICT images of any view in the Virtus WalkThrough 1.1.3 model can be made by using the *Snapshot* option found under the *File Menu*. When the *Snapshot* option is held down by the mouse, a pop-out menu displays several ways the image can be captured. The active window determines the kind of image recorded: if the *Top View Design Window* is active, then an image of the floor plan as a line drawing is captured; if the *WalkThrough Window* is active, a three-dimensional view is captured using the *Snapshot-PICT* option in the *File Menu*. The *PICT* option captures images in TeachText file formats. This is a general format that can be opened in many other graphics programs that read PICT files. Under System 7, TeachText files can be opened in the TeachText application for viewing only; they cannot, however, be edited in any way.

Virtus WalkThrough 1.1.3 PICT files are not bit-mapped images. They are, rather, complex objects composed of the individual planes of models visible in the *WalkThrough Window* when the *Snapshot* image is made. When PICT images are imported into other programs—such as Canvas 3.5 or FreeHand 4.0—the individual planes of these models can be altered in ways consistent with the program: that is, lines can be changed in weight; surfaces can be colored, textured, or shaded; individual polygons can be reshaped or grouped into larger units. One should realize, however, that these models can have numerous parts that the computer must individually calculate. It is not uncommon for a PICT model image to have, in fact, hundreds of separate planes, each of which must be redrawn on the screen when the composite image is moved or when the screen is scrolled. Large numbers of polygon planes invariably tax a computer's memory; the printing out of PICT files with many polygon planes slows printing times considerably. One of peculiarities of PICT files made from Virtus WalkThrough 1.1.3 models is that the *Snapshot-PICT* option captures along with all visible planes some hidden ones as well. These can be identified and removed if the draw program to which the PICT model is brought is capable of viewing objects as wire-frame images. (In the wire-frame mode, only object outlines are displayed; all planes are displayed as lines, including those hidden in the normal view.) In Canvas 3.5 this mode is accessed through the *Command-1* keystroke; to return to the regular image view, the *Command-2* keystroke is used. In FreeHand 4.0, the wire-frame mode is accessed by the *Command-K* keystroke; the same keystroke combination returns the image to the normal view.

Before examining some of the ways basic models are used in making scenographic sketches, it is necessary to list the various options scenographers have to display PICT model images. These are:

1. *Directly on the computer screen*. Files can be individually opened for study. In some programs—such as Canvas 3.5—a series of renderings can be put into a single file known as a slide show. The *Slides* command in the *Layout Menu* gives a dialog box that controls the setup of this feature.

2. *As PICT images created with Virtus WalkThrough 1.1.3's Snapshot option*. These images are opened—and modified, if desired—with other graphics programs that support PICT files. These modified images are viewed on the scenographer's own computer or copied onto floppy disks to be viewed on computers that have identical graphics programs installed.

3. *As 35-mm slides*. Any graphics file can be made into a 35-mm slide. This is only possible, however, by sending the files to organizations—such as commercial service bureaus—that have slide-making printers. These printers are too expensive for most users. Even commercially made slides range in cost from $5 to $25 per unit. (These costs will inevitably drop and the number of service bureaus increase.) It is possible to send graphic files by modem to service bureaus if slide-making facilities are not available locally.

4. *As hardcopy printouts*. Although any scenographic drawing or model can be viewed in color on color monitors, it is more likely that most scenographers will print their work as black-and-white line drawings and gray-scale shaded images rather than as color prints. The reason for this choice is the present high cost of most color printing. Although color printing will inevitably become less costly, for the foreseeable future it remains an option most scenographers cannot regularly afford. For the development stages of scenographic design—and that is, of course, our main focus in this book—black and white printing is probably the better choice, since form and spatial arrangement are made sharper when color options are reduced.

Figure 105 shows a Virtus WalkThrough 1.1.3 image in two printing modes. Figure 105*A* has graduated fills available in FreeHand 4.0; figure 105*B* was saved as a .5 point line graphic with white fills. These models (not shown) can also be printed as wire-frame images; that is, as a transparent skeletal structures consisting of black frames without fills. Printing models in the wire-frame mode is not recommended, since these views provide little indication as to position or the placement of planes; the three-dimensional form of a wire-frame model becomes lost in the maze of overlapping lines.

Figure 117 shows a scenographic sketch not derived from a model PICT image but from separate scanned images assembled into a single file and modified with specialized functions of the host program. For instance, gradient fills—such as those shown in both figure 117 and figure 118—are made possible using programs like FreeHand 4.0. Figure 118 shows how proportions of black to white in a shade are determined and how direction of the gradient's shading is set. Figure 119 also demonstrates how the gradients in FreeHand 4.0 are used to make PICT line drawings into more solid-looking images. The

IMAGE FROM BIT MAP LIBRARY

IMAGE MADE WITH OFOTO PROGRAM

A N T I G O N E   DARWIN REID PAYNE

Fig. 117. Scenographic sketch using FreeHand 4.0

method shown in figure 119 is perhaps the fastest way to turn Virtus WalkThrough PICT model images from black-and-white line drawings into shaded images. The steps required are these:

1. Open a new FreeHand 4.0 file.
2. Open a PICT WalkThrough model image.
3. Select all planes by using the *Command-A* keystroke.
4. Use the *Command-E* keystroke to bring up the *Fill and Line* dialog box.

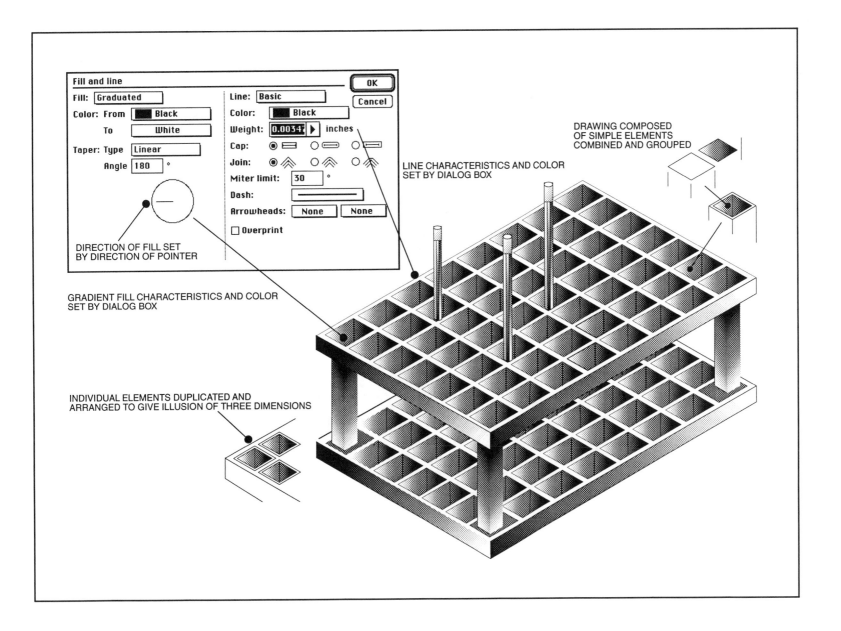

Fill and line

Fill: Graduated
Color: From ▨ Black
To □ White
Taper: Type Linear
Angle 180 °

Line: Basic
Color: ▨ Black
Weight: 0.0034 ▶ inches
Cap: ◉ ▭ ○ ▭ ○ ▭
Join: ◉ ⋀ ○ ⋀ ○ ⋀
Miter limit: 30 °
Dash: ▭
Arrowheads: None None
□ Overprint

OK
Cancel

DIRECTION OF FILL SET
BY DIRECTION OF POINTER

GRADIENT FILL CHARACTERISTICS AND COLOR
SET BY DIALOG BOX

LINE CHARACTERISTICS AND COLOR
SET BY DIALOG BOX

DRAWING COMPOSED
OF SIMPLE ELEMENTS
COMBINED AND GROUPED

INDIVIDUAL ELEMENTS DUPLICATED AND
ARRANGED TO GIVE ILLUSION OF THREE DIMENSIONS

Fig. 118. High-resolution graphic construction

5. Set the options desired; that is, determine what colors or shades of gray are to be blended into what other colors or shades of gray. (Figures 118 and 119 show how dialog boxes are set.)

6. Set the line widths desired before closing main dialog box.

7. Return to main screen. Gradient shading will appear.

These steps produce images where all planes are shaded in the same direction and to the same angle degree. It is possible, however, to reset both the angle and direction of shading

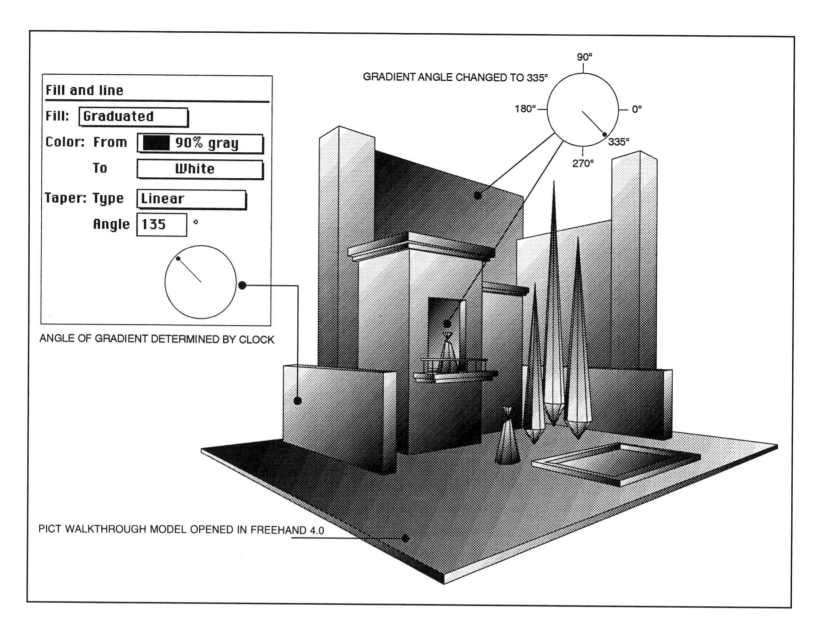

Fill and line

Fill: [Graduated]

Color: From [██ 90% gray]

To [White]

Taper: Type [Linear]

Angle [135] °

ANGLE OF GRADIENT DETERMINED BY CLOCK

GRADIENT ANGLE CHANGED TO 335°

90°

180° — — 0°

335°

270°

PICT WALKTHROUGH MODEL OPENED IN FREEHAND 4.0

Fig. 119. High-resolution graphic construction

for individually selected planes by using the degree clock shown at the top-right side of figure 119.

WalkThrough PICT models not only can be given gradient shadings like those shown in figures 105, 117, 118, and 119 but can also be used in tandem with other kinds of PICT images. For example, the setting shown in figure 108 combines the a Virtus WalkThrough 1.1.3 PICT model image from figure 99 with a scanned PICT bit-mapped image placed behind the pillars. In effect, the basic pillar arrangement shown in figure 99 becomes an electronic equivalent of the unit setting one constructs on actual theater stages. These computer unit settings only work interactively, however, with object-oriented programs, not in paint applications. One of the distinct advantages of computer scenographic modelmaking is that PICT images of any model view can be saved, exported to other graphics programs and changed into scenographic renderings like those shown in figures 93 and 108 above. In the following section—"Rendering Scenographic PICT Images on the Computer"—similar kinds of unit-setting design possibilities are shown for bit-mapped programs.

A WORD OF CAUTION: When the original Virtus WalkThrough PICT is opened, all planes have come into the new file document in two separate parts: an object outline and a fill without outlines. This situation is not apparent to the naked eye. When the planes are given gradient fills and line weights are set, both parts are acted upon equally. In effect, the drawing now consists of a double set of planes, making the file twice as big as it needs to be. While these redundant planes can be left, doing so makes printing take considerably longer and file sizes much larger. It is prudent, therefore, to remove these unneeded objects. This is done simply by selecting each plane in order and hitting the *Backspace* key.

5. *As perspective guidelines for manual scenographic renderings*. Many scenographers, during the past thirty years, have all but abandoned scenographic rendering, citing the indisputable fact that physical models more closely represent the true nature of settings on the stage. These scenographers further hold that scenographic renderings actually impede communication between them and others by creating false impressions as to what is possible to achieve in the theater. To a great extent, however, computer-generated model views assure that two-dimensional images derived from them represent photographically correct images of what is possible. These views, moreover, have two distinct advantages over the traditionally made perspective drawings: (1) they are more accurate than manually constructed perspective images, and (2) they provide scenographers with outline views of settings usable as guidelines for renderings. For these two reasons, I am including here a suggestion as to how electronic drawing is used for manual scenographic renderings using traditional tools and materials—illustration boards, watercolor papers, inks, watercolors, pastels—shown in figure 120. Figure 121 demonstrates the basic steps necessary for making and using perspective guidelines from model views. These are:

1. Create model in Virtus WalkThrough 1.1.3.
2. Save selected view as PICT.
3. Open draw program where outline is to be modified and scaled. Canvas 3.5 is a suitable program for this work, but other object-oriented programs can be used.
4. Edit image if necessary. Group all objects into single unit.
5. Scale to desired size.
6. Print drawing. The new scale of the outline may take more than one printer page. If this is the case, the image will be cut into parts; these must be aligned and glued together. Rubber cement is the recommended material for this work.
7. The outline drawing must now be made into a type of transfer paper. This is done by rubbing soft pastel or chalk onto the back of the assembled outline.

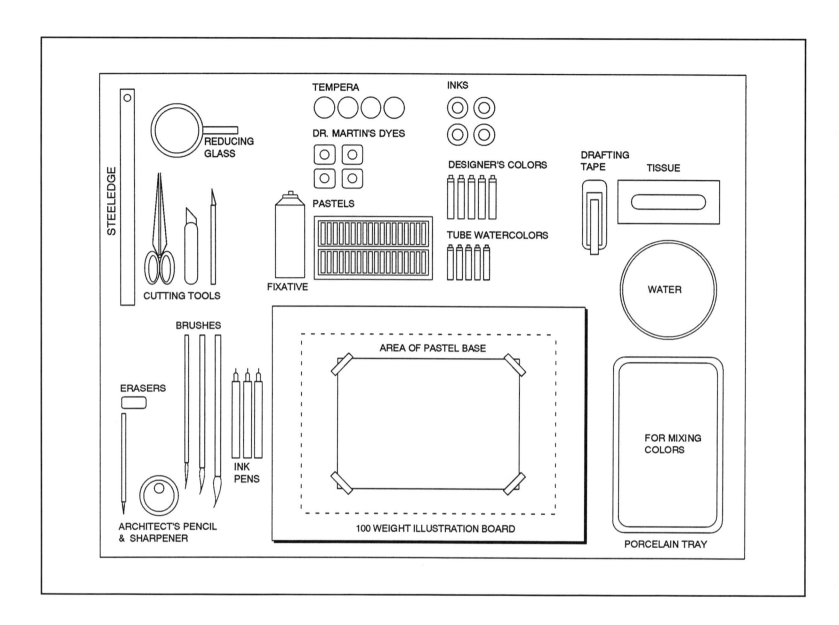

TEMPERA

INKS

DR. MARTIN'S DYES

DESIGNER'S COLORS

DRAFTING TAPE

TISSUE

REDUCING GLASS

STEELEDGE

PASTELS

TUBE WATERCOLORS

WATER

FIXATIVE

CUTTING TOOLS

BRUSHES

AREA OF PASTEL BASE

ERASERS

INK PENS

FOR MIXING COLORS

ARCHITECT'S PENCIL & SHARPENER

100 WEIGHT ILLUSTRATION BOARD

PORCELAIN TRAY

Fig. 120. Diagram of materials for scenographic renderings

8. The perspective outline can now be traced onto the board or paper of the rendering.
9. It is advisable to ink all transfer lines before rendering material is applied.

Rendering Scenographic PICT Images on the Computer

Creating atmospheric drawings is not the intention of most modeling programs. In the development stage of a scenographic design, clearly defined images are more valuable to scenographers—and those who work with them—than is the creation of shadowy scenes; clear representation of forms, as well as their placement on the stage, is crucial

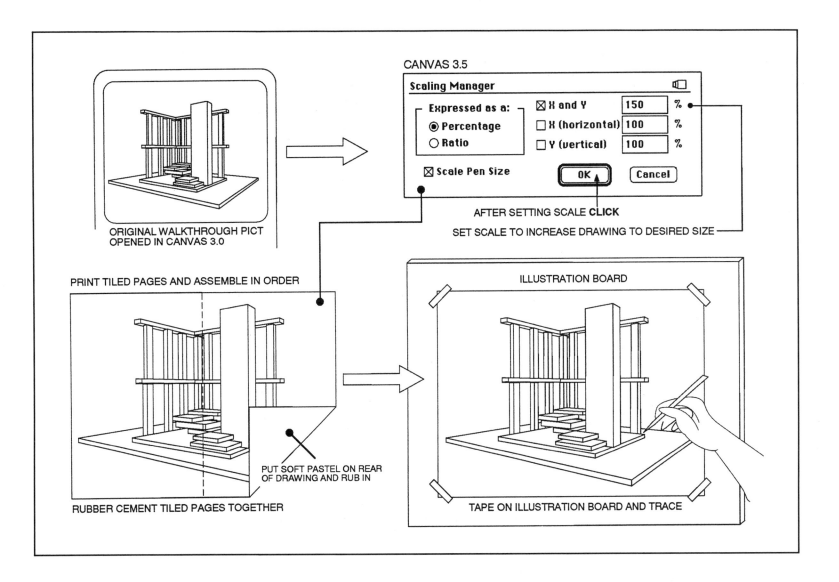

CANVAS 3.5

Scaling Manager

Expressed as a:
- ● Percentage
- ○ Ratio

☒ Scale Pen Size

☒ X and Y   150   %
☐ X (horizontal) 100   %
☐ Y (vertical)   100   %

[OK]   [Cancel]

AFTER SETTING SCALE **CLICK**

SET SCALE TO INCREASE DRAWING TO DESIRED SIZE

ORIGINAL WALKTHROUGH PICT
OPENED IN CANVAS 3.0

PRINT TILED PAGES AND ASSEMBLE IN ORDER

PUT SOFT PASTEL ON REAR
OF DRAWING AND RUB IN

RUBBER CEMENT TILED PAGES TOGETHER

ILLUSTRATION BOARD

TAPE ON ILLUSTRATION BOARD AND TRACE

to scenographic design. Nevertheless, an ability to modify computer models into more "artistic" drawings has psychological values for both director and scenographer that go beyond mere informational content.

Although images of model views can be printed immediately from Virtus WalkThrough 1.1.3 without use of the Snapshot feature in the File Menu, it is necessary to invoke this option if further graphic manipulation of the image is desired. Once having captured and saved the selected view as a PICT image, it is then possible to use it in any graphics program that supports PICT files. How the image is manipulated depends on the program's basic nature; the PICT file can be opened in both draw programs and paint programs. In Canvas 3.5, for instance, when the file opens, images exist as grouped objects. When ungrouped, individual planes can be separated and have outlines changed

Fig. 121. Diagram for scenographic sketches from PICT images

Fig. 122. Scenographic model rendered as
object-oriented graphics

in color and weight and fills altered in color, pattern, or gradient shading. In programs such as Adobe Photoshop 2.5 or Painter 2.0, the entire image can be altered to resemble other mediums: watercolor, pen and ink, chalk or charcoal. Other transformations are made using resident, or third-party, *filters*. Filters change the basic nature of images to which they are applied. In other words, if the watercolor filter from Gallery Effects—an application specifically designed for use within other programs such as Adobe Photoshop 2.5 and Painter 2.0—is applied to a Virtus WalkThrough 1.1.3 PICT imported into Adobe

Photoshop 2.5, the image changes from hard-edged objects like those seen in figure 122 to the more fluidlike images seen in figures 29, 124, and 125. Adobe Photoshop 2.5 images can be further manipulated in other paint programs such as Painter 2.0. Figure 123 shows a photograph of a scenographic model by Gordon Craig for a production of *Hamlet*. Scanned into Adobe PhotoShop 2.5, this basic image can be modified into any number of entirely new drawings. In effect, Craig's static photograph becomes a changeable unit setting. In figure 124 the basic setting has been altered using third-party filters—called *plug-in tools*—to give light and shadow (accomplished using the program's resident capabilities to lighten and darken selected areas), to make the floor plane reflective like polished marble (accomplished with the Andromeda Software *Reflection* filter), to texture the walls and floor (accomplished with the Aldus Gallery Effects *Watercolor* filter), and to sharpen the entire image (accomplished with the HSC Software Kai's Power Tools *Sharpen Intensity* filter). Figure 125 is another image consisting of elements from the original model scan (fig. 123) and altered by the same filters used for figure 124. Figure 126 shows a filter from Aldus Gallery Effects Volume 2 collection of filters. Called the *Texturizer*, this filter applies various kinds of textures to existing graphic images such as those shown in figure 127. The bottom image of figure 127 demonstrates how single textures—in this case the brick texture—can be scaled to differing sizes (see bottom-left window in figure 126 for the scaling devices used to effect these changes).

Another way to use PICT outlines from Virtus WalkThrough 1.1.3 models is to print them on transparent stock used for making overhead graphics. These transparencies

Fig. 123. Adobe PhotoShop 2.5 scan of Gordon Craig model: Hamlet

Fig. 124. Adobe PhotoShop 2.5 variation of Gordon Craig model: Hamlet

Animating Computer Scenographic Models

provide valuable guidelines for full-scale scenic-painting projects; using this method the traditional griding of painter's elevations is avoided. Figure 128 shows how this process would be implemented in the scenic painting studio.

There is little doubt that if technology progresses at the rate it has from 1980 until the year 2000, designers will have capabilities undreamed of now. Among those capabilities will be desktop computer animation. In the near future, however, it is neither prudent nor cost-effective to attempt high-end animation on the computers most of us now have. There are few programs that make it possible for scenographers to make elaborate animated files.

Although interactive modelmaking usually presupposes that the scenographer and the director are in the same place at the same time looking at the same screen, there are instances when planning must be carried on in different locations. Many scenographers design for more than one theater, only occasionally meeting with the director or technical staff. What, then, if the scenographer wishes to send files to a director or to a technical

Fig. 125. Adobe PhotoShop 2.5 variation of
Gordon Craig model: Hamlet

director in another place? In most cases, the recipient of the files could not open them, simply because the creating program would not be installed. Scenographers can, of course, send printed views of the model; but what if there is a need for those distant workers to explore the model as scenographers do in their own studios? One would assume the only way to accomplish this would be to ship a copy of the main application to those prospective users. This is not recommended for several reasons not the least being that distributing software in this way is unethical as well as illegal. There is, however, an alternative option; Virtus Corporation has provided a means for scenographers to provide legal copies of three-dimensional models that can be fully explored.

Virtus Voyager is an inexpensive program developed by Virtus that works in tandem with Virtus WalkThrough 1.1.3. Using this program scenographers can send animated models of their designs to those without the original program. Figure 129 shows the main screen of a Voyager file. Also included in figure 129 are the basic ways Voyager files are constructed. At the bottom the various operational features of the program are shown.

Virtus Voyager is a module of Virtus WalkThrough 1.1.3 by which three-dimensional

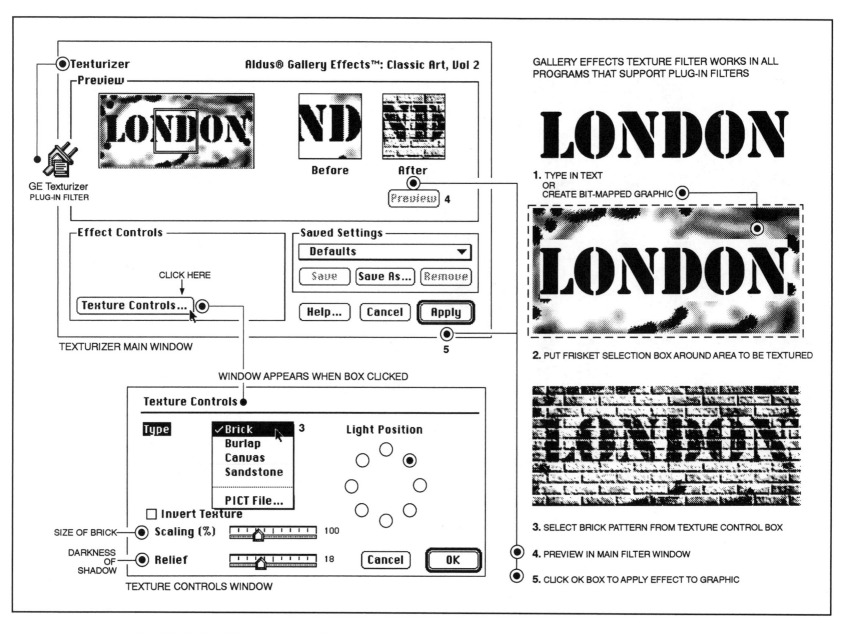

Fig. 126. Gallery Effects Texturizer filter

models originally created in the main program can be used by nonowners of Virtus WalkThrough 1.1.3. With Voyager, scenographers can convert any model into independent self-playing documents easily accessible to any Macintosh users who understand its basic graphical interface.

The main features of a Voyager models are:

1. The capability to explore a scenographer's model without having the Virtus WalkThrough 1.1.3 application installed

GALLERY EFFECTS CANVAS FILTER

GALLERY EFFECTS BURLAP FILTER

GALLERY EFFECTS SANDSTONE FILTER

BRICK TEXTURE SCALED TO VARIOUS SIZES

Fig. 127. Gallery Effects alternate Texturizer images

2. The capability to view with the click of a button preselected views of a model (front view, top view, right-side view, left-side view, back view, etc.)
3. The capability to watch prerecorded Virtus WalkThrough 1.1.3 animations of model views either as a single viewing or as a continuous loop of viewings

Even for those not familiar with computer graphics interfaces, navigation of a Voyager model is simple. Using the Novice option, the ability to move in and around a model

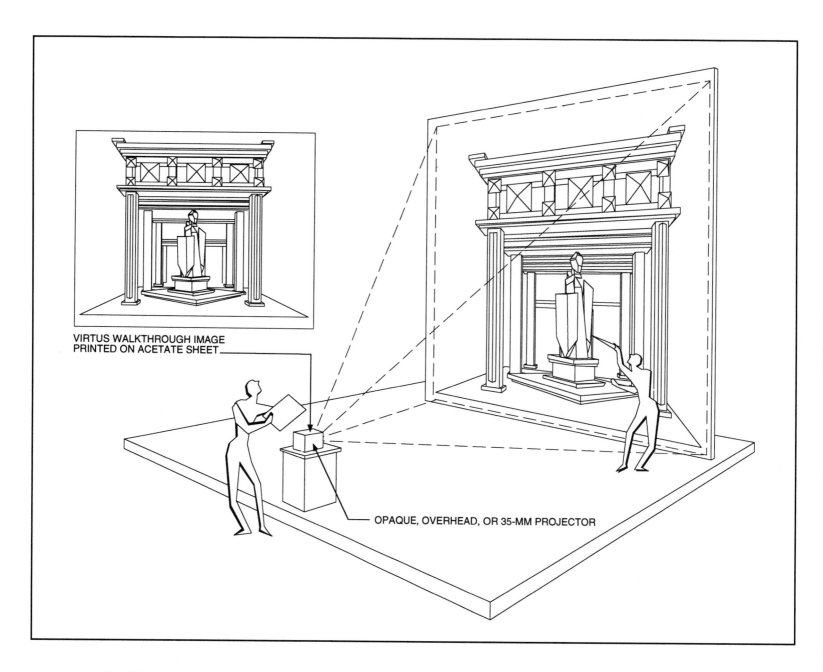

VIRTUS WALKTHROUGH IMAGE
PRINTED ON ACETATE SHEET

OPAQUE, OVERHEAD, OR 35-MM PROJECTOR

Fig. 128. Overhead projection of Virtus WalkThrough images

can be mastered in approximately ten to twenty minutes. Changes cannot be made with these documents; their main function is to demonstrate what has been created up to a certain point. Having such a model, however, allows the director or technical director to see exactly what the scenographer proposes. Phone conferences no longer are a matter of describing images in words; directors are able to make specific recommendations from what they see on their own screens.

While Virtus Corporation recommends a Macintosh II series computer with a color

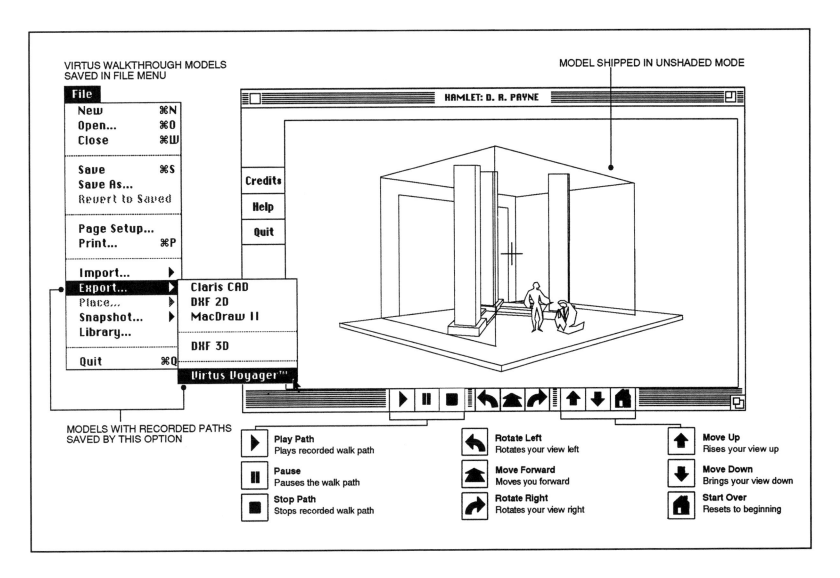

Fig. 129. Diagram of Virtus Voyager options

monitor as the basic workstation configuration, this feature runs on lesser models. It is important to note that while Voyager will run on a Mac Plus, a Mac Classic, or a Mac SE, a PICT cannot be viewed in Virtus Voyager unless the publication was created on a Mac Plus, Mac Classic, or Mac SE.

TECHNICAL NOTE: There are two kinds of PICT formats: PICT1 and PICT2. The difference is PICT2 allows color. Virtus Voyager checks which PICT reader you have and will not allow a PICT2 to be viewed with a PICT1 viewer. (If this is attempted, nothing happens.) Mac Plus, Mac Classic, and Mac SE machines have a PICT1 viewer unless the ROM has been updated.

Since Virtus Voyager publishes personal designs, the program is structured so that it is not possible for anyone to alter a publication. For this reason, it is important to create publications with all attributes carefully considered; the display attributes must be part of the model before publishing. One must, therefore, know what kind of Macintosh the prospective viewer(s) has. A model created with 24-bit color on your Quadra, for instance, may not look as good or walk as fast on a viewer's 1-bit Mac Classic.

As the author of a Virtus Voyager model, the scenographer has total responsibility for what viewers experience. Though Virtus Voyager uses the same navigation techniques as Virtus WalkThrough 1.1.3, many viewers will not be familiar with Virtus WalkThrough 1.1.3 technique. For this reason, Virtus includes with their basic Virtus Voyager package a number of small instruction cards to be sent along with the disk containing the model.

Three crucial questions makers of Virtus Voyager model file must consider are:

1. Is there information *about* the model that needs to be included in the publication? Virtus Voyager allows an informational PICT to be included as an integral part of the Voyager publication that a viewer can access. The scenographer can, using this feature, send a copy of the floor plan created in a technical-drawing program. This allows the viewer to know precise sizes of areas and dimensions of items not easily discernible from the model.

2. Is a recorded walk path to be included for the viewer(s) to play back? A recorded walk path can be included if there is something specific the viewer needs to see within the model. Other attributes of the publication to consider are shading, aspect ratio, lens focal length, fill and frame, cross hair, velocity grid, and basically anything in the Preferences/Navigation and Preferences/Rendering dialog. None of these are accessible to the viewer of a Voyager model; the scenographer has total control as to what the viewer sees. Preferences selected by the scenographer cannot be altered once the Virtus Voyager publication is exported. For most scenographic work at the level suggested here, Voyager models should be created as black-and-white graphics that have black frames to object edges and white fills. Although colored or shaded are seductive when viewed on computer screens, both have major drawbacks: shaded and/or colored models are considerably slower than unshaded black and white graphics.

3. Does the scenographer want the viewer to copy images of the model as hard copy? If the scenographer wants to keep such materials proprietary, then ability to print can be deleted from the model file sent.

Conclusion

As a scenographer's career progresses, it is natural that working environments change. Most of these changes are incremental; some, however, profoundly alter basic approaches and ways of working, some require radical changes in modes of thought. As adventurous as Leonardo and Michelangelo were in their visions, the technological basis of their practice changed little during their lifetimes. Nor have materials and techniques changed all that much for most graphic artists. Unfortunately for those who employ computers in their work, the technology that gives new possibilities changes radically in ever-increasingly smaller time spans. Most changes in an artist's working patterns, of course, result from expanding amounts of work they do. But it is also likely that scenographers using computers in their work will only become more skilled by employing newer programs and devices as they are made available. Although it is not possible to speculate completely on what will be available in ten years, the advice and guidance given here should remain current during the changes that inevitably will occur.

I have attempted to show that a computer's phenomenal speed and reliability can blind us to the ways these machines aid in exploring possibilities of vision and thinking central to creative work. I hope, therefore, that those who have read thus far not only begin to see the outlines of the possible present but also gain some guidelines for the probable future. Although it is possible to create an entire production on the computer, it is not likely that many scenographers will use computers exclusively in the preparation of their designs. Most of us, I continue to believe, still place value on those manual drawing and painting skills we have learned over time. The direct pen or brush stroke leaves personal marks that through trial and error we have come to trust; few graphic designers willingly forego that intimate interaction of hand and mind using the physical tools and materials. Seductive as the precision and speed of computer graphics are, they do not replace those feelings of accomplishment experienced when renderings turn out well, or finished models surprise us with new insights into the design on which we have been working.

As we finish this book some questions remain. Do scenographers who master computer graphics complete projects more quickly and more effectively than those who do not? Do computers really save us time? Are computer-generated productions inherently better conceived and executed than those relying on practices of the past? These questions certainly cannot be answered easily; maybe they cannot be answered ever. If the "saving of time"—a dubious concept at best—is the prime concern of the scenographer, it is likely that the answer will be *no*. Most artistic works, in fact, have built into them internal clocks that often begin before the actual physical beginnings of a project, and that run until after the project is done. To determine whether time is saved or ill-spent depends more on the effectiveness of the outcome than it does with arbitrary assignments of time allocations to steps in the process. Hypothetical stopwatches by which steps in the design process are measured do not exist, and if they did exist they would not really apply to the scenographer's art. The real question we should ask is how will computers aid the scenographer to demonstrate creative thought in communicative form, and—more important still—to what extent are resulting images modifiable as necessity demands. The real value of computers lies not in their ability to save hypothetical quantities of time but in the possible ways they allow design information to be effectively incorporated into scenographic design projects.

In less than a decade a new millennium starts. The rapid pace of technological advance during the last quarter of the twentieth century has been such that it is difficult to speculate with any degree of assurance what the future might bring. Certainly we can expect computers to have more programs incorporating artificial intelligence factors. How this area of research will develop in the future—and to what extent those developments will influence the scenographer's art—is a subject that must be continually monitored for any substantive information. If predictions of the past give any indication of what that future holds, it might be best to heed Dylan Thomas's advice that "the business of posterity is to look after itself."

It has been necessary to include in this book a great deal of technical data; many of the terms used, procedures described, and recommendations made have been specific in nature, sometimes bewildering in explanation. It has been my constant intention, however, that those new to this emerging area of graphics be given some useful directions and helpful advice. Since I am of that somewhat suspect class known as "rational humanists," it has been my underlying purpose to keep a human face on the subject at hand. I have attempted, for this main reason, to show how the vast powers of the computer are still guided by the considered instruction of the human mind, showing also, whenever possible, that the computer at its most useful is an extension of that mind. I have tried to demonstrate that the graphics we generate by computer are in direct contact with the motions of the imagination; this is something easy to state but difficult to demonstrate. Imagination is, of course, only another aspect of intelligence; the two cannot be independently considered.

As we end this book on the possibilities of our new way of working, let us take a moment to consider what we *cannot* expect for the foreseeable future. Some few others, besides myself, have voiced apprehension concerning the often mindless claims for a computer's abilities to outstrip the human intellect in performance and output. In terms of mathematical calculation, no human can match the speed or accuracy of the computer; but we should never confuse its often admirable powers with the fabrication of ideas. This area is likely to remain our sole preserve for some time to come, if not forever.

One of those important voices who have spoken out on the differences between the computer and the human mind is the noted historian-writer Theodore Roszak. In *The Cult of Information*—a book highly recommended to all who work with computers—he makes these wise observations:

> We can self-consciously connect idea with idea, comparing and contrasting as we go, plotting out the course of a deductive sequence. But when we try to get behind the ideas to grasp the elusive interplay of experience, memory, insight that bubbles up into consciousness as a whole though, we are apt to come away from the effort dizzy and confounded—as if we had tried to read a message that was traveling past us at blinding speed. Thinking up ideas is so spontaneous—one might almost say so *instinctive*—an action, that it defies capture and analysis. We cannot slow the mind down sufficiently to see the thing happening step by step. Picking our thoughts apart at this primitive, preconscious level is rather like one of those deliberately baffling exercises the Zen Buddhist masters use to dazzle the mind so that it may experience the unutterable void. When it comes to understanding where the mind gets its idea, perhaps the best we can do is to say, with Descartes, "An angel told me." But then is there any need to go farther than this? Mentality is the gift of our human nature. We may use it, enjoy it, extend and elaborate it without being able to explain it. (Theodore Roszak, *The Cult of Information: The Folklore of Computers and the True Art of Thinking* [New York: Pantheon, 1987])

It lies within this area, then—the *use, extension,* and *elaboration* of our mind-generated ideas—that the computer will best serve us; its attendant speed and accuracy, its precision of image generation, are welcome to our practice but should not be our entire concern.

Will the computer play a significant role in theater design of tomorrow? Undoubtedly it will. In what ways will it change the work or role of the scenographer? I cannot tell. What do I say to those—and there are many—who do not share my fascination with a technology that is admittedly in its primal stages of development? I have few answers except those presented in this book and to emulate that incurable state of curiosity Thomas Jefferson proclaimed two hundred years ago when he said, *"I am captivated more by dreams of the future than by the history of the past."*

Index

Index

Abbott, George, 137

Abbott Systems, 127

ACTA, 55

ADB trackball, 32

Adobe Illustrator 5.0, 38, 49, 51, 90, 121, 152

Adobe PhotoShop 2.5, 45–47, 50, 69, 71, 172, 186, 216–17

Adobe Premiere, 208

Adobe Streamline 3.0, 51–52, 78, 85, 152

Adobe Systems, 8

Albarn, Keith, 101

Alberti, Leon Baptista, 1

Aldus FreeHand 4.0, 34, 38, 45, 49, 51, 64, 69, 82–83, 90, 98, 116, 120–21, 123, 208–10

Aldus Gallery Effects filters, 217

Aldus IntelliDraw 2.0, 123, 131–33, 135–36

Aldus SuperPaint, 48–49

Alsoft, 127

American Zoetrope, 210

Andromeda Software filter, 217

Animation, and modelmaking, 218–24. *See also* Modelmaking

Anti-aliasing, 45

Appia, Adolphe, 157–58

Apple ADB mouse, 30–32

Apple Adjustable Keyboard, 30, 60

AppleCD 300i CD-ROM drive, 25

Apple Extended Keyboard, 30

Apple ImageWriter II, 29

Apple LaserWriter Pro 600, 29

Apple Macintosh One-Page (Portrait) Display, 25

Apple OneScanner Flatbed, 35

Apple StyleWriter, 29

Apple 13″ RGB Monitor, 27

Art of Human-Computer Interface, The, 39

Art of Measurement, The (Dürer), 1

Art of Teaching, The (Highet), 67

Atkinson, William, 16–17

AutoCad, 47. *See also* CAD programs

Automatic alignment, 122–24

Axonometric drawings, 109, 167

Barsacq, Léon, 200

Bates, Roger D., 53

Batista, Ricardo, 53

Bézier curves, 86, 91, 113–14, 123, 128

Bézier object, 90

Bird's eye views, 176–77

Bit map image. *See* Bit-mapped graphics

Bit-mapped graphics, 37, 41, 44–47, 49, 51–52, 69–70, 72, 74–75, 77–79, 81–85, 94–95, 98, 103, 111–12, 120–21, 152, 161, 208, 212–13

Bit-mapped images. *See* Bit-mapped graphics

Bounding lines, 111–12

Brook, Peter, 5, 187

Brooks, Frederick, 62

Brunelleschi, Filippo, 1

CAD (computer-aided design) programs, 23,

25, 27, 33, 37, 40–41, 44, 47–48, 50–51, 53, 92, 112, 116, 118, 120, 122–23, 127, 132–33, 138, 152, 155–56, 158, 171. *See also* AutoCad; Claris CAD 2.0; Mini-Cad+ 5.0; PowerDraw

CADD (computer-aided design and drafting) programs, 37, 115

CAE (computer-aided engineering) programs, 115

Calc+, 127

Calculator, 127

Calculator+, 127

Caligari's Cabinet and Other Grand Illusions (Barsacq), 200

CAM programs, 33

Canvas 3.5, 41–43, 45, 47–50, 64–65, 69–70, 75, 78, 80, 90, 95, 98, 100, 104, 110, 112, 116–17, 120–23, 125–26, 128–34, 138–40, 142–45, 147–48, 155, 165, 194, 208–9, 213, 215

Capture 4.0, 51

Carpal tunnel syndrome (CTS), 60

CDEVs, 53

CD-ROM drive, 24–25

Ceres Software, 103

Cinema and television: computer graphics and, 199–214

Claris CAD 2.0, 47, 54, 122, 138, 156. *See also* CAD programs

Clip art, 74, 81, 85–89, 98, 104

Cocteau, Jean, 174–75

Collier, David, 55–57

Collier's Rules for Desktop Design and Typography (Collier), 55–56

Color control, 27

Computer Dictionary (Microsoft Press), 8, 126

Computer drawing board, 38, 96–156

Computer files, management of, 57

Computer floor plans, 110; advantages of, 137, 139, 142–44; development of, 137–41; generic templates for, 139–40; and interactive drawing, 144; and multilayers, 138–43, 146, 148; and pivoted scenic units, 147–48; and revolving stages, 146, 47; and scenic changes, 144–48; and scenic unit rotation, 144–45; theater-specific templates for, 140–41

Computer graphics: advantages of, 63–70, 98–101, 103, 119–20, 124–25, 137, 139, 142–44, 150–51, 155–56, 162, 168, 171–72, 225–27; for building shapes and forms, 127–33; concept and technology of, xii; and guidelines for scenographers, 45; and lighting plots, 153–56; limits of, 63–70; and lines, 111–12, 119–20; and the role of play, 65–69; and speed, 4–5, 88; technical requirements and concepts of, 9–61; and theater work, 43–44

Computer graphics programs, 37–61; basic considerations of, 40–42; capabilities of 97–133; selection of, 41; types of 37, 40–41; and upgrades, 47–48

Computer graphics workstation, 12, 17–22; ergonomics of, 60; tools of 20–21. *See also* Computer studio; Electronic studios

Computer lighting plots, 110, 153–56

Computer monitors, 25–28; and color, 27–28

Computers: and the artist's conceptual process, 4, 72–73; and auxiliary hardware, 27–29; as basic hardware and equipment in a scenographic workstation, 22–37; and calculation, 127–28; and design experimentation, xii; as design research tools, 62–95; graphic programs for, 47–53; and health considerations, 58–61; and input devices, 29–36; keyboards for, 29–30; Macintosh recommendations for, 23–25; memory of, 25, 57, 64; and modelmaking, xii, 51, 149–50, 157–224; mythology of 4–5, 63; and new model purchases, 22–23; and printers, 29

Computer safety. *See* Ergonomics; Health considerations

Computer scenographics: automatic alignment with, 122–24; definition of, xi; precision of, 119–20; size and accuracy of, 124–25, 151–52; steps for mastery, 42

Computer studio, xii, 9–10. *See also* Computer graphics workstation; Electronic studios

Computer turntables, and revolving stages, 146–47

Control points, 113, 131, 133, 136

Covington, Michael, 19
Craig, Gordon, 157–58, 217
Cult of Information, The (Roszak), 227
Cumulative trauma disorders, 60

DataDesk SwitchBoard Keyboard, 30
Defaults, 134–35
Defragmenting, 53, 126–27
Deneba Systems, Inc., 41
Descartes, Réne, 162, 227
Detail construction drawings, 10, 167
Diagram (Albarn), 101
Diagrammatic drawings, 101–3
Dictionary of Computer Terms (Downing
    and Covington), 18–19
Digital drawing tablets. *See* Graphics tablets
Dingbats, 90. *See also* Text ornaments
DiskDup+ 2.21, 53–54
Disk Express II, 127
Dorn, Dennis, 111
Dot-matrix printers, 29
Downing, Douglas, 19
Dracula, 201
Drafting for the Theatre (Dorn and Shanda),
    111
Drawing Systems (Dubery and Willats), 2–3
Draw objects. *See* Object-oriented graphics
Dubery, Fred, 2–3
Dudley, William, 6–7
Dürer, Albrecht, 1–2

Electronic cinema, 201
Electronic materials, management of, 55–58
Electronic models, 149–50. *See also* Mod-
    elmaking
Electronic studios, 9–10, 57
Elements of Friendly Software Design, The
    (Heckel), 39
Elevations, as working drawings, 108–10,
    167
Empty Space, The (Brook), 5, 187
Engineered Software, 49
EPS, 90
Ergonomics, 10, 60–61
Excursions to the Far Side of the Mind
    (Rheingold), 62–63
Exhibition models, 167–68, 172. *See also*
    Modelmaking

Experimental models, 167–68. *See also* Mod-
    elmaking
Extended keyboards, 30, 52, 126. *See also*
    Keyboard
Extensions Manager 1.5, 53

Faired curve, 117
File formats, 46, 64, 77–78, 94–95, 156
Floor plans. *See* Computer floor plans
Fractal Design Painter 2.0, 45, 50, 69, 186
Fractal Design Sketcher 1.0, 50
Full-scale drawing: methods of, for graphic
    outlines, 152–53
Furniture libraries: value of, 141–42; cre-
    ation of, 142–43. *See also* Library files

Graphics tablets, 30, 32–34, 63, 69, 81, 96,
    120–21

Hairline, 111
Hard-disk drives, 28–29
Harwin, Dr. Ronald, 59
Haynes, Colin, 59
Health considerations, and using computers,
    58–61. *See also* Ergonomics
Healthy Computing (Harwin and Haynes),
    59
Heckel, Paul, 39
Hierarchial File System (HFS), 57–58
Highet, Gilbert, 67
High-resolution graphics. *See* High-resolu-
    tion images
High-resolution images, 51, 63, 70–71, 78,
    84–87, 98, 152. *See also* PICT images
HSC Software Kai's Power Tools, 217

Ideas on Design (Mayle), 74
Illustrative drawings, 101, 103
Images with Impact 1, 87
Images with Impact 2, 87
Infini-D, 160, 187–88
INITs, 53, 55
Ink-jet printers, 29, 172
Input devices, 29–36, 63, 81, 112–13. *See
    also* Keyboard; Mouse; Pointing devices;
    Scanner; Stylus; Trackball
Inspiration 4.0, 55, 103

Interactive drawing, 144. *See also* Interactive scenographics

Interactive scenographics, 7; image files for, 71–95; and modelmaking, 165–69, 177–78, 212

Interface, 42, 44, 156, 182–83, 188, 221; definition of, 38, 40; and Macintosh metaphorical graphics, 40, 122, 125; study of, 69

Interface: The Door to Computer Worlds, 122

Interior fills, 111–12

Isometric drawings, 49, 159

Johnston, Rob, 54

Jones, Robert Edmund, 154

Judson, Horace Freeland, 166–67

Katz, Steven D., 203

Keyboard, 29–30, 52, 60, 126

Key Caps, 53

Keyfinder, 53

"King's seat, the," as viewpoint, 172

Koh-I-Noor, 13

Laser printers, 29, 93, 172

Library files, 78–89, 95, 101, 126, 139–44, 150, 155–56, 186, 194–96

Lighting Energy Management for Offices and Office Buildings (National Lighting Bureau), 17

Line weights, 120–21

Little Mouse ADB, 32

Mac Classic, 27, 223–24

Mac Classic II, 50

MacDraw, 48

Macintosh, LC II, 23

Macintosh SE, 23, 25–26, 223

Macintosh SE/30, 23, 27

Macintosh IIci, xiii, 23–25

Macintosh IIfx, 24

Macintosh IIsi, xiii, 23–25

Macmillan Visual Dictionary, The, 89

MacPaint, 48, 51–52

Mac Plus, 223

Macro files, 79–81, 126, 140–42, 155, 194–95

MacroMind Director, 208

Macros. *See* Macro files

MacUser, 27, 35, 47, 59

MacWorld, 27, 59

Manual graphics studio, 10–13

Mayle, Peter, 74

Memory interleaving, 24

Michelangelo, 225

Mielziner, Jo, 154

Mind maps, 55

MiniCad+ 5.0, 42–43, 47, 49–50, 98, 114, 116, 122–23, 127, 129–30, 138, 142, 152, 155–56, 158–60, 170–71, 188. *See also* CAD programs

Mirror object, 132–33, 136

Mirror VS300, 75–76

Modelmaking, xii, 11, 16, 51, 149–50, 157–224; animation of 218–24; for cinema and television, 199–214; and virtual reality, 191–99; and Virtus WalkThrough 1.1.3, 187–99

Monitors. *See* Computer monitors

Motorola 68040 processors, 22

Mouse, 29–33, 60

Multigon Manager, 128–29

Multilayered drawings, 79, 98–99, 104, 138–43, 146, 148, 155–56, 183

National Lighting Bureau, 17

Norton Utilities, 52–53, 127

Object-fill patterns. *See* Interior fills

Object-oriented graphics, 37, 41, 44–47, 49, 70, 78, 81–86, 90, 111–12, 115, 120–21, 123, 128–31, 142, 152, 161, 194, 212–13

Object-oriented image. *See* Object-oriented graphics

Oblique cabinet projections, 37, 159

Oblique cavalier projections, 37, 159

Ofoto, 35, 77–78, 84

One-dimensional lines, 108

OneScanner, 77

Organizational programs, 55

Orthogonal projections, 37, 159

PACO Producers, 208

PageMaker 5.0, 207

Painter 2.0, 216

Peliz, David L., 47
Perspective drawings, 37, 49, 101, 103–5, 165, 167
Perspectograph, 1
PICS, 208
PICT files, 50, 84, 90, 103, 208–9, 215
PICT format, 46, 75, 77
PICT images, 16, 45, 50–52, 64, 70–71, 79, 95, 150, 186, 191, 195, 208–27. *See also* High-resolution images
Pivoting scenic units, 147–48
Pixel, 8, 29, 112, 123, 148; definition of, 46, 120; and scaling, 94; and scanning, 75–76
Pixel patterns, 84
Plans, as working drawings, 108–9
Plotter, 125–26, 171–72
Point, 106, 120
Pointing devices, 29
Polygons, 112–13, 117, 123, 127, 208
PostScript, 8, 29, 51, 121
PowerBook, 50
PowerDraw 5.0, 42–43, 45, 47, 49–50, 98, 114, 116–18, 123, 129–32, 138, 142, 152, 155–56, 158. *See also* CAD programs
Power users, 125–27; definition of, 126; steps to becoming, 126, strategies of, 126–27
Printers, 29, 67, 93, 172
Public-domain programs, 53–55. *See also* Shareware
Publish It Easy 3.0, 207

Quadra 800, 24–25, 50
Quadra 700, 24, 50
Quadra 650, 24, 50
Quadra 610, 24, 50
Quantum drives, 289
QuickKeys, 30, 40, 52, 69, 126, 132, 146–47
QuickTime, 208
Qume Crystalprint Publisher, 29

Radial object, 132–33, 136
Radius Monochrome Two-Page Display, 26–27
Rand, Paul 66–67

Rapidograph 3165 Technical Pens, 13
Real-world coordinate systems, 162
Repetitive stress injuries (RSI), 60
Rheingold, Howard, 62–63
Roszak, Theodore, 227
Ruskin, 69

Scaled models, 164–69, 174–75, 201. *See also* Modelmaking
Scaling images, 67, 92–95, 97, 115, 130, 142, 217
Scanner, 29, 32, 34–36, 96; as an image duplicator, 73–74, 88, 150; as a research archiver, 74; steps in using, 75–78; as a template maker, 74, types of, 74–75
Scanner resolution, 74–75, 77, 84
Scenic units: and computer pivoting, 147–48; and moving by arrow keys, 148
Scenographer, xi; and the advantages of using computer graphics, 63–70, 98–101, 103, 119–20, 124–25, 137, 139, 142–44, 150–51, 155–56, 162, 168, 171–72, 225–27; and computers, xi–xii; 5–7; and drawing on the computer, 115; and guidelines for using computer graphics, 4, 45; and learning computer graphics, 42–44, 95; and manual skills, 4, 158; and organizational programs, 55; as power users, 125–27; reasons for using CAD programs, 38, 64, 92; and tools, 3–4; and types of drawings, 101–11; and using database capabilities, 127, 155; and working environment, 9–10, 60–61
Scenographic, xi
Scenographic drawing, categories of, 44
Scenographic projects, phases of, 149
Scenographic renderings: manual production of, 213–14; computer-generated, 214–25
Scenographics: and cinema and television, 199–214; computer programs for, 42–43, 47–53; computer studio for, 9–10; defined, xi
Scenographic sketches, failures of, 157–58
Scenographic studio: and computer upgrading, 36–37; equipment and materials of, 13–16; and expendable materials, 16; lighting of, 16–17, 60; and permanent tools,

13–16; physical layout of, 10–13; requirement for, 10–60

Scenographic workstation: basic hardware and equipment of, 22–37; and computers, 22–37; requirements for, 22–60

Scenography, xi; and graphics programs, 37–61; recommended computer programs for, 47–53; requirements of, xi

Search for Solutions, The (Judson), 166–67

Shanda, Mark, 111

Shot by Shot (Katz), 203–5

Shareware, 53, 127. *See also* Public-domain programs

SIMM, 24

Simonson, Lee, 96–98

Softdisk Publishing, 53

Solitude (Storr), 68–69

Specular, 187

Speed Disk, 127

Stage Is Set, The (Simonson), 96–97

Star Manager, 129

Storr, Anthony, 69

Storyboard, 201, 203–7

Strata Vision 3D, 160

Styli, 45, 63, 69, 120–21. *See also* Graphics tablets; Stylus

Stylus, 32–33, 69, 83, 112, 121. *See also* Graphics tablets; Styli

SuperPaint 3.5, 69–70, 78, 81. *See also* Bit-mapped graphics

Sutherland, Ivan E., 161

Swivel 3-D, 188

Swivel 3-D Professional, 160, 188

Symantec Corporation, 53

Symmetrigon tool, 49, 132

System 7.0, 57, 139

Tear-off menus, 126

Technical specification drawings, 37, 42, 49, 95, 98, 111, 150

Templates, xii, 74, 78, 81, 101, 104, 133–56, 165; basis for, 135; definition of, 135; for furniture libraries, 141–44; of generic floor plans, 139–40, 145–46; and interactive drawing, 144; and multilayered floor plans, 138–43, 146, 148, 155, 157; as stationary files, 188; of theater-specific

floor plans, 130–41, 146; use of 136–37, 148, 155–56

Text ornaments: conversion steps for, 90–91; definition of, 90; as an image resource, 90–92

Three-dimensional computer graphics, 161–99

Three-dimensional object creation, 37, 42, 49, 67, 87, 104, 108, 120, 157–59, 209, 219–20. *See also* Three-dimensional computer graphics

3G Graphics, Inc., 87

3165 Jewel Pen, 13

Thunderscan, 34–35, 74

TIFF, 51–52

Tiling, 124–25

Tilles, Denise, 6

Trackball, 29–33

Two-dimensional design, 29, 42, 67, 104, 108, 157–59, 161, 166, 172, 213

Two-dimensional images. *See* Two-dimensional design

Typist, 75

Uccello, Paolo, 103–4

University of North Carolina Virtual Reality Research Center, 62

Vasari, Giorgio, 103–4

Vectors, 47, 112, 120

Vertex point. *See* Vertices

Vertices, 113, 123, 133

Vinci, Leonardo da, 1–2, 106–8, 225

Virtual reality, xii, 16, 51, 103, 161, 177–79, 182, 188, 191–99, 201–2. *See also* Virtus WalkThrough 1.1.3

Virtus Corporation, 179, 219, 222

Virtus Professional, 51, 187

Virtus Voyager 1.0, 51, 208, 219–24

Virtus WalkThrough 1.1.3, 16, 42–43, 49–51, 71, 103, 151, 162, 170–72, 176, 180, 182–99, 201, 205, 207–20, 224

Wacom SD-510C digital electronic tablet, 32–33, 45, 69, 83, 120. *See also* Graphics tablets

Willats, John, 2–3

WindowShade 1.2, 53–55

Wire-frame images, 208–9
Working at Home (Atkinson), 16–17
Working drawings, 101, 105–11, 153
Working models, 167–68. *See also* Modelmaking
Workstation: definition of, 19. *See also* Computer graphics workstation. Scenographic workstation

X coordinate, 162

Y coordinate, 162

Z coordinate, 162
Zero-dimensional points, 108
ZoomBar 1.7, 55
Zuberano, Maurice, 203

Darwin Reid Payne is an adjunct professor of scenography at Wake Forest University at Winston-Salem, North Carolina, and also a lecturer in scenographic modelmaking at the North Carolina School of the Arts. He was formerly chairman of the theater department of Southern Illinois University at Carbondale. In addition to designing and directing at regional theaters throughout the United Stages and Canada, he is writing a book on the integration of traditional scenographic rendering techniques with computer graphics technology.